Dear Monika,

I want to thank you for your beautiful soul! You are just lovely!

I really enjoy your meditations both before and after Lee's channeling.

Your generosity in allowing me to use your work with Kryon in "Gaia and the Universe," and "Ancient Lemuria," enabled me to do this project and publish it with integrity.

This work asked to be included!

I thank you for making it possible to publish as it was guided.

In deep appreciation!

Deborah

WISDOM FROM
KRYON

WORDS OF THE TEMPLE

WORKING TOWARD WORLD PEACE

A NEW HUMANITY
BOOK 1

INTERNATIONAL
BEST
SELLING
BOOK

DEBORAH SADLER

FOREWORD BY MICHAEL BERNARD BECKWITH

FOUNDER & SPIRITUAL DIRECTOR, AGAPE INTERNATIONAL SPIRITUAL CENTER
AUTHOR, *LIFE VISIONING* AND *SPIRITUAL LIBERATION*

Praise for Words of the Temple

Deborah's clairaudient work inscribing messages from the celestial beings she calls "The Team" puts her among the pantheon of individuals who've answered the call to be a loving usher during this time, as we emerge into the expanded awareness of our Eternal Nature and Oneness with the I AM Presence and All That Is. To bring Spiritual insight and perspective to what's happening in our world.

—**Michael Bernard Beckwith**, Founder & Spiritual Director,
Agape International Spiritual Center,
Author, *Life Visioning* and *Spiritual Liberation*

Deborah Sadler who has dedicated her life to the children of the world, joins in the march to help birth the new humanity. Her multidimensional awareness expressed in, Words of the Temple will help move the reader toward a more compassionate and loving way of being. This book will help this world make the shift from a sense of separation to the interconnectedness of all life - The Unity Consciousness.

—**Christian Sorensen, D. D.,** Spiritual Lead of
the Seaside Center for Spiritual Living

A significant story told through the prism of a skilled restorative justice practitioner. The reader will challenge critical thinking skills and will be rewarded if read with an open mind.

—**Steven M. Luttbeg JD.,** Host of LetsRocPodcast.com

Deborah, I loved your book. It was so insightful. I am sure it will help millions move through these changing times with ease and grace. Your eloquent phrasing was so interesting, it kept me totally engrossed from beginning to end. I am honored to be a part of the inspiration connected with your wonderful creation. It is definitely a page-turner. I look forward to the 2ⁿᵈ and 3ʳᵈ books in the trilogy.

—**Marilyn Harper**, Channel for Adironnda & Council of Light

I enjoyed reading the journey that Deb took from point A to point B, very revealing of the action of Spirit and Deb's willingness to trust the journey. The information that is given in Book One stimulates the excitement for Book Two and Three, the treasures that are yet to be revealed.

—**Kathryn F Boggio**, RScP and ALSP Emeritus

Deborah Sadler is an emerging thought leader, healer, educator, advocate and rebel writer with a unique perspective and rhythm to her channeled messages so relevant for these extreme, never before experienced changing times. With her new powerfully channeled book, Words of the Temple, Working Toward World Peace, the 1ˢᵗ book in her new trilogy series, she tells us about the birthing of a New Earth and a New Human. Her gift is helping us understand the past and how it has set the stage for "a time of great transition as humanity awakens to the Oneness of ALL...We have lived through the separation for millennia and now we are awakening to our Oneness as humanity." While there are many different layers to this book, I was particularly moved as she vividly showed the dichotomies of the current draconian world of our male energy dominated society that has predominated global culture for eons. In contrast we are also shown why it is no longer working as it is starting to be dismantled by a more feminine energy dominated society where restorative practices, cooperation, healing and open-hearted caring for all humans starts to be the norm. One example that stands out for me is her perspective on the Black Lives Matter movement, demonstrating how as we all sheltered in place during the 2020 - 2021 Pandemic, we were given a new lens to view the world at large and our own lives in the process. An opportunity to be with what we were witnessing, and to perhaps make new choices about what we choose to see, how we choose to act, how we choose to know peace for all beings. To co-create a new world where, as Deborah notes, "This is the shift, and the oneness of our experience has provided the time and energy to protest the thousand-year-long injustice of prejudice and discrimination falsely separating us when we have always been ONE." (p 26). This is just one example of why this book is such an important read for everyone committed to being part of the change, supported by the lineage of our past and the hope of our future. Deborah Sadler, who walks the walk and talks the talk, hits a home run with this book. You will never look at life the same afterwards and perhaps you will be inspired to act as part of the change.

—Harmony Sedona, Creator of *Writer Whispering*
and *SoulStreaming*

I am by birth Acjachemen. I have been trained for more than 20 years by Star Mother, as was Deborah Sadler.

—Rev. Sam Jaffe (aka Moyel Tukwaa),
Leader of the Eagle/Dove Clan

WORDS OF THE TEMPLE

*Working Toward
World Peace*

A New Humanity
Book 1

Deborah Sadler

GLOBAL WELLNESS MEDIA
STRATEGIC EDGE INNOVATIONS PUBLISHING
LOS ANGELES, TORONTO, MONTREAL

First Edition. Published by:
Global Wellness Media
Strategic Edge Innovations Publishing
340 S Lemon Ave #2027
Walnut, California 91789-2706
(866) 467-9090
StrategicEdgeInnovations.com

Publisher's Note: The views expressed in this work are solely those of the authors and do not necessarily reflect the views of the publisher, and the publisher hereby disclaims any responsibilities for them.

Editor: Bobbie Walton
Cover and illustrations: Eric D. Groleau
Book design: Global Wellness Media
Pictures: Harmony Sedona (Deborah Sadler), Brenda Bell (Rep. John Lewis), MerlinFoof [reddit] (Breonna Taylor), Ale Mi/DepositPhoto.com (Greta Thunberg /284343488).

Words of the Temple Book 1 / Deborah Sadler. -- 1st ed.
ISBN: 978-1-957343-01-3 (Kindle)
ISBN: 978-1-957343-00-6 (Paperback)

To my students

Table of Content

Foreword

As many of us know and can feel, humanity—individually and collectively—has been undergoing a Great Awakening. A Great Awakening of the heart, of the mind, of the body, and of the Spirit. A Great Awakening to love, to peace, to joy, to compassion, to equanimity. In essence, we are birthing a new humanity, a new Earth, a world that works for the highest and best for everyone. And at a soul level, we have all chosen to be here at this particular time to midwife this expanded consciousness into Earthly expression.

But in order to be reborn, we must die. Die to our old ways of thinking, our old ways of doing, our old ways of being in the world. We must die to the illusion of separation, of fear, doubt, worry, jealousy, envy, avarice, and lack and the various ways it plagues our planet and afflicts humanity through the myriad of social, political, economic, and environmental issues our world faces, as well as our interpersonal dealings and relationships. These afflictions of the heart and mind exist because we have forgotten our True nature as energetic extensions of the one Spirit, the one Mind, the one Presence, and the one Intelligence that imbues all Life everywhere.

However, as we begin to wake up to our innate Spiritual essence and become aware of our power of conscious creation, we align our thoughts, emotions, lives, and destinies with the laws, order, and processes of the Universe. We are restored back to our original, magnificent whole, and Love becomes our sole purpose and focus. We transmute and transcend any and every affliction, issue, problem, situation, or circumstance, and recognize that the one Idea that knows only Love, only joy, only peace, only well-being, only abundance, and only generosity are our true identities. But we must answer the call, the evolutionary impulse within all of us to emerge into this next iteration of humanity; to be a conduit for bringing Heaven to Earth, according to our own unique gifts and talents.

Deborah Sadler is one such conduit.

Deborah's clairaudient work inscribing messages from the celestial beings she calls "The Team" puts her among the pantheon of individuals who've answered the call to be a loving usher during this time, as we emerge into the expanded awareness of our Eternal Nature and Oneness with the I AM Presence and All That Is. To bring Spiritual insight and perspective to what's happening in our world now so that it shifts us well beyond our current paradigms and ways of seeing, thinking, knowing, and being, and freeing us to powerfully create a more loving, peaceful, and just planet. These times might seem chaotic now, but there's always a Universal order underlying the chaos. Allow this book to be your companion during this time.

Peace & Richest Blessings,

Michael Bernard Beckwith

Founder & Spiritual Director,
Agape International Spiritual Center
Author, *Life Visioning* and *Spiritual Liberation*

Introduction

On the first weekend of March 2020, a friend of mine and I went to a psychic fair in a place called Harmony Grove Spiritual Center in Escondido, California. We met to enjoy the beautiful oak covered grounds and to experience the psychic fair on my birthday. I purchased a ticket for one service.

I chose to have a reading with a woman named Maryann. She told me right away that I would be writing a book. I would definitely be writing a book. The book was going to be about common sense because in her words, "There is no common sense on this planet right now." She also saw me in a past life as a monk or a head nun, where I had privileges beyond those of a nun, and that I was able to create opportunities for the nuns I worked with. I also had a lot of freedom for the times.

On April 1st 2020, I had my annual reading with Jaqueline Valdez, which I have been doing since I went with my sister 10 years ago. Since that time, I go every year, usually around my birthday. It's like an annual check-up.

In the reading, she said, "yes," I would be writing a book, "and then another and then another. It would just become a process." Covid-19 struck our consciousness the week after the psychic fair at Harmony Grove and two weeks before my reading with Jacqueline. Little did I know I was about to become a monk, or nun, sheltered in my townhouse along with my husband Jim, of 46 years, to stay safe and healthy and avoid contact with this potentially deadly virus.

On May 30th and 31st, 2020, I participated in a virtual *Kryon Los Angeles Meeting*. Lee Carroll has been channeling this entity since 1989. One of the participants in the meeting was Marilyn Harper who channels Adironnda at Kryon events. She also does a one-day class the Monday following the Kryon meetings on "How to Channel." I signed up and took what Marilyn calls "How to Channel 2.0," an updated version. The first chapter of this book is what I wrote during the guided writing time provided in the workshop.

Marilyn instructed us to continue writing every day for at least 21 days because that is how long it takes to establish a new habit. I took the class on June 1st. I had also participated in a writer's summit with Park Point Press. At that summit they stated that you can write a book in 90 days.

This book is the culmination of these encounters. I wrote the book in 92 days. Every morning I RPM (rise, pee, meditate). Instead of listening to Kryon channelings I began to pray myself in, which is doing an affirmative prayer. I started by connecting with the heartbeat of Earth Mother and then called in many guides and helpers in the seen and unseen realms as part of my affirmation. Then I wrote.

Part way into the book, I was told it was a part of a trilogy. I was also told to resuscitate the title for a trilogy I wrote 30 years ago entitled, *Heal Your Mother, The Words of the Temple, Working for World Peace.* In a reading with an entity named Malachi channeled by Katherine Torres, over 30 years ago, he told me, "You know you need to put it into writing, the words of the temple." Back then, I took the time to transcribe my cassette recording of the reading. I recall reading over the transcript understanding everything, except the part about "the words of the temple."

Shortly after that, I began writing a book following the loss of a stillborn baby girl named Lily Rose. The first chapter was called "A Mother's Day Story," where I wrote about this life-altering experience from a spiritual point of view. I was compelled as part of my healing to write. I then wrote a chapter for each holiday. At one point I realized, "I think I'm writing the words of the temple." A friend of mine had written on the sand at the beach, here in Cardiff-by-the-Sea, California,

"Heal Your Mother." I borrowed it and it became my mantra and my license plate (HEALRMA) and it became the title of my trilogy.

One of the messages that came out of this profound loss was that I was now freed up to take the time that would have gone to Lily Rose and devote myself to children in general. I did take a year to mourn the loss of our daughter and tend to our three children. When a mailer came providing opportunities to volunteer at my children's elementary school. I decided to jump in and became the chair for a program called, "Project Self-Esteem." This opened a door that eventually led to three teaching credentials and a master's degree in education that has spanned the last 30 years, which is a full Saturn cycle. It takes Saturn 29 and a half years to go around the sun. Saturn rules the business of our lives.

This book is a full circle. While I have had all of these experiences in the last 30 years, "The Words of the Temple," are again available for the New Earth and the New Human who are emerging as us. This trilogy is Aquarian — it is unique, and it is the message of unity that is upon us. Although it is linear in time in its structure, this book is a multidimensional examination of where we are going, moving humanity from the children's creation story to a more adult understanding of where we came from and what it is ours to do now in this time of radical transition and transformation.

I consider the content to be guided writing. The Team, as I call them, work for about an hour or a little more every morning, and then they are done. At that point, my hands don't move correctly, or my typing becomes totally inaccurate.

This is a trilogy about the shift taking place on Earth and in humanity. It also documents what is happening in real time to highlight that the shift is happening now. As someone who was introduced to astrology at the age of 25, I have rediscovered its power to tell the story of our personal and collective lives. As a result, we show how the movement of the planets and the meaning ascribed to them determined over millennia not only impacts our lives but directs where we are and where we are going as a planet and as humanity.

There is so much more going on than we have been taught. This applies to our spiritual systems as much as to our science. In retirement I discovered Kryon on YouTube, searching for Abraham, whom I love. I have become a Kryon follower. Kryon is an angelic entity from the other side of the veil channeled by Lee Carroll. Through Kryon we see the BIG Picture, the universal lens, which I tap into heavily as guided by the Team.

Who are we? Where did we come from? What is our role in the Universe? How big is the Universe? What is our purpose? Why are we here? These are age-old questions that the Team attempts to explain through Kryon channelings, through current news sources that document the shift, and through the astrological aspects or relationships that define what is happening on a universal scale.

We are in the "in between," between the past and the not-yet-future. We are at the cusp of a shift that takes place galactically every 26,000 years called the precession of the equinoxes. Each of us is here because we stood in line to be part of this major transition to a New Earth and a New Humanity. This trilogy is a real-time exploration of this profound journey on our way, toward world peace.

I am grateful to the Team for the ease and grace they bring to this project to bring clarity to the chaos and gyrations moving us into our personal and collective divinity. We are each a flower blossoming into the sunshine of infinite love, beauty, and compassion. This is our destiny. I say we grab it now!

Cardiff-by-the-Sea, CA
December 20, 2020

Preface

Guided Writing - Adironnda

6/1/2020

Beloveds—we have been waiting for the opportunity for a long, long time and we are so thrilled that you have agreed to open this connection. We are light beings from the stars, and we honor your spiritual commitment to yourself, your family, friends, community, state, nation, world, and all of the stars in the galaxy and universe beyond.

We are here to assist you to communicate spiritual truth to humanity in a way that is clear, practical and healing. As the Reader Maryanne communicated to you—we have a book to write about spiritual common sense. It is a time where humanity's foundations have and continue to crumble beneath our very feet.

This is a time of death and rebirth—of the renewal of the partnership between humanity, Earth Mother and the very cosmos that creates All That Is.

Your message is our message because the truth is that "We Are ONE"—and this truth needs to be shared.

We have been waiting for this activation for the many years that you have been out in the world putting these spiritual truths into practice. We are infinitely grateful for your wonderful service with the Indigo children—and the wait has been worthwhile as those experiences triggered compassionate action on a daily basis that you may have not even been aware of. Your contribution to the life of your students is an opening in the cosmos to social and economic justice for ALL!

1

The teachings we bring support this essential work—and it is time for it to go out into the world

(Guided Writing, 6/1/2020 at *"How to Channel 2.0,"* with Adironnda, Marilyn Harper and Joeaux Robey, virtual all-day class)

Chapter 1

Beyond the Children's Story

6/2/2020

The Story we have been told by our past and contemporary cultures about *Life* is the children's story. In this book we are going to share the adult story which is much grander and more elegant. Through audio recordings and books, Kryon, who is channeled by Lee Carroll, illuminates the distinction between the children's and adult creation stories in a way that is comprehensive. This knowledge is known by many sources and has been on my personal radar screen for over three decades. The purpose of this book is to focus on moving from seeing ourselves as limited and powerless victims to realizing and recognizing ourselves as infinite, wondrous and powerful creators.

This information is from Kryon, which Lee Carroll has generously made available on his website Kryon.com and for this trilogy. This information is supplemented by the Kryon books as well as the work of Monika Muranyi, who is the archivist of the Kryon material. In addition, Dr. Amber Wolf who has been part of the Kryon Team for many years wrote with Muranyi, *The Women of Lemuria, Ancient Wisdom for Modern Times* from which much of this information is derived. Relevant sources and current news feeds are woven into the Kryon and other spiritual teachings to reveal that we are going through a shift in humanity, right now!

How we got here

Yet, it is from these powerful resources we learn humanity as we recognize it came from the stars. We are stardust literally and metaphorically. The Star Mothers from the Pleiades star system arrived on Earth approximately 200,000 years ago. They look like us because there is a commonality throughout our universe of how people look, think and live.

They come not by spaceship but by working with the laws of physics that we have yet to discover on Earth. They mated with the humans of the time for the purposes of implanting a piece of Creative Source into our human DNA. This process took place over many thousands of years until all the other lines of humans died out and there remained the Sacred Human connected to the Great Central Sun in the universe. These new humans have 23 chromosomes instead of the 24 chromosomes of all other animal life on Earth.

Science corroborates this, noting that 200,000 years ago one human species emerged out of the many that had gone before (Weaver). The way evolution works is to create a wonderful variety within each species. Think about how many monkey species are on our planet, or cats or dogs, or horses, or even lions and tigers. There is great variety. However, there is only one form of humans.

Our Creation Story in the West about Adam and Eve is about an intervention. An angel appears and suddenly they have the knowledge of good and evil, light, and dark. Where did this knowledge come from?

Spirit is everywhere and humans were given the opportunity to choose light or dark in how we live our lives and how we perceive events. This is what the Pleiadian Star Mothers gave us; the knowledge of Creative Source inside so that we as humans have the choice to discover and connect with this infinite power, or not to.

We live in a quantum universe that is infinite in its possibilities which means that we as creative beings have infinite potential to create a world that works for everyone. We are born magnificent because we have been seeded with the infinite potential of Creative Source.

4

We are not born dirty as some spiritual systems tell us. There is no such thing as sin and hell; if it is anything, it is merely a state of mind.

Our universe is teeming with life — much of it has life that looks like us. However, we are the new kids on the block. We are the youth of the universe for we are surrounded by Star Families from other galaxies who seeded the Pleiadians.

There is a system of creation whereby beings on planets raise their consciousness individually and collectively to move from separation consciousness to unity consciousness. This is called Ascension. And when a planet and its inhabitants reach a place of peace, harmony, and unity they then go and seed another planet in our galaxy, to go through the same process of moving toward Ascension.

Passing the Marker

This is what is taking place on our Earth right now, at this time. We have passed the marker of December 21, 2012, noted by the Mayan calendar and we are now in Ascension. We are moving from what the Native Americans referred to as the Fourth World of Separation to the Fifth World of Peace as prophesied by our Indigenous people on Earth.

We are birthing a New Earth and a New Human. This is a time of great transition as humanity awakens to the Oneness of ALL. We live in a quantum universe where all is entangled which means it is connected.

We have lived through the illusion of separation for millennia and now we are awakening to our Oneness as humanity. We are increasingly linked by technology which is a part of moving into the Aquarian Age. Aquarius rules technology and all things electrical. Aquarius is also ruled by the planet Uranus which signifies fast and unexpected change. We live on the cusp of this age and change is upon us in ways that are unexpected and seem to be moving at the speed of light.

The Virus

As I write this on June 3, 2020, humanity is literally in the midst of shifting. First the coronavirus, Covid-19, descended upon us before we could even understand or comprehend the depth of transformation it would usher into our personal and collective lives. Before we knew it, we were sheltered in place first country by country until it expanded to include the entire planet and almost all of humanity.

When governments and states began to reopen, there was a sense of relief. In a matter of a few months, our entire way of living on this planet transformed as we worked to remain safe and healthy, avoiding the sometimes-life-threatening symptoms of this virus that includes death.

We have no immunity to this virus because it is novel or new. The entirety of humanity is vulnerable to this sometimes-deadly microbe. In this we see and begin to comprehend that we share the same air, that we are all vulnerable and that we must not only protect ourselves, but we must protect one another through the choices we make.

Millennial adults have pressed upon their Baby Boomer parents to shelter in place, and to stay there. While what this means for teenagers is an even greater challenge due to their natural need to socialize and interact.

Schools around the globe have even shuttered and students sent home from universities and colleges. And we have made these shifts almost immediately.

Technology has been our friend as we are set up for this, it turns out. The universe always provides and so now we connect by Zoom and FaceTime. Much of the workforce is performing their jobs from home, while schools are teaching students remotely from the instructor's home to the student's.

People are taking yoga on Instagram and Zoom. Conferences and workshops that normally take place in convention halls and hotels are now online—often at reduced prices which allows more individuals to learn and grow, right from home.

Social Justice

And then the killings of African Americans by white supremacists and police continued and the tipping point was met. It wasn't the killing of just one man or woman but the weekly march toward a point where the entire world watched when a Minneapolis policeman put his knee on the neck of George Floyd, an African American man, for over eight minutes as the man said, "I can't breathe." Bystanders begged for mercy as three other police officers just stood by, as this man laid on the street without struggle—to die in front of us, over and over and over again, through our media feeds.

As much as our press selects gore as the leading stories, this man's death by police is the camel that broke the proverbial back, not just in Minnesota, or even the United States, but all over the globe. People now march for equality; they march for justice as they march for a new humanity, and they march with masks on their faces as they hold their handmade cardboard signs and sing their chants of freedom and change.

In June 2020 we are in the shift that has been prophesied. We were moving toward a more compassionate and loving human family where we lift one another up, and where the paradigms of the past no longer work for an entire planet.

What has always been, is no longer acceptable to the global humanity. Marchers self-police themselves and form human chains to protect property.

"When we see death, we are seeking birth, when we see destruction, we are seeing reconstruction, and when we see the headlines, we are seeing the Old Guard lose its grip,"—these words of modern-day mystic and teacher, Matt Kahn, describe the transition that is upon us now, as Matt shares in a YouTube interview with Michael Sandler (*Inspired Nation* 4/1/2020).

We have transitioned from a very masculine based energy where we were all out in the world doing, driving, shopping, visiting, eating out at restaurants, attending sporting events, stuck in traffic, going to and from work and school, unable to abate our use of fossil fuels, always going, going, going. A world where everyone was exhausted, overwhelmed, and separated from ourselves in the intensity of our doingness, doingness, doingness.

And within the matter of a week or two in most parts of the planet we sheltered in place and went within. And so, we shifted from masculine out in the world energy to feminine going-within vibration of self-reflection, free time, open choices, and the absence of our frantic, madcap world. And many of us have found this to be restorative, to be renewing. Families are with their families, children and parents are home. Neighbors help neighbors and light workers volunteer at food giveaways while merchants shift to sales on-line and restaurants make the move to take out.

This is the shift, and the oneness of our experience has provided the time and energy to protest the thousand-year-long injustice of prejudice and discrimination falsely separating us when we have always been ONE.

As individuals pour into the streets and gather to protest the death of yet another innocent Black man, our planet moves into Ascension. We peel away from the Old Earth as a eucalyptus tree sheds its outer bark or a snake its skin.

For these global citizens are an army of the light. This time in our story, history and herstory merge to create a new story of Peace on Earth.

We witness the old guard as it loses its grip on an anachronistic cry for law and order when in fact, law and order and social justice is exactly what the lightworkers around the world are demanding. And to magnify their statement of the need for social justice, they are marching in a global pandemic where physical distancing is advised. In other words, they are putting their lives on the line for a cry for social and economic justice for ALL on a global level from Minnesota to New Zealand.

Chapter 2

Lemuria

6/4/2020

In *The Women of Lemuria: Ancient Wisdom for Modern Times,* by Kryon, Monika Muranyi and Dr. Amber Wolf we learn the following information about our Creation story.

The Pleiadian Star Mothers arrived in many places on Earth Mother to starseed the planet. This is the way the cosmos, planets and star systems that have reached Ascension status birth new life to continue the expansion of consciousness in the universe.

Just as other star families seeded the Pleiadians, specifically the Octurians, and the Orions and Syrians before them, the Pleiadians were directed to seed the Earth with the consciousness of the Divine Creator. The second and third DNA strands were merged through this process, in humans on Earth. The second DNA strand contains the consciousness of love, compassion and Oneness, the very attributes that separate us from the animal world.

And so, 200,000 years ago the human race was starseeded with the consciousness of Creative Source, or a piece of God. This resulted in humans having 23 chromosomes while the entirety of animal life on this planet has 24 chromosomes.

In fact, we do have 24 chromosomes, but the 24th chromosome given to us by our Pleiadian Star Mothers is quantum and cannot yet be measured by our current science and technology.

Although the Star Mothers landed many places, the area where their core teachings were focused was Lemuria, which is located where the

Hawaiian Islands are today. These islands rest upon a hot spot underneath the ocean which in that time raised the islands so that they contained the largest mountain on Earth. Lemuria was a place where individual humans incarnated for one lifetime to learn the core teachings directly from the Star Mothers. After this, individuals had lifetimes in other places on Earth, but returned to their new lifetimes with the teachings from the Star Mothers in their personal Akash, or life records.

Life in the Garden of Eden

Lemuria was the Garden of Eden. What made the teachings so powerful is the fact that as an island, this culture was isolated, and so for over one hundred thousand years the teachings remained pure. The transference of the DNA from the Star Mothers to the population took approximately 100,000 years around the globe.

In Lemuria, the culture was at its peak from 50,000 to 15,000 years ago. Women were honored as the Divine Life-Giving Feminine with a recognition that women are the Life-Givers.

The women were the Spiritual teachers as taught by the Star Mothers who remained actively teaching the women and children throughout the time of Lemuria. Women assisted one another in giving birth which was done in the warm waters on the shores of this small continent and Edenic Island.

The women gathered food from the Island/continent while the men fished for food from the sea. The men honored the life-giving power of the women and their shamanic and spiritual knowledge. Though the men did the fishing, the women directed them where to find the fish in the sea. The men honored and followed the direction of the women to find the fish and safely return to land.

The men always cooked the fish. They caught it, prepared it and served it. This was not a technologically driven society; life was simple.

Yet, there were scientific activities that took place at the top of the highest mountain called the Temple of Rejuvenation.

In the deep cold of this isolated place, individuals underwent treatments that healed their bodies and extended their lives so that they could continue to gather wisdom from the Pleiadian Star Mothers, in their own life in Lemuria.

The children went to school and were taught by those who had been taught and trained by the Star Mothers themselves, who still reside in these islands. Some Lemurians were taught directly by the Star Mothers—and the teachings were fun and joy-filled. The mothers accompanied their children in their education, supporting the purity of the culture and the teachings from the Pleiadians.

The children were instructed about love, about compassion, about joy, about the creative process where our thoughts, feelings, and actions create our reality. By controlling our thoughts, we can consciously create a society built upon the foundation of love, honoring and respect for all life, including Earth Mother.

Earth Mother was revered as the opulent provider and support for all life on the planet. Lemurians lived in harmony with Gaia and performed ceremonies throughout the year to demonstrate their appreciation and respect for the life-giving home that Gaia provides for humanity.

This was done through ceremony. The women and men each had their own separate ceremonies as well as ceremonies where both genders participated in the honoring. The children had ceremonies as well—each blessing and giving thanks for the nurturing and life-giving Earth.

The teachings included that the Lemurians had been seeded by the Pleiadians with a piece of the consciousness of the Creator. It was this information that distinguishes humans from this point forward from the animals of the Earth.

This story broadly matches the Creation story of much of humanity—that an angel came down to the Garden of Eden and gave Adam and Eve, who were naked like the animals, the knowledge of the light and dark or good and evil, and the ability to have free knowledge was given to Adam and Eve in the same way the Pleiadians planted the 24th chromosome into humanity—or the God seed of Divinity.

We are all connected to the Creative Source, or ALL That Is, through Divine intervention. This means we are connected to and are a part of the Creator of All That Is. We are Divine. We have been given the choice to discover the light within us, or to dismiss it. This freedom of choice is open to each of us—to see the Divinity inside us and inside of every human we encounter. Or we can choose not to recognize or acknowledge our sacred lineage and inheritance.

We are at such a place as humanity in 2020, a year of great upheaval and lightning quick change. The protest marches suggest there is a quickening in the awakening of humanity to our common magnificence and to creating a world that works for everyone.

This is the promise of the prophecy of the Mayan calendar that the marker of December 12, 2012, when met and passed, leads us to world peace. This is just the beginning of a brilliant and expressive awakening to the truth that we are Spirit expressing in a physical body whose DNA is directly linked to and contains the Light of the Central Sun and Creator.

Chapter 3

It is Always in the Stars

6/4/2020

The precession of the equinoxes is a 26,000-year cycle of our solar system's sun's orbit around Alcyone, the brightest star in the Pleiadian constellation known as the Seven Sisters. The precession occurs when the wobble of the Earth returns to make one revolution. At the 26,000-year point, the wobble is centered, balanced, before continuing our sun's solar system's orbit, again, around Alcyone, beginning the wobble anew.

> Since our Earth is not completely rigid, as it rotates on its axis, centrifugal force causes the equator to bulge. This is the same force that causes you to fling to the side of a giant spinning wheel in a theme park. The non-uniform gravitational force of the Sun and Moon will pull on this bulge and cause the Earth to wobble as it spins around its axis, just like a spinning top that is almost falling off (*Mydarksky.org*).

Another description of this phenomenon is:

> This wobble causes the axis of the Earth to create a 360-degree circle in space over the course of 26,000 years.
> Through this rotation the axis of the earth moves through all twelve constellations of the zodiac during this cycle, also referred to as a Platonic year (ancient-wisdom.com).

Each age lasts for 2,160 years. Earth is now shifting to the Aquarian Age.

Aquarius is ruled by Uranus, a planet that represents electric energy and so it rules technology. It is also a higher vibration of the mental plane and allows us to tune to higher frequencies. Aquarius also signifies civilization coming together in a way that honors all groups and all paths to the Divine.

The Piscean Age, which is coming to a close, began with the period around the life of Jesus Christ. This age has been the age of love and consciousness; that we are all the children of Spirit—as Christ stated: "These things that I do, you too can do even greater" (John 14:12). He also taught us that: what we believe is reflected back to us in our lives; "It is done unto you as you believe" (Matthew 8:13), or the cosmic law of cause and effect.

The Wobble / Earth's Axis

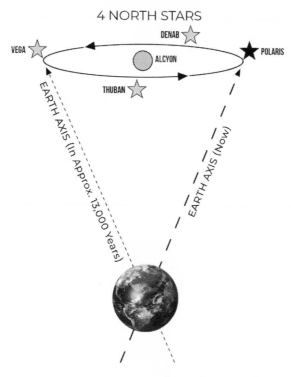

(Adaped from MyDarkSky.org)

The Precession of the Equinoxes

The Mayan calendar is based upon the precession of the equinoxes which it describes as the "long count." This cycle ended on December 21st 2012, and began a new cycle. For the Gregorian calendar 2000 CE was predicted to be Armageddon or the end of an aeon.

This is why there is so much disturbance in the field at this time on Earth. We are ending a 26,000-year cycle and beginning a new 26,000-year cycle. Each of us on the planet chose to be here at this time to assist with and participate in this cosmic shift.

Formal religion that grew out of the Christian Era and prevailed throughout the last 2000 years is in transition as humanity shifts to a higher consciousness that recognizes the magnificence of every person and strives to create a world that works for everyone.

In astrology the symbol for the Earth is a circle with a cross inside. This shape mimics the precession of the equinoxes through the 26,000-year cycle.

According to the website lunarplanner.com "The precessional orientation of Earth's polar axis relative to the galactic plane reveals exactly where we are in the unfolding spiral in consciousness. It defines the timing of this cycle."

The Earth's Precessional Cycle

Nick Anthony Firenze who authored the lunarplanner.com website describes this as: "The Earth's Precessional Cycle; The Sacred Geometry of Global Change." He also describes this as: "The Cycle of Earth's Precessional Cross and Evolutionary. Cycle of the Soul" (lunarplanner.com)

One Platonic Year (26,000 years)

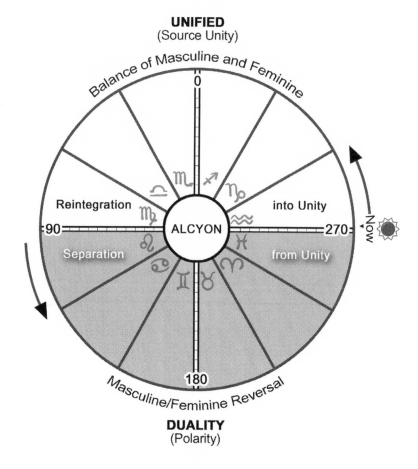

UNIFIED
(Source Unity)

Balance of Masculine and Feminine

0

Reintegration   into Unity

90   ALCYON   270

Separation   from Unity

Now

180

Masculine/Feminine Reversal

DUALITY
(Polarity)

Notice that the diagram of the precession of the equinoxes includes a cross, as noted, the astrological symbol of Earth. Fiorenza states that this is often referred to as the "Holy Cross," or "Heavenly Cross," which refers to a cross found in the heavens, such as in the diagram of the cosmos.

The cross has been a dominant symbol in the Piscean Age, from which we are emerging, as the primary image of the past 2000 years has been the crucifixion of Jesus the Christ, on a Roman cross.

As you can see in the diagram below, one cross occurred 13,000 years ago, and another cross appears now.

Earth's Precessional Cross

2160 YEARS AGO
30° TO ERECT

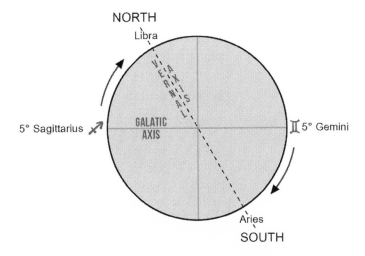

2000 AD (NOW)
ERECT CROSS

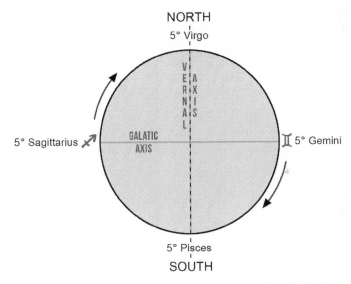

(Adaped from Nick Anthony Fiorenza)

It is clear that we are in a time of great cosmic change and shift. In looking at The Platonic Year Diagram, we can see that for the past 13,000 years, humanity has been in a part of our 26,000-year Earth cycle where we experienced separation from Divinity 13,000 years ago. During this time the masculine force came to dominate and a reversal of the "matriarchal/patriarchal" paradigm took place. At the marker of 180 degrees, we experienced the "epitome of polarity," or opposites.

Alcyone Star Cluster (Seven Sisters)

The Great Flood

Therefore, 13,000 years ago we lost contact with our unity. This can be interpreted as "The Fall," in Biblical terms when humanity left our innocence or sense of unity for the duality of male and female and the knowledge of light and dark along with the ability and power to choose, or express free will. This is also the time of the great flood, or Noah's Ark when the ice age ended and the planet warmed, melting glaciers worldwide, flooding the lands of the planet. So, implicit in this diagram of "The Great World Cycle," are significant geophysical events triggered by specific transition points (Ibid.). Fiorenza states:

The more we examine this dynamic astrophysical geometry, the easier it becomes to acknowledge it is the underlying time piece governing our Earthian experience.

He goes on to assert:

The phase transitions occurring within the Great World Cycle create an intelligently ordered progression of evolutionary unfoldment in consciousness—an evolutionary spiral supporting the maturing and spiritual fulfillment of incarnating souls (Ibid.).

Fiorenza continues:

The evolutionary spiral occurs in the relationship of the astrophysical and gravitational vectors that determine our temporal experience as durative and evolving souls participating in the spiritual unfoldment of Divine Intelligence...

The precessional orientation of Earth's polar axis (Earth's Precessional Cross) relative to the galactic plane reveals exactly where we are in the unfolding spiral in consciousness; it defines the timing of this cycle.... This specific cross now marks a primary phase transition in this embracing precessional cycle. This specific cross creates a paradigm shift in Earth's natural evolutionary unfoldment of consciousness. As Earth's pole now reorients back toward the galactic plane, the precessional cross becomes active. It marks a time where we return from 12,000 years of darkness, from our experience in duality consciousness, from the separation of the feminine and masculine principles to a reunification in consciousness. What emerge is the Divine Feminine and Divine Masculine principles on Earth. We can now demonstrate the Divine Union of the feminine and masculine, both within ourselves and in our relations with each other and with all life. This transition has just

begun—2000 A.D., and so too, our return journey into
unified field awareness" (Ibid.).

According to Fiorenza, "Nested within a geometry of rotating astrophysical spheres of Cosmic Intelligence, Earth's precessional cycle governs the 'Evolutionary Cycle of the Soul'—a natural cycle that directs the spiritual unfoldment of Earth's entire soul collective" (Ibid.).

He describes how this plays out.

> Approximately 12,000 years ago, the previous erect cross
> (and at the time of the Great Flood), the pole of the Earth in
> local space began to tilt away from the Galactic Plane—
> away from our source of illuminating light. At that time we
> began a 12,000-year period of temporal darkness—
> apparently separate from the unified galactic awareness. For
> the duration of this time, humanity experienced a tormenting
> shear within the masculine and feminine principle which is
> now being healed in the direction of balance between both
> powerful and creative forces.

"Black Lives Matter"

Fiorenza's explanation of the precession of the equinoxes, eloquently describes the shift in which we find ourselves today, June 6, 2020. As I write this, peaceful protests around the globe ignited by the video of a white police officer, pressing a knee on the neck of George Floyd, a Black man, for almost nine minutes resulting in his death on May 25th, Memorial Day, are taking place. This is the tenth day of protests across America and in cities and rural towns.

For nine days people have been marching in countries from around the world and the Mayor of Washington, D.C., had "BLACK LIVES MATTER," painted across and down the entire street leading to the White House in bright and bold yellow paint. She also had the street renamed, "Black Lives Matter."

We are cosmically at the juncture of "Integration into Divinity," depicted by the Platonic Year diagram, moving every day a little further away from the "Epitome of Polarity," and the "Matriarchal/Patriarchal Reversal," which we have experienced for the last 12,000 to 13,000 years. We are now in the "Transition Re-Integration" quadrant where we begin to remember our origin from Source and unity, as the spiritual truth of our cosmos.

Political forces are hanging on to the past of hyper-masculinity. Their rejection of the feminine principles (compassion, nurturing, nourishing) as tools of governing represents our past. They are struggling to hold onto patterns that have served a limited number of people at the expense of much of humanity that in turn has been discriminated against, suppressed, punished, and ostracized for millennia.

Today, the citizens of the globe have come together to not only counter the pandemic through two to three months of shelter-in-place but have birthed what has become an international movement of peace marches. We are declaring the end of the separation that has dominated the past 13,000 years. We are moving literally as a planet into the physical galactic light where we remember, we reawaken to our common humanity.

We can see this on our media feeds, news broadcasts and social media around our globe. This is not an anomaly; it is our first step into a future where we live in peace together as one planetary Earth Soul Family, which is the spiritual truth of who we are and where we are going.

In a New York Times article on 6/6/2020, titled *Huge Crowds Around the Globe March in Solidarity Against Police Brutality,* by Damien Cave, Livia Albeck-Ripka and Iliana Magra, updated June 9, 2020:

> Tens of thousands turned out in Australia, Britain, France, Germany and other nations in support of U.S. protests

against the death of George Floyd, while denouncing racism in their own countries.

We as a planet and humanity are physically moving into the galactic light in our universe. We have been in the dark for the past 13,000 years. We forgot our Oneness with all life and with each other. And so, these years have been dominated by wars of division where humanity has been in a pattern of killing one another over and over and over.

Because life is eternal, we also are eternal. Many of us have lived thousands of lives on this planet as both male and female. We have had multiple experiences of killing others and being killed. Division and separation have marked these 13,000 years.

But now we find ourselves at the time of the erect cross in the heavens and light is beginning to be shed upon much of the darkness that we have inherited from our multiple lives as humans on planet Earth.

The Feminine force is rising as there is a growing global consciousness about the health of Earth Mother and the health of humanity. We have been awakening to the power and grace of the feminine principle in our focus upon the cycle of global climate change which, in fact, is the natural rhythm of our home. Our modern-day pollutants make our air unsafe to breathe in many places on Earth. The awareness that we cannot dominate our planet wantonly is an awakening to our Oneness with the Earth and our interdependence.

The notion of dominance which has been the way, particularly of the past 200 years reflects the dominating male force during this 13,000-year cycle. The epitome of polarity is to perceive the Earth and its weather as a force to be controlled and managed, when in fact, there is an inherent intelligence in the Earth that Westerners, in particular, have failed to recognize or acknowledge.

The Indigenous Always Remembered

The Indigenous around the Earth have maintained the memory and knowledge of the Oneness of all life as well as the sacred balance of the feminine and masculine. While dominant elite culture fell under the spell of "The Fall," with the loss of the knowledge of our Oneness, the Indigenous held these sacred truths through the millennium. And though the Indigenous have been marginalized and their populations and land minimized, they continue to retain the cosmic connection to spiritual and universal truth today.

At a *Kryon Homeroom* meeting in Laguna Hills, California, I attended on July 14, 2019, Lee Carroll and Monika Muranyi presented the following information based upon their personal research and experiences in traveling to Uluru in Australia, and Rapa Nui, also known as Easter Island. Aborigines in Australia trace their DNA lineage back 50,000 years. They are the longest known Indigenous bloodline on the planet currently. They trace their ancestry back to the Seven Sisters star system, or the Pleiades. The same is true for the Rapa Nui on what we know as Easter Island. There are nearly 1,000 moai, or large stone figures of torsos with heads that were built and placed by the early Rapa Nui people. Seven of these moai face outwards near the sea, facing the direction of the Hawaiian Islands. There are seven of them suggesting the Rapa Nui recognized their ancestry from the Hawaiian Islands and the constellation of the Seven Sisters.

Lemuria was the Hawaiian Islands combined into one mini-continent. The Star Mothers taught those who incarnated there the divinity within each one of us.

According to Kryon, a multidimensional angelic being from the other side of the veil, channeled by Lee Carroll since 1989, those who incarnated in Lemuria did so for only one lifetime. Later they were reborn in other places on Earth, spreading the teachings of our Divine heritage from the stars.

Much of the information shared here has been derived from the many channels Lee Carroll has been doing around our globe for the past

30 years. This information is consistent and beautiful. It is also corroborated by many others.

The Pleiades

I first was exposed to the knowledge about the Pleiadians seeding Earth when I read *Starseed Transmissions* by Ken Carey in the 1990s. I also had an experience that came to me in the form of a medicine dream, or at least that is how I perceived them.

In 1989 I gave birth to a baby girl who was stillborn. She was the fourth child in our family. Not long after this life-halting experience, I stood at the cash register of a New Age bookstore and noticed I was standing next to Katherine Torres, who channeled an entity named Malachi. She was purchasing a book named, *What if God is a Woman?* I shared with her my sad news and said I would call to set up an appointment for a reading with Malachi.

I had been to Malachi before who used a phrase I cherish: "Let me give you a little giggle." However, in this reading I was going for comfort and resolution. During the reading Malachi said, "She didn't come in because of the soil, it was too contaminated for her. She came for a close examination of the Earth, but she is waiting to come in, at a time when the soil of the Earth is cleaner."

"The soil?" I said incredulously, and then I shared with Katherine/Malachi that her name is Lily Rose, flowers that grow in the soil. It is for this reason I have remained open to multidimensional sources of information. How else do you get information like that that just feels right and synchronizes even with the name? I found this information healing and reassuring.

For many months following Lily Rose's transition back into formlessness, I had what I thought of as a medicine dream that just kept repeating: "The Pleiades, the Pleiades, the Pleiades, the Pleiades!" It was then that I began to buy books about the Pleiades and to really connect with this constellation.

I also began to study with a Native American. I was introduced to her by Katherine Torres. She did the first "Sacred Passages for Women" retreat with Star Mother (the spiritual leader of the Acjachemen tribe of Orange County) on Star Mother's land in the mountains. Katherine moved away, but I remained a student of Star Mother, who taught us Earth studies as well as astrophysics for nearly twenty years.

We use Star Mother's spirit name, since she passed on, rather than her given name. This is seen by the indigenous as a sign of respect.

Through Ken Carey's book I was already convinced that we came from the stars and that we are stardust!

Chapter 4

Astrology 101

6/8/2020

When I was 25 years old, a friend gave me a paperback book by Linda Goodman called *Linda Goodman's Sun Signs.* I devoured this book and then began reading her book, *Linda Goodman Love Signs,* and everything else I could find about astrology. Within a few months, my friend and I were doing astrology charts for money.

I continued to do astrology chart readings, but other avenues of life took my energy, although I have continued to follow the progressions and regressions of the star systems for the past 40 years. My torn and tattered Ephemeris from the 20th century and another for the first half of the 21st century tell the story of their use. I did my first-born child's astrology chart before he was a week old, and I took my astrology calculating books and Ephemeris with me to the hospital when I gave birth to my second son. By the time our daughter arrived, this was standard procedure.

My first child, I planned astrologically to be a Pisces girl, I guess like me. He arrived as an Aries boy. He was past his due date when I was instructed to go to the clinic in a nearby town to get a non-stress test. During the test his heartbeat went down a few times and so we were asked to go to the hospital where I was to give birth in San Diego about 35 miles away from the clinic.

It was the afternoon on a full moon, and I was not in labor. I was aware that up to two thirds of births occur on the full moon and I did not want my baby to be born on the full moon. University Hospital, at the time, was an aging teaching hospital.

When my husband and I arrived all the birthing rooms were full, so they put me in a recovery room. The nurses hooked my belly and me up to monitors. doctors came in and kept checking how many centimeters my cervix had opened.

I repeatedly told them that I was fine and so was the baby, and I wanted to go home. I also explained that I did not want my baby on the full moon. This was in 1983 and the doctors and nurses were curious to know why I didn't want my baby born on the full moon.

I patiently described to them that I did not want my baby's sun to be opposite their moon, that this configuration creates conflict and challenges. They accepted my theory/belief. After much poking and prodding, the doctor came in and told me that I could go home, but that they wanted me to return the next day.

At that very moment I had a huge, powerful, and long contraction. "I don't want to go home," I disappointedly replied. "I am having a huge contraction."

"What about the full moon?" my husband Jim said. "Forget about the full moon," was my reply.

Two and a half hours later I gave birth in a delivery room where my husband barely made it into scrubs, the baby came so fast.

So, now I had my beautiful son in my arms, healthy, while the women who were occupying the birthing rooms when I arrived five hours earlier were still in labor. With a sun in Aries and a moon in Libra, our son Jesse is a natural leader (Aries) who knows how to work well (Libra) with all kinds of people and personalities. He has a PhD in European History from UCLA [proud smile].

We understand as a modern society that astrology and astronomy were sacred for the ancients. The pyramids in Egypt and places like Stonehenge and Machu Picchu are aligned with equinoxes and solstices in an exactness that defies our contemporary imaginations, on three different continents.

Consider that for millennia humanity lived in nomadic tribes, under the evening stars. By following the cycles of the stars, they could determine when to plant seeds and when to harvest. They saw shapes in the stars of men and horses and bows and arrows. They felt the meaning of the constellations through an Earthly and cosmic remembrance.

The Indigenous around our world knew they came from the stars. They had the knowledge that the planets, including Earth, revolved around the sun. When Galileo announced his discovery in the 1600s that the Earth was not the center of our solar system he was arrested and identified as a heretic, defying the accepted belief that the Earth was the center of the solar system.

We Forgot

As we lost the knowledge of our unity and Divinity 12,000–13,000 years ago, we lost the knowledge of our birth from the stars. The Native Americans call this the *Fourth World of Separation,* and this is where we have been for this transit through the Duality half of our 26,000-year cycle or Platonic year.

And so, humanity has warred and conquered, reinforcing this separation. We created separate nations and warred over the borders which through killing and conquest shifted and moved in an endless dynamic of death and despair for humanity.

We formed spiritual systems based upon a God that was separate from us—up in the sky somewhere, in a place we call heaven in much of the world. The first formal belief system, Hinduism, emphasizes the Unity of all life, as well as reincarnation. Those spiritual systems that followed focused in a greater way on differences and the separation of God from humanity.

John Randolph Price, a visionary and philosopher wrote in his pocket sized, *The Abundance Book,* about how the message of Jesus Christ was one of Oneness and Unity. But through the efforts of those in power, this truth was subverted and repressed.

Price writes about those who came after Jesus and their efforts to keep alive the spiritual truth of our Oneness with all life and with Creative Source.

> The Mystery Schools of Asia, Egypt, Persia and Greece provided an invaluable service to humankind by reawakening the spiritual powers in a core group of dedicated men and women. And this knowledge of harmony and fulfillment continued in sacred books and secret teachings… in the Hebrew Qabbalah, by Hindu and Buddhist Mystics, in the Gnostic writing or early Christianity, and in certain passages not removed from the Bible (3).

It is clear that throughout the cycle of the Fall from Unity consciousness, 13,000 years ago, that the cosmic truth of our origin and Unity with Source includes our Divinity. This knowledge was retained by the Mystery schools and secret societies as well as by the Indigenous.

John Price describes how these teachings of Jesus Christ such as John 10:13, "I and the Father are one, and John 14:12, "Truly, truly I say to you, whoever believes in me will also do the works that I do; and greater works than these will he do, because I am going to the Father," was reframed by those in power at the time.

Through the inspiration and teachings of Jesus, the Gnostics (from the Greek word "gnosis" meaning "Knowledge") continued the esoteric teachings. Their writings emphasized the Oneness of God and man, the divinity of the individual, and the creative power of each man to rise above limitation (3).

As a Licensed Religious Science Spiritual Practitioner since 2015, through Seaside Center for Spiritual Living, I recognize these as precisely the teachings of Ernest Holmes who published his *Science of Mind* book in 1926. But to many, even in the 21st century—these are blasphemous words—that we are Divine expressions of Spirit and that like Spirit we too can consciously create as Jesus did.

The spiritual truth is that we are all co-creators in an infinite universe full of infinite potential and possibilities. We are coming from a three-dimensional world bound by our consciousness of space. But this is an extremely limited perception of reality that has kept us bound within the walls of our senses and our logical mind.

Remembering Our Divinity

Again, these are contemporary beliefs of the New Thought movement that was birthed by the Transcendentalist Movement in America in the 19th century, based on the thoughts and writings of Ralph Waldo Emerson.

In his famous essay, "Self-Reliance," Emerson opens with a poem:
Ne te quaesiveris extra.

Man is his own star; and the soul that can
Render an honest and a perfect man,
Commands all light, all influence, all fate;
Nothing to him falls early or too late.
Our acts our angels are, or good or ill,
Our fatal shadows that walk by us still.
Epilogue to Beaumont and Fletcher's Honest Man's Fortune
(Emerson's Essays, 31)

Humans are individual stars who can bring in the light and create a life of perfection and balance in accord with the angels, if we choose. In the opening paragraph of his essay *Self-Reliance,* Emerson boldly declares: "To believe in your own thought, to believe that what is true for all men—that is genius" (Ibid. 31).

After almost two millennia of thought control through the structure of Western theology, Emerson restates the teachings of Jesus and the Gnostics who then codified Jesus' teachings into their belief system. In fact, Emerson refers to the accepted and established beliefs of his time to the worshipping of thought leaders from the past. "Familiar as the voice of mind is to each, the highest merit we ascribe to Moses, Plato and Milton is that they set at naught books and traditions, and spoke not what men, but what they thought" (Ibid. 32). Emerson continues: "A man should learn to detect and watch that gleam of light which flashes across his mind from within, more than the luster of the firmament of bards and sages" (Ibid. 32).

 He advises his readers that we should look within to our own sparks and flashes of insight, instead of aligning our lives with the thoughts and teachings of others, no matter how great. We need to look within for wisdom as did the thought leaders who came before us.

Emerson continues as he points out why this is essential; to honor oneself first. "Yet he dismisses without notice his thought, because it is his. In every work of genius, we recognize our own rejected thoughts; they come back to us with a certain alienated majesty" (Ibid.).

If we don't heed our intuition and thoughts, we miss great opportunities. We all know that feeling of recognizing in a creation what we had thought of doing but didn't because we had no faith in our connection to the Divine—believing it existed only in others of greatness.

One of Emerson's most quoted lines from this essay is: "There is a time in every man's education when he arrives at the convictions that envy is ignorance; that imitation is suicide" (Ibid.). Not much later in the text Emerson declares; "Trust thyself" (33). This message matches the teachings of Jesus Christ and the Gnostics. But the nearly two millennia that separated these gentlemen in time was filled with a different message that discounted and denied the Divinity within each of us, as a way to maintain power and control over a still awakening humanity.

How We Got Here

At the beginning of the Piscean age a new belief system emerged called Christianity, named after Christ. The Gnostics were honoring the Christ consciousness teachings to "love thy neighbor as thyself." However, this spiritual truth was subverted when, according to John Randolph Price in *The Abundance Book:*

> In A.D. 180, Irenaeus, Bishop of Lyons, attacked
> independent thinking and all teachings related to the
> Oneness of God and man. Believing that a spiritual
> consciousness and a personal union with God would
> undermine the authority of the Priests, he directed his wrath
> upon Gnosticism... The shift in mind direction from within
> to without had begun, and the innate power of the individual
> was gradually given to an outer structure and a lower
> authority (5).

After this, Emperor Theodosius declared Christianity as the official religion of the state in 395. The result was the "Institution assumed complete control over individual minds, and humanity entered the thousand-year period referred to as the Dark Ages" (5). Price states, "The Western mind was kept in the dark until the institutional structure began to crack in the 1500s and the eternal principles of Oneness and Unity began to surface" (5).

When Moses returned with the Ten Commandments, he found his people worshiping a false God in the form of a golden calf. This calf represents the bull symbolized by the Age of Taurus. Moses' rejection of the golden calf signified the end of the Age of Taurus and ushered in the Age of Aries or the Ram. Christ was often depicted as the "lamb" of God referring to the ram.

Secret Societies such as the Rosicrucians, known as "Fraternity of the Rosy Cross," remained underground until 1614 when they published the "Order's Manifesto," challenging the religious intolerance of the time. Freemasonry—"more ancient than any of the world's living religions," according to Albert Pike—continued the chain of Sacred Mysteries" (7).

And so, the promise of the all-loving Christ consciousness united in Oneness with Creative Source, which Jesus defined as the "Father," slipped into a state of oblivion for one thousand years. Price states, "In fact, the first 400 years of this period is considered the "Barren Age" in Europe, as few advances in literature, science, and education were contrived for the future of the race" (5).

Not only are we seeded by the stars with the Divinity of Creative Source of All That Is, but we reincarnate as the Buddhists and Hindus understood, over and over. Kryon states that we have lived many lives on the Earth, and lives in other constellations and planets in the universe. So, we are our own ancestors. We lived during this long period known as the "Dark Ages."

Man co-opted the message of infinite and unconditional love for all life, taught by Jesus the Christ, for political purposes of maintaining power over the populations they ruled. This dominance blocked the light of the Christ that we are all One, and that we too can become the Masters of our own lives, as Christ demonstrated in multiple miracles he performed.

These miracles went beyond the limitations of three dimensions, tapping into a higher frequency of physics, feeding thousands of people with a few fish and loaves, walking on water, raising Lazarus from the dead, healing the blind and crippled right on the spot where he stood.

We find ourselves now at the threshold of a new Age in the zodiac. Each of the twelve signs of the zodiac takes 2160 years to move through before it goes into the next sign. We are on the cusp of the Age of Aquarius, which is about the coming together of the greater community of humanity.

And so, we find ourselves in 2020, in the midst of a global pandemic with the Covid-19 virus. In addition, a global groundswell of largely peaceful protests are declaring the Oneness of humankind and rejecting our history of separation by skin color. Price addresses how the New Thought Movement that erupted in the 1800s, "moved across Europe and the United States like a tidal wave." He described the blossoming of what he describes as "esoteric philosophy and practical mysticism" (7).

The Transcendental movement begun by Emerson was followed by the Metaphysical Movement led by Phineas Quimby. Mary Baker Eddy founded Christian Science followed by the New Thought Movement led by Charles and Myrtle Fillmore of Unity, Nona Brooks of Divine Science, Emma Curtis Hopkins who was considered to be the "teacher of teachers," and Ernest Holmes of Religious Science. Paramahansa Yogananda founded the Self-Realization Fellowship, introducing an Eastern influence on these alternate pathways to formal religion.

A New light of spirituality is flowering in the shadow of the emerging New Age of Aquarius. Despite the 1,000-year-long repression of the spiritual truths of prosperity and the Oneness of all life through the institutions of organized religion, the light began to emerge. It happened first with the birth of Protestantism in the 1500s, and then the explosion of the New Thought movement in the 1800s in America.

We find ourselves not only on the cusp of the Aquarian Age but at the marker of our solar system's sun's 26,000-year revolution around Alcyone—to a time of seismic change of Integration into our Divinity, consciously and collectively!

We call this, "THE SHIFT!

Chapter 5

The Lockdown and Social Justice

6/11/2020

During what has become known as the global "lockdown," which saved hundreds of millions of virus cases and millions of lives, and continues today, we as global citizens have had the opportunity to go within. There are remarkable photos from around the world.

The first image sent to me by my Vietnamese manicurist, Nancy, was of the Shibuya Crossing in Tokyo, which was almost vacant. In June of 2019, CNN identified this intersection as the busiest in the world. In fact, "approximately 2,500 pedestrians cross at a time coming from all directions at once" (3/5/2018 world atlas.com).

We went to the Shibuya intersection on the first day of sightseeing with my son Brendon and daughter Ada, at the end of his junior year abroad. Later, our entire family experienced this wild intersection and saw that between the cars going and the people walking, there is a brief moment when the multi-intersection is eerily empty, and then the action begins. It was so odd to see this scene almost empty due to the global lockdown.

This shows the degree to which we have adapted and shown resilience as a species and as humanity. We have learned to physically distance. Almost all of us wear masks in public and masks are required in most places to enter a store. The 11 days of peaceful protests that followed the videos of the murder of George Floyd have been a source of hope and upliftment for humanity's renewal. As people have marched across the globe in cities and towns and hamlets, most are wearing masks to protect others.

Masks

When we were in Tokyo with our family, we observed many people wearing masks. Rell, a veterinary doctor, kept reminding us that the mask does not protect people from getting sick, but it does protect others from getting germs or viruses from the wearer of the mask.

This conversation we had in Tokyo became an international topic in March and April of 2020. As Dr. Anthony Fauci stated, who has served as the director of the National Institute of Allergy and Infectious Diseases. "Wearing a mask is a sign of respect. I respect you and you respect me" (television news broadcast).

And so, we have gone within. We have returned to the womb, which is our home, our nest, a safe retreat for most of us, away from the threat of catching Covid-19. Those succumbing to the virus, for the most part, are elderly and those in assisted living. Elder care facilities have been hit particularly hard. Over 100,000 lives have been lost to this disease.

But going within saved millions of lives and kept millions out of hospitals and ICU's. Humanity has come together in a way no one could have imagined before this invisible microbe began circulating round our world. Dr. Anthony Fauci states that this virus was his "greatest nightmare, a virus that took only one month to bring the entire world onto our knees" (news broadcast).

Football's Mea Culpa

And so we are on our knees, and taking a knee is a sign of protest first taken by Colin Kaepernick, the quarterback for the San Francisco 49ers, in August of 2016, during the national anthem played before the game. At the time he stated, "I am not going to stand up to show pride in a flag for a country that oppresses Black people and people of color.... To me, this is bigger than football and it would be selfish on my part to look the other way. There are bodies in the street and people getting paid leave and getting away with murder" (NFL Media 8, 2016). Kaepernick, who is biracial, was adopted and raised by parents who are white (*ESPN.com News Service,* August 27, 2016).

Kaepernick went on to say in an interview with ESPN, "I have to stand up for people that are oppressed…. If they take football away, my endorsements from me, I know I stood up for what is right." In 2016, Kaepernick's contract wasn't renewed, and he became a free agent who has not played professional football since, because he was rejected by the football team owners in concert for his stance on social justice.

Ironically, an announcement by Roger Goodall who presided over football during the time of Kaepernick's ostracization as the NFL Commissioner, on June 5, 2020, in a video from his home (we are all on Zoom) that stated, "We were wrong for not listening to NFL players earlier."

He went on to say in his 90 second statement:

> We, the National Football League, condemn racism and the systematic oppression of Black people. We, the National Football League, admit we were wrong for not listening to NFL players earlier and encourage all to speak out and peacefully protest.
>
> We, the National Football League, believe Black Lives Matter. I personally protest with you and want to be part of the much-needed change in this country. Without Black players, there would be no National Football League. And the protests around the country are emblematic of the centuries of silence, inequality and oppression of Black players, coaches, fans and staff (Yahoo/sports, Jasen Owens, June 5, 2020, 3:45 p.m., Roger Goodall: NFL admits "We were wrong."

The police force in Coral Gables, Florida who all took a knee during the protest march in their town, also wore masks. It is obvious that this police force has received restorative practices training in contrast to the police in Washington, D.C, who drove peaceful protesters away with tear gas, batons, and outright violence. All this, to create a path for the president of the United States to get a photo-op, in front of the historical St. John's Episcopal Church, holding a Bible upside down.

In restorative practices, those in authority do things "with" those they serve as opposed to "to," them. The Coral Gables police wore masks as a sign of respect that they did not want to get anyone sick. By taking a knee as a group, they showed the protesters they were "with" them. And you know what? The protesters stopped, took a knee, and joined the police. This showed the protesters were "with" law enforcement.

In Flint, Michigan on May 31st, Sheriff Christopher R. Swanson of Genesee County demonstrated restorative practices in action. A 27-year veteran of the sheriff's office, he showed Americans "another way." "We want to be with you for real," Sheriff Swanson said, addressing the demonstrators who gathered in Flint, Mich., according to footage from WEYI-TV" (New York Times, *Michigan Sheriff Took Off His Helmet and Marched with Protesters,* by Mariel Padilla, May 23, 2020).

Restorative Justice in Law Enforcement

"I took my helmet off and put down the batons," he said of his riot gear. He stood in the midst of the crowd and told them, "These cops love you—that cop over there hugs people," he said pointing at the officer.

And on the video, you see him looking around for the leader of the protest and when he found him he said, "What do you want? I want to make this a parade, not a protest." When Officer Swanson asked the protesters, "What else do you need?" The crowd began to chant; "Walk with us, walk with us, walk with us," so the people and law enforcement walked in unity for a mile and a half (WEYI-TV).

Sheriff Swanson said this was probably the worst tactical decision he has ever made, by taking off all the protection and going into the crowd, but the benefit far outweighed the risk… "That was the best decision to show that I am not going to create a divide, I am going to show vulnerability and walk in the crowd and make the first move." He stated that his decision to chuck the gear was spontaneous because he could feel the frustration and there had already been a confrontation with a police officer.

Sheriff Swanson let the crowd know that he and his fellow police members were not the kind of cops they had seen in Minneapolis or Washington D. C.

According to the New York Times article, "Sheriff Swanson was among several law enforcement officials who in the past few days have engaged with marchers and shown solidarity either by marching, kneeling or publicly denouncing the death of Mr. Floyd.

"I believe we saved lives last night," Sheriff Swanson said at a news conference on Sunday… Quajuan Adams, one of the protesters, also spoke at the news conference. He said the protest was not just about the George Floyds and Eric Garners of the world—it was about everyone.

"All the police forces need to make sure they are doing things the right way," he said. "They need to focus on the training, policies, what is considered being combative, what is not being combative and what forces need to be taken in certain situations"

Sheriff Swanson said people of all ages and backgrounds came from as far as Detroit and Indiana to voice their frustrations about what happened in Minneapolis. But that episode, he said, was not a reflection on all 80,000 police officers in the country.

"We became the beacon of light last night, and so we are calling for a national night of peace," he said. "It starts from law enforcement: Lay down your swords."

Over 1,000 people have been fatally shot by the police in the past year, according to the Washington Post.

Around the country, law enforcement officials have joined demonstrators protesting police brutality and the death of Mr. Floyd.

In Camden, N.J., a police chief carried a banner and led a peaceful march. In Schenectady, N.Y., police officers marched with protesters through the city's downtown area. And in Santa Cruz, Calif., police officers knelt with hundreds of protesters to honor Mr. Floyd and bring attention to police violence against Black people.

In New York City, officers took a knee in Queens and in Times Square as crowds cheered.

And in Houston, where Mr. Floyd grew up, the police chief denounced police brutality in an emotional speech.

The chief, Art Acevedo, has marched with demonstrators and has called for charges to be filed against the four officers in Minneapolis who were involved in taking Mr. Floyd into custody.

… "We have a man, a son, a brother, an uncle, a cousin, a Houstonian, a child of God that was killed by servants that are supposed to be servants of God and they showed no mercy when they put their knee of his neck," he said of Mr. Floyd (New York Times, *Michigan Sheriff Took Off His Helmet and Marched With Protesters*).

In another instance, a platoon of National Guard from Georgia, danced the Macarena alongside peaceful protesters in Atlanta, George. The protesters joined in the dance de-escalating and uniting the National Guard and protesters in unity. In restorative practices, we use a model called the "Social Discipline Window. This simple diagram of four squares within a square describes different modes of discipline.

Social Discipline Window

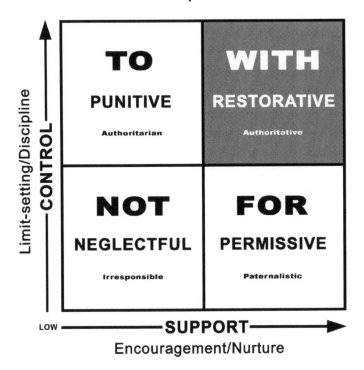

(Based on work from www.iirp.edu)

We can see in the diagram from the International Institute of Restorative Practices four different approaches to discipline. At the bottom part of the model, we see that "Not" disciplining is "neglectful," and "irresponsible." It provides low "support and encouragement." The "For" square is "permissive," but maintains a higher level of support, encouragement, and nurturing. Yet, it is described as paternalistic—believing the authority knows best how to do the activity. We also see from the vertical axis that these two bottom quadrants are low on "control" and "limit setting for discipline."

In the top two quadrants, the "To," although it is "punitive" and "authoritarian," provides much more control and limit setting outcomes than "Not" disciplining or the more permissive "For." This is the model of our race consciousness. This is the model for before the marker of

December 21, 2012. This is our known and recognized history. This is our legacy.

The "With" pane of the window is "restorative" and "authoritative" while providing "limit setting discipline" resulting in control. This is what Sheriff Swanson, the dancing National Guard, and the masked police officers in Coral Gables who took a unified knee, were practicing. They let the frustrated and angry protesters know they were "with" them.

The result was total de-escalation of the building negative energy that Sheriff Swanson stated he felt. His intuition told him that going into the crowd with riot gear was only going to escalate the situation. He had already witnessed a tussle between an individual and a police officer. He described his decision as "spontaneous." In following his gut, he took a risk, literally threw aside everything he had been taught, opened his heart and showed the world an alternate approach. It worked beyond his wildest dream.

In the YouTube video, you can see him asking the leader when he found him, "What do you want?" In doing this he let the protesters know he was deferring to their leader; he was showing mutual respect.

The response makes me weep, "Walk with us, walk with us, walk with us!" And out of this the world saw restorative practices as a positive and healthy way to bring discipline and control to a potentially out of control and even violent situation.

"The International Institute of Restorative Practices (IIRP) is a graduate school founded by Ted and Susan Wachtel based on their work at "Buxmont Academy," which served at-risk youth during the 1980s. IIRP have trained more than 100,000 professionals from 85 countries around the world (data from 2006–2018 academic years (iirp.edu).

Their website states:

> Our entire institution is guided by the premise that "people are happier, more cooperative, more productive and more likely to make positive changes when those in authority do things "with" them, rather than "to" them or "for" them (Ibid.).

We saw this on our newsfeeds. When those in positions of authority are wearing a mask or taking a knee, or throwing down their helmets or batons, or just bursting into song and dance they can de-escalate a frustrated and angry crowd. The crowds went from angry to happy.

This is the model of our entry into unity consciousness after 13,000 years of losing touch or being separate from the spiritual truth—that our origin is unity with the Source of All That Is. We are awakening, we are remembering, we are quickening to our Divinity and union with all life, not just here on Earth, but in our universe. The truth is, we are One Soul Family as Earthlings. This is what we are being initiated into.

In "Defining Restorative Practices," by the IIRP, they describe the ultimate practical applications of this view on discipline:

> The social discipline window also defines restorative
> practices as a "leadership" model for parents in families,
> teachers in classrooms, administrators and managers in
> organizations, police and social workers in communities and
> judges and officials in government (Ibid.).

For those who believe this approach is too "soft on crime," as the common political phrase goes, the wisdom of one of the initiators of this approach to discipline shares results from his research:

> The social discipline window reflects the seminal thinking of
> renowned Australian criminologist John Braithwaite, who
> has asserted that reliance on punishment as a social regulator
> is problematic because it shames and stigmatizes
> wrongdoers, pushes them into a negative societal subculture
> and fails to change their behavior (Braithwaite 1989)

Punishment does not change behavior. And we, in our country and the world, have used punishment as a way to alter behavior for millennia. It is a failed strategy, globally and historically.

Suspending a child in school once puts them into the school-to-prison pipeline, literally. This is the opposite of the intent of public and private education.

As the facts are explored, my guess is that it was the violence from the authorities that resulted in the few instances of violence or rioting on the part of the protesters. It's like as a culture, we drew a line. As one headline said, it was the "Police who were rioting," against peaceful protesters. Data later showed that 93 percent of the Black Lives Matter protesters were peaceful during the summer of 2020 in America (*TIME Magazine*, Sept 5, 2020).

The Armed Conflict Location & Event Date Project (ACLED) analyzed more than 7,750 Black Lives Matter demonstrations in all 50 states and Washington, D.C., that took place in the wake of George Floyd's death between May 26 and August 22.

Their report states that more than 2,400 locations reported peaceful protests, while fewer than 220 reported 'violent demonstrations.' The authors define violent demonstrations as including 'Acts targeting other individuals, property, businesses, other rioting groups or armed actors.' … In cities where protests did turn violent— these demonstrators are 'largely confined to specific blocks,' the report says. ACLED also highlights a 'violent government response,' in which authorities 'used force more often than not' when they are present at protests and they 'disproportionally used force while intervening in demonstrations associated with the BLM movement, relative to other types of demonstrations.' The report also references 'dozens of car-ramming attacks' on protesters by various individuals, some of whom have ties to hate groups like the Ku Klux Klan.

...The authors of the report say the Trump administration has exacerbated tensions caused by racial inequality and police brutality. President Donald Trump and high-ranking members of his administration have frequently generalized protests as violent anarchists (Ibid.).

This is not defensible in a new world where unity is our driving force. What we have is the crash of the Age of Pisces careening into the Age of Aquarius. The realm of organized religion is bucking up against a much freer and more independent vibration of the Aquarian Age where we are One. We are moving from the upper left quadrant of the Social Discipline Window, where control or limit setting discipline is done "To" us in a punitive way, to the upper right pane where discipline is expressed as a "With" action and is restorative.

This is playing out in our politics as the president of the United States urged the nation's Governors to "Dominate," the mostly peaceful protesters. In contrast, Democratic leaders joined the leader, or Speaker of the House of Representatives, Nancy Pelosi, in taking a knee for 8 minutes and 46 seconds in the rotunda of the U.S. Capitol. That is how long the Minneapolis police officer had his knee on George Floyd's neck. This was to show they were "with" him and his people.

We have made this shift in education in many school districts across America.

Chapter 6

Restorative Practices in Schools

6/14/2020

In a dark and dingy Engineering and Construction classroom at Kearny High School in San Diego, my colleagues and I met daily for the first 12 days after the end of the school year to create and develop a "project" for our students to do the following school year. We were part of what the California Department of Education refers to as a "California Partnership Academies," or career theme based small schools within a school.

After imploding economically in the summer of 1993, in a California financial crash, I took our three children camping in the Southwest for three weeks while my husband Jim stayed in his shop— where we had set up camp. Though we did this because we were broke, and in between living situations, and I thought, "If we don't get a place to live right away, we can go on a cool vacation," and so we did.

Every summer for several years we repeated this new family tradition that emerged out of going broke, including going to Zion and Bryce Canyons, the Grand Tetons, Yellowstone and eventually to Glacier National Park among many other places like the California, Oregon, and Washington coast. We would also visit our friend Tim in Baker, Oregon and drive an hour and a half back into logging roads to stay at a primitive cabin on a scenic river with two fishing ponds, with no electricity.

In 1996, I drove our children cross-country and back to see the sights and visit friends, family, and some great National Parks.

On the way back West, I heard on the radio, probably around Iowa, that Governor Pete Wilson announced that he was reducing class size in elementary school. A little voice in my head said, "Why don't you get a teaching credential?" Sounds like they will need more teachers.

I had been inspired especially by the teaching of two of my children who were in a multi-age classroom, of first, second and third graders in the Cardiff School District, where we live. The teachers had trained at the San Diego Area Writing Project at the University of California, San Diego, and their program had kids writing in new and innovative ways. My oldest son had one of these teachers in second grade, the summer after she completed her first training at San Diego Writing Project.

And so, I listened to that voice and began the long journey of taking tests to get admitted to the program at California State University San Marcos, along with two prerequisite classes. December 1999, I had my multiple subject credential, and felt ready for the new millennium. I was making a shift in my life in my mid-forties.

I substitute taught from Del Mar to Oceanside for three and a half years. I taught computers in the Cardiff District and Title 1. I also attended several summer institutes at San Diego Area Writing Project, some even from these very teachers who inspired me. My son Brendon and daughter Ada also attended their Student Summer Institute one year.

But, when I went to my daughter Ada's back-to-school night at her middle school, she had a new English teacher who also taught physical education. He said that night, "I told the student they could bring things from home to put on the classroom walls, to make the class look nice." I thought to myself, "Why doesn't he assign a writing task or group chart work to enliven the classroom walls?" On my way out of the driveway of Oak Crest Middle School a little voice said, "Why don't you get an English credential?" and I immediately thought to myself, "Why didn't I think of that first; I could teach reading and writing all day. *Oh, and I wouldn't have to teach math.*"

And so, I headed back to Cal State San Marcos and earned a credential in Single Subject in English. I took another class at San Diego Area Writing Project, which was my third summer of attending the program called, "Assessment, Assessment, Assessment." One of the facilitators was a teacher at Ada Harris Elementary where I taught computers and where my children attended from fourth to sixth grade.

Liz Goldman lived inland from me and suggested we drive in together to UCSD. At the end of the two weeks one of the facilitators, Karen Wroblewski, who had accepted the position as Literacy Administrator at San Diego High School, was stepping into the role of administrator, or what we fondly refer to as "the dark side," approached me.

San Diego High had just completed adding a large three-story building to make room for ninth graders and they were hiring 50 teachers. On the last day of the workshop, Karen asked me if I was interested in a job at San Diego High teaching 9th or 10th graders English. Wow! I had just received my secondary credential in English.

It took over a month for me to consider getting out of my beach-town bubble. Spurred on by the beginning of a new school year, I eventually called Karen and began my English teaching career. I began teaching on the 17th day of school due to my reluctance and seesawing emotions. I taught at San Diego High School for two years. Karen brought me into her small school the next year, where she was the principal. "The School of International Studies," became the International Baccalaureate school, within a cluster of six themed small schools.

This new model was an education reform movement embraced by Bill and Melinda Gates regarding small schools. The belief was that if high schools were broken up into theme based small schools, academic achievement would rise in areas which were challenged with low achievement scores. The notion was that small schools would create a greater level of personalization for students and would result in higher test scores based upon deeper relationships between students and staff.

In my first year of teaching high school English at San Diego High School in 2003–2004, we spent our professional development time planning for small schools. At the end of that second year at San Diego High, I was bumped by a teacher with more seniority coming from a school that was closing and went charter.

This is how I ended up at Crawford High School of Law and Business the following year. At Crawford, I replaced a teacher who had quit after a few weeks at the beginning of the school year because the students were so hard to manage. My job was teaching English as a Second Language (ESL), Beginner, Intermediate and Advanced. Crawford, like San Diego High, had small, themed schools and the ESL classes were composed of students from all four small schools. I was hired by the principal of the School of Law and Business in 2005, who insisted I observe the classes before accepting the position. The next day I showed up to observe but no substitute arrived, so I taught the classes the first day as a substitute.

Some years later the Area Superintendent asked us to apply for a grant to become a Law Academy, as a California Partnership Academy (CPA). The State Department of Education was issuing six grants in partnership with the California Bar Association, across the state where only one school in a county could qualify. No other schools in San Diego County applied for the grant, so we got it.

We then came under the umbrella of CPA's and began attending the annual CPA conference in Sacramento. There, 2500 educators teaching in small career academies around the state, meet and share best practices. Eventually, our team became presenters providing the attendees the experience of being in a community building circle following a group PowerPoint presentation. Every year, the coordinators gave us a larger room to present in, our breakout sessions were so well attended.

Our interest in restorative practices all began in the summer planning work in 2013 at Kearny High School. This site was selected because it had air conditioning for our summer work. In addition, it was the high school of a principal who was a strong leader of a career-based learning environment.

The law teacher who began the Academy of Law, along with me as the English teacher, and another Social Studies teacher as well as another English and Social Studies teacher, gathered in this dark, cool room. Steve Luttbeg, the law teacher, was a retired attorney who had graduated from Crawford High School in 1965 when it served a mostly white, Jewish student body.

In its current form, Crawford is the most diverse high school in California. Located in the City Heights area of San Diego, this high school serves immigrants, refugees, and African Americans. Over 38 languages are spoken, and students come from all parts of the planet. City Heights is where refugees are located when they first arrive. Therefore, the school is rich with students from East and Central Africa, Myanmar, and many countries in the Southeast, as well as Russia, Syria, and other war-torn zones. This is what made teaching all English as a Second Language (ESL), or more accurately, other languages, so interesting my first year at Crawford.

Steve was passionate about social justice and continues to be to this day. He taught his students that in 1975 there were 24,131 prison inmates in federal prison. In 2020 that number is 225,000 (*Wikipedia*). Prisons had been privatized and these private prisons lobbied politicians to go tough on crime, so they could build more prisons and make more profit.

The state of California "has built 23 prisons since 1980. In the same period, the University of California system has opened one new campus... the state's spending per prison has increased five times faster than its spending per K-12 student in the last two decades" (*HuffPost*, 8/3/2013, Saki Knafo).

> California has more than 130,000 prisoners, a huge increase
> from the state's 1980 prison population of about 25,000.
> Prisons cost California taxpayers close to 10 billion,
> compared with $604 million in 1980... Despite the 21 new

prisons built since 1980, construction hasn't kept pace with
the growth of the inmate population, and CA's prison system
is one of the most crowded in the country (Ibid.).

Clearly, we have gone through a very dark period as a nation and as a state that we would value punishment over education.

When Steve became the law teacher at Crawford, he initiated a program called "Teen Court," a diversion program for youth run out of *Say San Diego*, an organization that focuses on youth and equity. In coordination with Juvenile Court, this program provides an opportunity for offenders to go to Teen Court and agree to the requirements of their peers. The other choice is to go to Juvenile Court and face the demands of a judge. In order to qualify for Teen Court, the offender must admit guilt ahead of time.

Steve trained our students from the Academy of Law in his law class to be the peer jurors. After a courtroom was built for us in a classroom, he oversaw Teen Court after school. Steve would preside as the judge, black gown and all, and the students would sit in the jury box and take notes. The individual charged with a crime would speak in the witness box and often their parents or guardians would speak as well.

The students would then gather while the youth offender, and their accompanying adult would step outside the classroom/courtroom. The students would determine what they felt would be fair, and often it was more than what a Juvenile Judge would require. Students set specific requirements for the offender to complete within six weeks. They might include community service, writing a letter of apology, or drug counseling among other steps to take.

If the youth offender completed what the student peers laid out for them in six weeks, the record is destroyed. Parents and youth overwhelmingly rate Teen Court Juvenile court by a large margin. For example, in a study conducted by the Urban Institute Justice Policy Center by Jeffrey A. Butts, Janeen Buck and Mark B. Coggeshall titled *The Impact of Teen Court On Young Offenders,* in a questionnaire on youth response before court, teens answered the question, "I wish I had gone to regular court, not teen court," they agreed at the following percentages: Alaska, 3%, Arizona, 5%, Maryland 3% and Missouri 4%. When parents filled out questionnaires and were asked the following questions, "My child will probably benefit from teen court," they agreed at the following percentages: Alaska, 97%, Arizona, 99%, Maryland, 98% and Missouri 93% (ojp.gov). Our students volunteered after school to participate in this program that supports youth in San Diego.

At our summer planning Steve had arranged for a few people to come as experts on social justice. One individual was Linda Williams, a retired elementary teacher who was passionate about restorative practices and was familiar with all the leadership in the San Diego Unified School District who wanted to shift the district away from zero tolerance. One individual who was a proponent of restorative justice was Chief Little John, who headed the district school police.

The other individual was a young woman who had received a master's degree at the University of San Diego in social justice, named Justine Darling. After speaking with the five of us she said, "You are going to have to meet my partner." In my mind, I thought she was referring to a partner who she did restorative practices with. But, in fact, she was referring to her romantic partner, who it turns out, had been on our Advisory Board since its inception. Small world, "Andrew? We know him!"

We developed a year-long project around community building circles, restorative practices, and Teen Court. Steve had a belief in the students *that was sincere and deep*. He began introducing these topics in his law class. Before we knew it, the students in the 11th grade were invited to present at a Bi-National Peace Conference held at the University of San Diego's (USD), Joan Kroc Peace Center. Included were students from Tijuana, Baja, California, and San Diego County. Those students went on to become leaders in restorative practices.

At the end of the school year, City Schools (San Diego Unified) has their California Partnership Academies (CPA's) and other project-oriented programs present at the Career College Technical Education (CCTE) Showcase. This is a district competition for the best projects. Students set up their props in booths. Leaders from various industries including science, engineering, culinary etc., walk around and judge the various projects, including interviewing participants. This is project-based learning at its best.

We had done a project on *To Kill a Mockingbird* in our first showcase. As the English teacher, I had students re-enact the courtroom scene, writing their own script from the text in the novel. They would do this re-enactment in the courtroom we had. At our first showcase, we won first prize in the Rookie category for this project.

In the later Showcase the students won first prize for the entire district for their project on restorative practices. In 2013, I began doing community building circles in my classroom every Monday, at the beginning of the year, in every class. The school was in the first phase of a major remodel, and I was moved to an art classroom that was large, so I set up a large oval of chairs on one side of the class.

When I retired in 2017 after being the Teacher of the Year at Crawford and a semi-finalist for the district teacher of the year (top 16), San Diego Unified officially became a restorative district, four years after our first meeting at Kearny High School. The district established a department to direct the program. The first director of the Restorative Justice Practices Department soon thereafter became the leader of Student Support Services at San Diego County Office of Education. This agency has now trained thousands of educators, para-educators, counselors, administrators, and youth support professionals in restorative practices.

What we began in 2013 in a dingy construction classroom has now blossomed into a full-blown movement that is a gift to humanity at this time in 2020. We do not need to invent new strategies for peaceful living but tap into what already exists and grow it in the realm of restorative practices.

We were not the only educators teaching restorative practices. However, our career theme focus on law and justice enabled our team of teachers, counselors and administrators to teach restorative practices across curriculum from English to Social Studies, and Science to Math.

The support we received from Justine Darling who ended up working for the National Conflict Resolution Center (NCRC) in San Diego, and the San Diego Unified School District, was invaluable. In the Law class, students were taught how to facilitate community building circles and how to do peer mediations between students to resolve conflict.

Over time, Justine was joined by the powerful teachers of restorative practices such as Jen Vermillion who has a master's degree in social justice from University of San Diego and also worked for NCRC. These restorative justice experts spent much time working with students and staff at Crawford and at Lincoln High School in San Diego Unified. Later, Lara Anderson first volunteered and then worked for NCRC providing much heartfelt support for our students and staff.

San Diego Unified now has a department dedicated to restorative practices that serves all schools. One of our colleagues from Crawford and the Academy of Law and Justice, Danielle Vincent-Griffith (VG), who taught Chemistry and was the Teacher of the Year at Crawford the year before me, as well as a finalist for District Teacher of the Year (top 12). She wrote curriculum for two years on positive behavior strategies before returning to the classroom. As a chemistry teacher she used community building circles in her classes. She also graduated from Reed College, which is my alma mater in Portland, Oregon. It is ironic that as Reedies we were teacher of the year back-to-back in the same high school, considering the two decades difference in age.

It is rewarding to see the implementation of and training in restorative practices taking place in education, including training students as facilitators. They are naturals! These strategies empower all stakeholders in education to raise the bar on how we interact with one another across communities and nations. San Diego Unified is committed to student agency and strategies for sharing and articulating various points of view in a managed environment where everyone's voice is valued.

Chapter 7

Moving Into Higher Dimensional Realities

6/17/2020

In the Crawford Academy of Law and Justice, we circle up when challenges arise. It can be something as simple as an experience with a substitute, or much more serious discussions such as theft. What is so remarkable from an educator's point of view is that the teacher or adult is no longer the mediator. Students solve common problems through sharing equal voices along with the teacher.

There is no hierarchy; the teacher's voice is equal to every other voice. This is where we get into the Indigenous model of the circle and the equality of all voices. Like technology in the classroom, this shifts the power dynamic from the teacher to the community. From an educator's perspective, there is nothing more beautiful than students taking accountability for situations and solving them in a safe community of peers.

Crawford High School is the lowest-performing High School in San Diego Unified. The reason it is low performing is because of the diversity of the campus. Many of our students need to learn English as a second or third language while learning high school curriculum. Crawford has 100% free and reduced lunch because when families filled out the federal survey it was determined over 90% were below the poverty level. The district/state provides 100% of the students with free morning breakfast, a mid-morning snack and lunch. At this high school, multiple cultures from all over the world come together on a peaceful and harmonious campus.

Yes, there are skirmishes, and yes, kids get high in the bathroom, and yes, we sometimes have behavior issues in our classrooms and on our campus.

When the Academy of Law and Justice students began doing Peer Mediation on campus, it was often following a confrontation. The model perplexed some of our first administrators because the mediation takes place guided by two students who have been trained in peer mediation. No adult is in the room, which is what confused administrators at first.

The way it worked at Crawford is that a Vice Principal would send the name of two or more students who had a confrontation or even a fight, along with the schedules of these students to a designated teacher at the Academy.

The teacher would ask students who would like to volunteer. Students always volunteer to do peer mediation, some more than others, but you always have eager folks. The two mediators each go to the classes to get one of the two (or more) students. The teacher then lets them into a room where the trained mediators set the intention for a win - win situation. Though neutral, each mediator is an advocate or support for one of the students.

I was the point of contact teacher my last two years teaching at Crawford. When the students who were in conflict come to an agreement, they sign a contract that is written by one or both peer mediators.

In my experience, the Vice-Principal would advise us before any real physical or verbal contact had gotten out of hand. So, often we mitigated conflict before an event occurred. There was a small teacher's lounge next to my classroom, and we used that for peer mediation, so I was right next door. It was always fun to see the look on the faces of the students who were in conflict when I would unlock the door of the small room, and then walk away as the adult. They were like "Where are you going?" And I would explain that it was their peers who would be doing the moderating.

When students from war-torn countries like Somalia, The Congo, Sudan, Myanmar, Muslims from Russia, and other regions of conflict, living in poverty, can teach Peace in America, we have a template that is moving from the third dimension to the fifth dimension. We have a model for peace that is multicultural and based upon simple principles of respect.

I studied for almost twenty years with a Native American whose tribe, the Acjachemen built the Mission at San Juan Capistrano. The Indigenous often speak about moving from the Fourth World of Separation to the Fifth World of Peace. Star Mother, like many Indigenous of our time, found herself honored by those outside of her tribe. So, she taught the sacred traditions of "her people," which for the Acjachemen are based upon the rainbow. I am honored and grateful to have been a recipient of these teachings as someone outside of this beautiful and ancient indigenous culture.

Like our community circles, we always sat in a circle with Star Mother. This is part of the wisdom of the ancients that has been borrowed by restorative practices, reinforcing the equality of all within the circle.

The fourth World of Separation is where we have been for a long time as a global culture. The Platonic Year diagram indicates we have been in this consciousness for 13,000 years. We have been separated and divided, as our history records, marked by a series of seemingly endless war and conflict. The prophecy, however, has always been that we will move into the Fifth World of Peace.

This is very much like moving from the third dimension of materiality and division to the fifth dimension of peace and harmony. The path is the fourth dimension which can be compared or described as "the dark night of the Soul."

Those of us who grew up in the 1960s remember the name of the rock group, the Fifth Dimension. In reading Kerry's *The Starseed*

Transmission, decades ago, one of the statements he added has stuck with me. I paraphrase, "That we (Baby Boomers) were the first generation to see the angels in over 2,000 years."

We see social unrest in June 2020 over the brutality of the police in our country, especially against Black men. This is a theme that has run through our American history from the dawn of this nation.

Our generation was awakened by the shocking and destabilizing assassination of President John F. Kennedy. I remember hearing about it in my fourth-grade classroom at Kings Highway Elementary School in Westport, Connecticut. A fifth or sixth grader told the teacher the news at the classroom door. It didn't really sink in until we all got home and began to watch the news that then went on for days.

Much like our contemporary global shutdown for the Covid-19 virus, the world came to a standstill and collectively mourned the murdering of hope and youth and a new vision for our country. Global leaders traveled to America for a funeral that was both tragic and historical.

I will always remember the image of a beautiful Jacqueline Kennedy dressed in black, with a light black veil over her face, walking beside Bobby Kennedy, the Attorney General and the president's younger brother. He gently held her hand as they followed the horse-drawn carriage carrying the casket of her husband, father of her children, and our president, on foot.

Just like today, there was the feeling of chaos. which only increased with the assassination of Dr. Martin Luther King, Jr. in Memphis, Tennessee and then Bobby Kennedy during a campaign stop in Los Angeles in a run for the presidency. As a young person in the 1960s, it felt as though everything was out of control, especially in America. There didn't seem to be any adults capable of taking charge of the situation. It was living in political limbo.

During his presidency, as a response to civil rights clashes in the cities, Kennedy submitted a weak civil rights bill to Congress that he did not actively support. It was the "Children's March," in Birmingham,

Alabama that shifted events. Birmingham was considered to be the most racist city in the United States and often referred to as "Bomingtown." The idea of the march was conceived in May of 1963.

As advisor to Dr. King and a leader of the Southern Christian Leadership Conference, Reverend James Bevel came up with the idea of a protest comprised of children. They initiated the Children's Crusade and began their march on Birmingham. On May 2nd, thousands of children left their classrooms through windows as many teachers turned their backs, giving tacit permission to join the march.

The children then walked to the 16th Street Baptist Church where they were released to march in groups of 50. When Dr. King spoke from the pulpit, he said, "I think it is a mighty fine thing for children, what you're doing because when you march, you're really standing up; because a man can't ride your back unless it's bent" (Daily Beast. Dottie L. Joiner, *How the Children of Birmingham Changed the Civil Rights Movement*. Pub. May 02, 2013).

According to child marcher Raymond Goolshy, who stood next to Dr. King as he gave his inspiring speech to the children, and who was in the first group of children sent out to march, "Our job was to decoy the police. We got arrested about a block and a half from the 16th Street" (Ibid.). The next day, the children reported to school, climbed out of the windows, and returned to the 16th Street Baptist Church, like the day before.

Again, children were released to march in groups of 50. But Bull Connor, an authoritarian commissioner of public safety [irony], "brought out fire hoses and attack dogs and turned them on the children" (Ibid.). This scene was covered by the press, and the images were shown on the national news along with headlines from around the world.

Marian Wright Edelman, founder and president of the Children's Defense Fund stated:

> Pictures of bravery and determination of the Birmingham
> children as they faced the brutal firehoses and vicious police

dogs were splashed on the front pages of newspapers across America and helped turn the tide of public opinion in support of the civil right movement's fight for justice (Ibid.).

The result was that the children were arrested, put in paddy wagons, and taken to jail. The Birmingham jails ran out of room, so the children were relocated to the fairground where they slept on cots and sang freedom songs while the movement's leaders raised money for their bail.

When the children were released from jail, they would return to the march the following day. Finally, under political pressure, "Birmingham negotiated a truce with King, and on May 10, Connor was removed from his position" (Ibid.).

According to Clayborn Carson, director of the Martin Luther King, Jr. Research and Education Institute of Stanford University, King "had never led a massive campaign of civil disobedience before, and there were not enough adults prepared to be arrested. So, the Children's Crusade turned the tide of the movement" (Ibid.).

In one account, King at first was reluctant to use children as protesters and was concerned for their safety. "He prayed and reflected and finally accepted that putting children in danger could help determine their future" (Washington Post, *Children have changed America before, braving firehoses & police dogs for civil rights*, Steven Livingston, 3/23/2018). Livingston states, "The 1963 children's crusade changed everything" (Ibid.). He described how." When the children kept coming, Connor turned firehoses on them, knocking the children to the ground and spinning them down the street" (Ibid.). Then the police gathered the children and put them in squad cars, paddy wagons and buses for their trip to jail.

By the end of the first day of the children's crusade, "More than 500 kids were behind bars charged with parading without a permit, some 75 youngsters crammed into cells meant for 8 adults" (Ibid.). This became national news and President Kennedy was now aware of the protest.

On May 3rd, the second day of the Children's March, and the next day, May 4, 1963:

> … The young protesters hit the streets en masse, confronting police armed with snarling German shepherds in addition to the water cannon blasts. To supercharge the water jets, firefighters had funneled the flow of two hoses into one nozzle, packing it with such a ballistic fury it dislodged bricks from buildings. These jets were driven across the kids' bodies, lacerating their flesh, tearing clothes off their backs, hitting elm trees in nearby Kelly Ingram Park, the blasts ripped off the bark. The children, knocked to the pavement, crawled away; some struggled to their feet with bloody noses and gashes on their faces (Ibid.).

The next morning the images of the children sliding down sidewalks and streets at the power of the firehoses, in newspapers across the nation, hit the president's breakfast table. Kennedy was disgusted by what he saw. His brother, Attorney General Bobby Kennedy stated, "What Bull Connor did down there and the dogs and the hoses and the pictures with Negroes, is what created a feeling in the United States that more needed to be done" (Ibid.). This march had finally galvanized the Kennedy administration to take proactive steps toward comprehensive civil rights legislation. For two and a half years, Kennedy did not directly address civil rights, focusing on issues of national security, the space program, and the economy. But the Children's March opened his eyes.

A month later Governor George Wallace, on June 11th, stood in the schoolhouse door to stop two qualified Black students from enrolling in the University of Alabama. It was that same evening that "Kennedy hastily went on national television to decry the immorality of segregation and to announce plans to introduce civil rights legislation" (Ibid.).

Kennedy and his brother Bobby were catalysts for change in race relations in the United States. Although President Kennedy was cautious in his approach to race, he "sent hundreds of U.S. Marshals to enforce a court order to admit African American, James Meredith, to the University of Mississippi. The marshals encountered fierce resistance from violent segregationists. In a melee, two people were killed and dozens injured" (pbs.org. African Experience).

But King had gambled and won with the children's bravery.

For King, the children's courage was pivotal for the civil rights movement.

"Looking back," King wrote later, "it is clear that the introduction of Birmingham's children into the campaign was one of the wisest moves we made. It brought a new impact to the crusade, the impetus that we needed to win the struggle" (Ibid.).

Four months after the Children's March, the Sixteenth Street Baptist Church was dynamited by the Ku Klux Klan, killing four Black girls (Ibid.). Six months following the assassination of Kennedy, President Johnson was able to pass the "Civil Right Act of 1964." President Lyndon Johnson was able to get the "Civil Rights Act of 1964," This was a landmark law.

Under the Civil rights Act of 1964, segregation on the grounds of race, religion or national origin was banned at all places of public accommodation, including courthouses, parks, restaurants, theaters, sports arenas and hotels. No longer could blacks and other minorities be denied service simply based on the color of their skin.

Title VII of the Civil rights Act barred race, religious, national origin and gender discrimination by employers and labor unions and created an Equal Employment Opportunity Commission with the power to file lawsuits on behalf of aggrieved workers (*History.com*).

On the heels of this landmark legislation came the "Voting Rights Act of 1965," which prohibits racial discrimination in voting

In addition to all the racial unrest at that time was the Vietnam War. This "first generation who could hear the angels sing," not only climbed out of classrooms to march for civil rights, but many youths protested the Vietnam War. For the first time in millennia, a generation said, "Hell, no, we won't go!"

This created protests and riots that were interwoven with the civil rights movement. When the end of the Vietnam War was announced, the American military had to flee Vietnam in a humiliating defeat. We wondered, "What is going to happen to the music?" The music of the 60's and 70's had been shaped by the upheaval of human rights and a sweeping embrace of no more war, an anti-war movement.

It did not look like it, but we were moving into higher levels of consciousness, away from war, towards unity and peace. The peace sign that was born in the mid '60s, along with the symbol of holding up our first two fingers in a "V," have been absorbed as global symbols of a generation that broke with war and saw a higher calling for humanity. We were moving in the direction of the Fifth World of Peace, after thousands of years of endless war and conquest!

Chapter 8

Ascension Status & the Indigo Children

6/22/2020

At this time of the precession of the equinox, the 26,000-year marker that we passed as humanity on December 12, 2012, we have moved into ascension status as a planet.

From the cosmic viewpoint, once we as a global civilization passed this marker without destroying ourselves or experiencing Armageddon, as our prophecies predicted, our cosmic path became one of world peace. Civilizations from planets who have achieved the full cycle of ascension around love, peace and conscious creation then seed new civilizations with the DNA of the Divine, or Spirit, or All That Is; whatever you may choose to name it.

The Harmonic Convergence occurred on August 16, and 17, 1987 and is the designation given "to the world's first synchronized global peace meditation indicated by historian Jose Arguelles, based upon the Mayan calendar and on the relatively rare alignment of the planets. (The Wild Rose.net).

The period in history known as Harmonic Convergence was defined by Jose Arguelles as,

> "...the point at which the counter-spin of history finally
> comes to a momentary halt, and the still imperceptible spin
> of post-history commences." It was the fulfillment of this
> prophecy of Quetzalcoatl known as the Thirteen Heavens

and Nine Hells. The prophecy stated that following the ninth hell, humanity would know and experience an unprecedented New Age of Peace. The Hell cycle ended on August 16, 1987; the Harmonic Convergence began on August 17. Thus began the projected twenty-five-year culmination of the 5,125-year Great Cycle of History, as well as the 26,000-year cycle of evolution, both slated to end in 2020 (Ibid.).

1987 Harmonic Convergence
(August 16–17)

⊙ Sun: 0° Virgo
☾ Moon: 0° Virgo
♀ Venus: 0° Virgo
♂ Mars: 0° Virgo
☿ Mercury: 4° Virgo (orb. of influence)

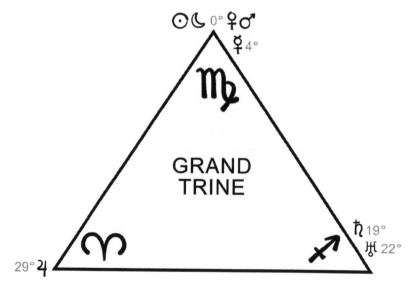

♃ Jupiter: 29° Aries   ♄ Saturn: 19° Sagittarius
                              ♅ Uranus: 22° Sagittarius

The astrological alignment is based upon a configuration known as a grand trine. A grand trine occurs when three planets are 125 degrees apart from one another forming an equilateral triangle in the cosmos. This is considered to be the highest vibration configuration in astrology.

On August 24th 1987, two luminaries and two planets were aligned at zero degrees Virgo, including the Sun, Moon, Venus, and Mars. Mercury was four degrees Virgo which is considered within the number of degrees of conjunction. So, five celestial bodies were in alignment. This five planet stellium (three planets in alignment or more in astrology), had a 125-degree positive relationship with Jupiter at 29 degrees Aries.

Uranus, on August 24th was 22 degrees Sagittarius while Saturn was 19 degrees Sagittarius, forming another conjunction. This resulted in a grand trine or a triangle, the most positive relationship between spheres.

Many people congregated at power centers and held meditations during this time. If you look at the triangle, it is a pyramid shape, the most stable geometric form, whose majesty is reflected in the pyramids of Egypt and Mayan pyramids in Mexico and Central America.

Jose Arguelles stated, "The Harmonic Convergence also began the final 25-year countdown to the end of the Mayan Long Count in 2012, which would be the so-called end of history and the beginning of a new 5,125-year cycle" (Wikipedia). This site continues:

> Evils in the modern world, e.g., war, materialism, violence, abuses, injustice, oppression, etc. would have ended with the birth of the 6th Sun and the 5th Earth on December 21, 2012. This is not known to have occurred."

But it is occurring as I write this on June 23, 2020.

On November 9, 1989, the Berlin Wall fell. On December 25, 1991, the Soviet Union fell.

Kryon, an angelic entity from the other side of the veil, came through Lee Carroll in 1989. Lee was an award-winning sound engineer, who met his second wife, Jan Tober, as she recorded the blues at his sound studio. She was involved with New Age activities at the time and asked him to come to a channeled reading for her birthday. Lee, who was a Christian when married to his first wife, did not believe in esoterica but went along because, well, it was Jan's birthday (*Kryon Homeroom Meeting,* July 2019).

At the reading Lee was told that "Kryon was trying to get a hold of him." Jan always had cassette tape audios of any readings she had done. When Lee got home, he remembered another channel had told him the same thing three years prior. Lee said at the Kryon meeting, "I had to get into Jan's stash to find that previous tape." And yes, a different channel had the same message, "Kryon is trying to contact you."

Lee heard this as "Krylon" is trying to get a hold of you and made jokes about rustproof paint trying to connect with him. As a total skeptic about all things unseen, Lee one day told Kryon that if he was real, he needed to show himself. So, Lee sat down in a chair, open (as much as he could be at the time) to receiving something.

As Lee tells it, he felt a grand love engulf his body, mind, and soul. He wept in the chair.

I discovered Kryon on YouTube after I retired from San Diego City Schools in June 2017. Now, I had the luxury of more time. I had long been aware of Abraham, a group of entities channeled through Esther Hicks, through my studies at Seaside Center for Spiritual Living.

I discovered Seaside Center for Spiritual Living after my mother passed away in Westport, Connecticut in March 2010. I went back to Connecticut for 13 days to pack up my mother's house with my sister. Janet had bought a ticket to return with me to vacation in California for three weeks. At the end of that time, she decided to stay in California. We have a close family friend who attended the Unity Center in San Diego, where she received much spiritual support in a metaphysical way, which I respected.

Seaside Center for Spiritual Living is a half a mile from my house and though I had been there for musical concerts I had never attended a Sunday service. I had looked at my sister's astrological chart and noticed she had several planets in the 12th house. She liked to hang out at bars, a 12ᵗʰ house activity, but spirituality is the foundation of this astrological house.

My thinking was that church was the same energy as the bar in terms of meeting spiritual and emotional wants and needs. So, one Sunday we went to Seaside, and we loved it. The music was amazing, anchored by a jazz band and an artistic director who blew the keys off the grand piano.

The message was positive, uplifting, and funny. Janet lived with us for a year and a half until she got herself on her feet in the midst of a huge economic recession. When she moved out of our house, she stopped going to Seaside, but I kept going. Janet would say, "I don't really know what he is saying, but I love his message anyway," of Dr. Christian Sorensen, the spiritual leader.

I began taking classes at Seaside and became a Licensed Spiritual Practitioner in Religious Science, or Science of Mind. This is a philosophy and a way of life created by Ernest Holmes in the spirit of the New Thought movement birthed by the American Transcendentalists. It is based upon the reality that our thoughts create our world. There is a large banner in what we refer to as the sanctuary that states: "Change your thinking, change your life." This was not a new idea to me, but I was hooked!

I had studied with Star Mother for almost 20 years, and when our studies seemed to come to an end, I relied upon that spiritual foundation. For two decades I had driven from Cardiff-by-the-Sea to Descanso, at the top of the mountains east of San Diego. Star Mother and her husband Dan had moved there from San Diego not long before I began my studies.

Finding Seaside as a spiritual home a half a mile away was like a cosmic joke. I am grateful to my sister Janet for being the conduit, the catalyst to get me through their doors.

I knew about the Indigo children through the draft of a book on color by Nancy Tappe, who lived in Encinitas, when we had our art business.

We worked with a local printer named Elroy Printing owned by a woman named Anna from the time we moved to Cardiff in 1977.

In the early '80s, she printed a draft of *Understanding Your Life Through Color* by Nancy Tappe. She experienced the metaphysical meaning of color through her senses. Her book addressed the Indigo children, who were just being born at the time. We were fortunate to get a first peek at this seminal work.

At the same time, Jan Tober and Lee Carroll were made aware of this work and they wrote three books in the 1980s on the Indigo children. In the early 1990s, when I began to study with Star Mother, she too taught us about the Indigo children.

When I learned about Kryon in 2017, and then Lee Carroll and Lee's authorship of books on Indigo children, I thought Jan and Lee must have learned about Nancy Tappe's work on color energies because they began their work in Del Mar, California back in the 1980s. When I finally began exploring Lee's website, *Kryon.com*, I discovered Nancy's name and reference.

The first Kryon event I attended was a "Homeroom" meeting, designated as such because it is in the area where Lee first channeled Kryon in the Newport Beach area of Orange County, in California. I drove up with my friend Katie, a Practitioner Emeritus, who at the time was a spry 88-year-old. I met her at Seaside when she moved down to San Diego from Los Angeles. We arrived early at the all-day event.

When the doors opened and we walked toward the front, I asked Katie where she would like to sit. "In the front row, of course," she replied and that's where we sat. Lee, who channels Kryon and travels all over the world doing Kryon meetings, is very approachable.

During a break we went up and spoke to him. We told him we were practitioners from Seaside Center. "I lost my contact there," Lee replied, as he shared, he knew the center and what a great place it is. In my mind, I wondered if that contact was Nancy Tappe, who made her transition in 2012.

At that meeting at the end of 2018, Kryon channeled at the end, as he always does. He told us, "Democracy in America is broken," and he was right. We see the results of this daily.

From her website, we learn what Nancy's process was for seeing life colors.

> Nancy saw a rainbow of colors around all living objects. These colors constantly move and change except for one color which is constant throughout an individual's life. That color shapes and defines the individual's personality and provides a focus for each person's unique perceptions.... *Understanding Your Life Through Color* presents her entire system of information thoroughly (nancytappe.com).

This is the book that we had the draft of in the early '80s, and we ate it up. Later Tappe wrote, *Indigos: The Quiet Storm.*

On her website Nancy writes, "Indigos are the bridge to the future."

"And then there are the crystals." I heard this from a woman I sat next to at my next Kryon event at a small metaphysical bookstore in Laguna Niguel called "Awakenings." It's owner, Brandon, hosts the Homeroom Kryon events. Generally, one meeting is in the summer in a small room at the bookstore, and another is held in a nearby hotel in a large conference room setting. This woman, a retired administrator in education, knew of Nancy's work. "Crystals come in during times of transformation to assist others in their lessons" (Ibid.).

Nancy Tappe's website, dated 2009, describes the Indigos:

> In the 1960s Nancy started to perceive a new life color appearing in infants. She saw it as the color 'indigo.' Today, most people under the age of 30 have this life color (Ibid.).

This means most global citizens below the age of 40 are Indigos now, in 2020.

In a New York Times article by John Leland, January 22, 2005, titled; *"Are They Here to Save the World?"* He described the impact of Nancy Tappe's work on the world.

Indigo children were first described in the 1970s by a San Diego parapsychologist, Nancy Ann Tappe, who noticed the emergence of children with an Indigo aura, a vibrational color she had never seen before. This color, she reasoned, coincided with a new consciousness.

The article goes on to describe Lee Carroll and Jan Tober books. In *The Indigo Children,* Mr. Carroll and Ms. Tober define the phenomenon. Indigos, they write, share traits like high IQ, acute intuition, self-confidence, resistance to authority and disruptive tendencies, which are often diagnosed as attention-deficit-disorder, known as ADD, or attention-deficit-hyperactivity disorder of ADHD.

… These children demand a new model in education and as adults in politics. In the view of Carroll and Tober these "children are overmedicated," and "schools are not creative environments" (Ibid.).

The article quotes a New Thought leader, Doreen Virtue, who states, "To me these children are the answers to the prayers we all have for peace." As a former psychotherapist for adolescents, she also wrote about the Indigo children whom she refers to as "a leap in human evolution" (Ibid.). She is quoted in the article. "They're vigilant about cleaning the earth of social ills and corruption, and increasing integrity," Ms. Virtue said. "Other generations tried, but then they became apathetic. This generation won't, unless we drug them into submission with Ritalin" (Ibid.).

One parent in this article describes her 10-year-old daughter Alexandra. "Ms. Piper said… 'She has trouble finishing work in her school and wants to argue with the teacher if she thinks she's right.'" (Ibid.).

As a parent and teacher of Indigos, I absolutely love this quality of not being intimidated by authority figures.

In this revealing article Marjorie Jackson, a tai chi and yoga teacher in Altadena, CA. says she sees many Indigos in her practice. She also sees it in her own son. She states:

> The purpose of the disruptive ones is to overload the system
> so the school will be inspired to change. She said that
> schools should treat children more like adults, rather than
> placing them in a "fear-based, constrictive, no-choice
> environments, where they explode (Ibid.).

At the close of the article, 14-year-old Jasmine calmly explains; "Like the women at the table she said that Indigos have a special purpose: 'To help the world come together again. If something bad happens, I always think I can fix it. Since we have these abilities, we can help the world' (Ibid.). This article is prescient of this time in our story. The Indigos have come-of-age, and they are the change we have been waiting for.

How does this relate to the ascension of the planet? A new Earth is being birthed out of the old Earth, and a new human is emerging from the former human.

Kryon explains that he came through Lee Carroll to support humanity through the transition of "passing the marker," or December 21, 2012. He speaks of a 36-year window, with 18 years before the marker and 18 years after the marker—to make the transition to an ascended planet.

The Armageddon prophecy stated that we would not make it past 2000 or 2012 without destroying ourselves. Up until the Harmonic Convergence, according to Kryon, we were on the trajectory of self-annihilation with the Soviet Union and the United States in a nuclear arms race. We are now eight years past the marker with another ten years to complete the shift from a global pattern and record of endless wars, to a new paradigm of Peace on Earth. We are moving toward ascension into higher consciousness that lifts the vibration of our planet, our solar system, our galaxy, and our universe.

This is what our star parents did, and their star parents before them. Once they achieved ascension status, they would go starseed a new planet with the spark of Divinity that the Pleiadians gave us. According to Kryon, Earth is the new kid on the block in our universe. We are the only planet of free choice; to choose the light or to choose the dark, within our galaxy.

Our galaxy and universe are teeming with life that is on a higher vibrational frequency, and these star families are assisting us in our shift from a paradigm of war to one of infinite peace. These other star families have experienced what we are moving through, and they are here to guide us.

Kryon describes us as "the new kids on the block." He says that we will, in all likelihood, change our calendar to resetting year 1, in 2012. The years before will be considered the "barbaric" era where all we did was war against one another. Bracha Goldsmith, an astrologer, believes 2020 may be the new year 1.

Kryon likes to point out we haven't had a major war for over 70 years. Yes, there have been wars such as the Korean War, Vietnam War, Iraq War, Afghanistan War, Syrian War, etc., but they have been localized—rather than consuming the world as in World War I and World War II.

And so, we have passed the marker which means we have made it to a new level of consciousness. This is because enough individuals on the planet shifted to a consciousness of peace and unity in the 1980s to set us on a path of renewal rather than destruction.

Chapter 9

The Shift is Upon Us

6/26/2020

We are moving at warp speed ushering in a new planet and a new human based upon the dispensation of compassion. When Moses came down from Mt. Sinai and scolded the Jews for worshipping a calf, or false God, that marked the end of the Taurus Age. It lasted from 4,000 BC to 2,000 BC. The ram is the symbol of this sign in the zodiac—ushering in the Age of Aries.

At the end of the Taurean Age, when Moses came down from the mountain to speak with the people and to greet them with the new commandments from God, he became angry when he found his people had become weak and restless in his absence, and so had created a golden calf to worship. This was a sign that they had reverted to the old ways of the Taurean age of worship because they thought Moses had deserted them. Moses then forbade them the old ways of worshipping the golden calf and made them learn the ways of the new commandments" (*undersea.tripod.com/The Age of Taurus*).

Through his commandments, Moses signaled the dispensation of Law into human consciousness. When Christ ushered in the Age of Pisces, he grounded the dispensation of Love into our planetary and human consciousness. As we move deeper into the Age of Aquarius, we are experiencing the dispensation of compassion, in the words of Kryon.

Kryon described the Ten Commandments as "The Ten Suggestions," [smile], but these were basic human laws to live by, introduced to humanity millennia ago.

The shift is upon us as reflected in yesterday's paper, in fact, it's in every day's newspaper. Areas of resistance for millennia are crumbling before our very eyes and the Indigos are right there, leading the charge. Here are a few headlines from the front page of the San Diego Union Tribune on June 25, 2020: *YOUTH AT RACIAL JUSTICE RALLY IN FOR THE MARATHON, Teens gather hundreds at Kate Sessions Park to call for change, keep momentum strong, New SDPD Policy on Use of Force Put in Place,* and *CALIFORNIA VOTERS TO DECIDE FATE OF AFFIRMATIVE ACTION BAN IN NOVEMBER.* In the meantime, Confederate statues are coming down across the South, monuments that have been in place for over 120 years in some cases, tumbled in a matter of weeks.

Just as the Berlin Wall fell in a matter of days, so the last stubborn vestiges of American slavery are being deconstructed. This is happening not only through the removal of statues and paintings, but also through changing the names of U.S. military bases named after Confederate leaders. We need to be reminded of the notion that those in the South fought against the United States Union Army.

On the front-page article about youth by Morgan Cook, the reporter writes:

> The organizer of the event, Yasmine Goley, 18, and Jaya
> Rivers, 17, said that if the government ignores their
> generation's calls for justice, the young people will make
> themselves heard at the ballot box.

Goley stated simply, "I know that I have the power to bring people together, and I wanted to just have a day where we could all preach oneness and appreciate each other and spread the true idea of love in all of us," she said. The article continues, "Speakers at the event said it would be a mistake for the people in power to dismiss recent rallies and protests for racial justice as a flash in the pan, because their movement is neither" (Ibid.).

Goley asserts, "We're in for the marathon. I love long distance" (*SDUT*, 6/25/2020). This is their time, and they are going to maximize their impact on our society and culture.

Deeper into the A Section of the Union Tribune from the same day is the headline; *MISSISSIPPI LAWMAKERS SUGGEST CHANGES TO THE FLAG, Replace Confederate battle emblem with "In God We Trust.* The first paragraph by Emily Wagster Pettus informs us:

Jackson, Miss.
Two of Mississippi's top elected Republicans proposed
Wednesday that the Confederate battle emblem be replaced
on the state flag, with the words 'In God We Trust,' seeking
a path toward unity in their state amid the backdrop of
national protests over racial injustice.

In quoting a statesman, Pettus adds, "Another Republican statewide elected official, Auditor Shad White, said Mississippi needs a flag that is more unifying than the one we have now." You can see the words "oneness" and "unifying" being used by youth and adult legislators from the Deep South.

In an article on page one by Teri Figuero, regarding the San Diego Police Department, the subtitle is, *"De-escalation, duty to intervene if excess force is the focus."* The article begins:

San Diego police now have a stand-alone policy for officers
to attempt to de-escalate encounters when they can, and a
new imperative that officers intervene if they see another
officer using unreasonable force, the mayor and police chief
announced Wednesday (Ibid.).

The article continues:

The changes come three weeks after city officials called
emergency meetings to address de-escalation and other
policies, following days of local and national protests
decrying police brutality and racial injustice (Ibid.).

Figuero later states that, "For two years the city's Community Review Board had pushed for such a measure." And now, it is done in a matter of weeks. We are on a fast track to Global Unity and World Peace that is youth driven.

What seemed impossible for the past 150 years is, within a matter of weeks, possible. Change is upon us. The sign of Aquarius is ruled by Uranus, a planet that represents science, technology, and sudden, unexpected changes. As the Piscean Age gives way to the Aquarian Age, the institutions of the past 2,000 years are crumbling.

The top half of the front page of the San Diego Union Tribune on June 25, 2020, contains the following two headlines, *US SUFFERING BIG RESURGENCE OF CORONAVIRUS, Wave of infections sweeping across South and West.* The other headline in bold is, **COUNTY POSTS ANOTHER RECORD FOR COVID CASES**, *Goal still to slow spread as officials reiterate need for masks, distancing.* With the void in leadership on the national level, we are left to use our own free will to shelter in place, wear masks, wash hands and socially distance, or not.

The final headline I want to highlight appears on Page A4 at the bottom. *"US MARSHALS TOLD TO PROTECT MONUMENTS, Trump vows stern punishment for vandalizing statues,"* by Devlin Barrett & Matt Zapotsky.

> US Marshals have been told they should prepare to protect national monuments across the country, according to an email directive viewed by the Washington Post, as President Donald Trump has vowed stern punishment for those who vandalize or destroy such structures as part of police violence protests.

The article continues:

> On Monday, protesters attempted to topple a statue of President Andrew Jackson in a park next to the White House, though police in riot gear intervened and stopped them. That night, Trump tweeted his dismay, and the next morning he wrote that he had 'authorized the Federal

Government to arrest anyone who vandalizes or destroys any monument, statue or other such Federal property in the US, with up to 10 years in prison, per the Veteran's Memorial Preservation Act, or other such laws that may be pertinent' (Ibid.).

Here, the model of punishment is embraced to protect the legacy of those who upheld slavery and were willing to destroy our country to maintain this toxic and unjust model for social and political life.

In an interview on April 1, 2020, following the murder of George Floyd, Matt Kahn, a mystic and metaphysical teacher, on *The Inspire Nation Show*, hosted by Michael Sandler on You Tube said:

"When you see death, you are seeing rebirth. When you see deconstruction you are seeing reconstruction, and when you see the headline you are seeing the Old Guard lose its grip."

Trump proudly represents the Old Guard. Kryon describes Trump as a "wildcard," which is a person or an event that is totally unexpected, and brings about radical change. The virus is also a wildcard. Just as nobody expected Donald Trump to win the election of 2016 for the presidency of the United States, including Donald Trump, nobody saw this global pandemic coming either.

Kryon says Trump is here "to stir the pot with a big stick." As the Piscean Age gives way to the Aquarian Age, the models and institutions of the past 2,000 years are falling apart, including the Catholic Church and the U.S. government and its limited democracy.

As Dr. Bruce Lipton reflects, everything needs to be destroyed to make way for what Dr. Joe Dispenza refers to as the "awakening of something far greater which is waiting to emerge." While 60 percent of Americans and most of the world bemoan the destructive impulses let loose in so many areas by Donald Trump, he is in effect speeding up our transition to a new Age.

Kryon says instead of taking two or three generations to bring about seismic change, we are doing this in a matter of months and years. The

36-year window we are in during this period of the precession of the equinox is primed for radical change.

The blatant corruption of the Trump administration is nothing new in politics. The difference, Kryon says, is that we are seeing it. In the past we couldn't see it even if we suspected and knew about it. It was hidden. Kryon reminds us that since we passed the 26,000-year precession of the equinox on December 21, 2012, the light has been winning over the dark.

As Donald Trump uses the power of the U.S. presidency for his personal aims and uses the power of the government to hide his actions, bury his tax returns, disclaim the Mueller report, he is making short-term gains. But given that we are now in the "Unity" part of the 26,000-year cycle, beginning anew, and in the galactic light, he and his administration don't stand a chance.

Currently Donald Trump trails Joe Biden by 14 percent in national polls and Joe Biden is not even campaigning other than to make a few public appearances, where he demonstrated that he is in step with the radical changes taking place in our world.

Donald Trump perceives our social justice focused youth as, "looters and thugs." Clearly, his views are unsustainable as our planet Earth, our solar system and galaxy move into new places in the Universe where we have not been before.

As the planets and astrological ages shift along with the profound ending of a 26,000-year cycle and beginning of a new 26,000-year cycle there is a collision. This then births an ascended planet. All the powers of the presidency that Donald Trump has waged will wither and ultimately disappear into the nothingness from where they came.

The old Piscean model of punishment has given way to a new model of respect and honoring in the tradition of the Indigenous. In restorative practices we don't punish the offender, we do something much more powerful, we demand that they "repair the harm," to those they offended.

Ask a student if they would rather be suspended for an infraction or repair the harm to the individual or community they offended, and they will select suspension every time. This is because repairing the harm requires humility, taking responsibility and making changes in one's attitude and actions. Being suspended requires none of these life-altering requirements.

This is where we *are* as a nation. According to the New York Times, *"Black Lives Matter May Be the Largest Movement in U.S. History."* In an article by Larry Buchanan, Quoctrung Bui and Jugal K. Patel, dated July 3, 2020, they report:

> The recent Black Lives Matter protests peaked on June 6, when half a million people turned out in nearly 550 places across the United States. That was a single day in more than a month of protests that still continue today.
>
> Four recent polls—including one released this week by Civis Analytics, a data science firm that works with businesses and Democratic campaigns—suggest that about 15 to 26 million people in the United States have participated in demonstrations over the death of George Floyd and others in recent weeks.

These figures would make the recent protests the largest movement in the country's history. This suggests that as a majority we have admitted we have done harm to African Americans as reflected in the number of citizens participating in these protests, in the middle of a pandemic no less. A consensus is forming that it is time for us to repair that harm.

I supported Marianne Williamson for president because her campaign was restorative. Her campaign motto was: "Repair, Restore, Renew," and she maintains that as a nation we need to admit the harm we have done to Native Americans and African Americans. She suggests reparations be paid to the Native Americans and African Americans as a way to repair the harm done to these Americans. In addition, she believes we did harm during the Vietnam War and the Iraq War and should apologize as a nation.

This is where we are going. One suspension in school puts a student on the school-to-prison pipeline, the opposite of our intention as educators. But when you ask a kid to sit down in the center of a circle and hear from peers the effects of their behavior on the community and ask them how they can repair the harm, they are not likely to want to re-experience this. As students have told us many times, "If you suspend me, I am just going to get a few days off to play video games at home and I have no reason not to reoffend. But, when you ask me to repair the harm in front of my peers, I am not going to reoffend.

With the youth uprising, all Donald Trump has to fall back on is more punishment. This is a weak and ineffective strategy against the Indigos who are here to transform our global society, despite the challenges and obstacles we face.

In Kryon Book Fourteen, titled; *The New Human, The Evolution of Humanity,"* Kryon, channeled by Lee Carroll states:

> The precession of the equinoxes and the end of 2012 marked the beginning of a Human consciousness that starts to go into maturity. This is the prophecy of the ancients. Next there is an age of getting used to it. I'm not going to tell you how long that's going to last. On other planets it was amazingly short. The potential is there for you to get through this quickly. Dear ones, you have paid the price for this. All of the lifetimes of working the puzzle have culminated to this point, and now you are having the freedom to see the end of it. It takes adjustment to move from the old to the new, and in the adjustment a recalibration of finding a new frequency is upon you. Getting out of fear is upon you (16).

He continues:

> The darkness will try to win now that the light has been turned on. They have one tool, which is potent—really potent. This tool can get to the highest of the high and ruin

them. It can get to the Light worker, the healer and the channeler. It's a four-letter word called fear. If you're afraid then they have won. I want you to think about that. They know this. Let your light shine through this in such an amazing way that there is no longer a horrible, controlling four-letter world. It doesn't even exist. March through these times and remember them, for you expected them and worked through them. Work toward the new four-letter word—LOVE (161–162).

Moving from Fear to Love. We see it playing out in our politics of the day. One headline inside the San Diego Union Tribune newspaper dated June 19th is, *PELOSI REMOVES PORTRAITS OF CONFEDERATE SPEAKERS, Lawmakers must lead by example, House leader says.*

The article by John Wagner and Paw Kane begins:

WASHINGTON. House Speaker Nancy Pelosi ordered the removal of the portraits of four of her predecessors who served in the Confederacy, a gesture that comes during a national reckoning on issues of racial injustice and police brutality.

Separately, Blunt is one of several Republicans who signaled support for a provision in a must-pass military policy bill that would require the Pentagon to strip bases and equipment of Confederate names, monuments or symbols in three years (A3).

The next paragraph states: "President Donald Trump has condemned the provision and said he would not even consider such changes" (Ibid.).

We can see the struggle between the dark and the light playing out in front of our very eyes. As one side embraces fear the other side is willing to put the light on the dark and condemn it to the past. This leads the way for an Age of Enlightenment for all of humanity as we raise our consciousness from fear to love, individually and collectively.

As Kryon explains in Book Fourteen, where he describes the new human:

> Here is the prophecy (again). Now listen: What I'm going to tell you is a summary and a generalization of the prophecy of the Indigenous of Earth. These are the ones who were here much earlier than anything that happened here, and it is written clearly in the Mayan Calendar. Listen: If the planet passed the marker of 2012, which is represented by the middle point of the wobble of the Earth—a cycle that is 26,000 years old, it would start the beginning of a new consciousness on the planet, and an evolution vibration. That is the prophecy. Remember my channeling of a day or so ago? Humanity would go from three to four to five and beyond! Human beings would begin to think differently, and the ascension of consciousness would begin in all of you (209).

Can you feel it? Can you see it? We are in the shift right now and we go from 3, the third dimension, through 4, the fourth dimension, to 5, the fifth dimension and beyond because when we get to the fifth dimension, we are now in multi-dimensions which are not linear. Kryon says there are two hundred dimensions, but once we get to 5, we are in all dimensions (Kryon channel, Vancouver, BC, Canada, August 22, 2020, *Your Divine Heritage*).

Kryon continues:

> Look to the children. At some level, it's possible that the change here will come through your children, who may not agree with you from one generation to another… They may turn away from the old way. It's going to happen through generations of birth. That's the channel. It's bigger than you think, yet the change is centered here (209–210).

As we say at Centers for Spiritual Living and as Kryon finishes every channel with, "And so it is!"

Chapter 10

Star Mother

6/28/2020

I am by birth Acjachemen. I have been trained for more than 20 years by Star Mother, as was Deborah Sadler.

—Rev. Sam Jaffe (aka Moyel Tukwaa),
Leader of the Eagle/Dove Clan

Star Mother was the Atiatich of her people, the Acjachemen, who resided in the Orange County area of California before the white man came. Father Junipero Serra coordinated the building of Catholic Missions from San Diego all the way up California to San Francisco. The missionaries referred to the Acjachemen as the Juaneño Band of Mission Indians. Star Mother called this their slave name.

The Atiatich is the spiritual leader of the tribe. When one crosses over in this teaching, the individual receives a spirit name. They are then referred to only as that name. Star Mother is the spirit name of my teacher. Her father, Yellow Eagle, had been the Atiatich until he made his transition. Star Mother's mother, whose spirit name is Star Dancer, was a Pueblo Native American, descendant of the Anasazi. She grew up in Albuquerque, New Mexico, and she was sent away from her home to an American boarding school. This was not a choice. All the children were sent away from their people to be indoctrinated into "American" culture.

Star Dancer was born in 1919 and made her transition in 2001.

I first met Star Mother through Katherine Torres who channeled Malachi. Katherine and Star Mother, who went by her given name at the time, did a Sacred Passage for Women that began on a Friday afternoon and was complete Sunday early evening.

Star Mother, and her husband Dan, had moved from a house in Southeast San Diego, just a few doors down from Star Dancer's house, to Descanso, at the top of the mountains east of San Diego.

Our retreat was on the land of their home. There were eight women paired up with each group of two sharing a tent and becoming star sisters (although we did not use that term then). I was paired with a woman named Lori who had grown up in the Bronx and had a strong New York accent. I grew up in Westport, Connecticut, 50 miles east of New York City and felt a connection with her right away.

We used her tent which she and her best friend growing up had used when they drove cross-country. The tent's name was "Saggy." It was an old canvas tent that leaned a lot, but it was bigger than the tent I brought. I remember we began the gathering inside the house in Star Mother's living room. One of her three sons, Gary, and his wife, had just given birth to twin boys. I remember their photos placed prominently on the dining room sideboard; Raymond (named after Yellow Eagle) and his twin brother.

Star Mother had been a welder at NASCO, the shipbuilding company in south San Diego. She met her second husband, Dan there. She would tell us that when she would see or pass Dan, she would say, "Hi Dan, how are you!" And he would say, "Fair to middling," every time. We thought that was funny.

We also concluded the weekend inside, but the remainder of the weekend was on the land. A woman had been hired to cook our food and to clean the Porta-Potties, bless her. The house was at the top of a hill that was fairly steep although it had some flat places.

Throughout the weekend we went through a series of ceremonies with our partner, one of which included getting into ocean water in a small tub and being rinsed in the dark and cold of the middle of the night. This ceremony included ocean seaweed too.

For later Sacred Passages for Women, I would have my husband Jim help me gather ocean water and seaweed and put it into plastic 20-gallon containers, to take up the mountain. We did these Sacred Passages for Women quarterly.

My three children were small and leaving them home with their father was a bold move because I would be gone over two days. Lori also had two small children. Her husband Marty was also from New York and was an accountant.

I had a sleeping bag but no pad underneath, and so I slept on the least rocky surface we could find, not having camped for years. One of the things we did was gather beautiful mountain sage, which grew all over the land. We used the sage for one of the ceremonies and to cleanse our auras or energy fields.

Star Mother knew all about fresh organic vegetarian food and always prepared a thorough menu for our weekend ceremonies and classes which I continued to participate in for almost 20 years. I was always amazed how I could get from where I live in Cardiff-by-the-Sea to Descanso, at the top of the mountains, in 60 minutes, from the sea to the summit. So, the food was always delicious.

Being on the land was hard. And the land was hard too. We had to climb up and down the hill. Temperatures in Descanso can be in the 90's and 100's in the summer and in the 40's and 50's in the winter. We did about six seasons of Sacred Passages for women, so we experienced the elements. One time we did a star passages ceremony, so our spiritual work was done over the course of the night. This meant that we slept during the day and did our ceremonies from sunset to sunrise.

I began taking classes with Star Mother beginning with "Song of Creation," a class where you get in touch with your primary power animal, other power animals, plants, trees, etc. We were always required to bring a "dream blanket," a notebook for notes, a payment for $80 and a "gift of the heart." At the end of the class, Star Mother would find a creative way for individuals to select from the wrapped gifts to exchange them.

My family adjusted to my trips up the mountain and when I would come in the door, my three children, Jesse, Brendon and Ada would immediately ask, "What did you get? What did you get?" They always wanted to know what I had received as a gift of the heart.

In my first classes with Star Mother doing Song of Creation, I see in my notes: "Polarity—discord on Earth—riots—need the expressions. Advances work of enlightened ones" (6/20/1992). These notes refer to the Rodney King riots in South-Central Los Angeles in 1992. Star Mother was saying that riots occur when there is too much polarity, and the discord needs to be expressed. In her teaching, riots can advance the work of enlightened ones.

I was a volunteer through a Reed College project called "Take Charge," where I worked with a co-volunteer with students at Markham Middle School in Watts, Los Angeles. The riots happened right where the school is located. My co-volunteer and I went up to see the students that we had worked with for the past two years, following the riots. They were 8th graders.

These students were in 6th grade when we first began working with them. They would say calmly, "There are drugs, there are guns, there are killin's." Most students had seen someone die by gunfire by the age of 12. When we drove up to Markham Middle School after the riots, my co-volunteer, also a Reedie, and I got off the 405 freeway at Imperial Avenue to be greeted by National Guardsmen and tanks lining the Avenue. He had recently purchased a used police car and so we opted to drive my car this time.

When we met with the students, we sat in a circle and passed around a talking piece. Many of their families got them out of town and away from the mayhem during the riots. Stores around the school had been looted and the Martin Luther King Jr. Center had even been damaged.

The most poignant part of that experience was at the end of the circle, the students said, "We have a question for you." We welcomed their questions and the first one was, "Weren't you afraid to come today?" That they were thinking of our safety when they led lives of little or no safety was heart opening. We replied, "No, we feel totally safe," and the truth is, with the National Guard everywhere, we, at the time, were safe.

And so, this take on riots by Star Mother is present today. Riots advance consciousness. They are the result of polarity or oppositions that pop from the pressure and give way to an expression of "enough."

These riots occurred after four Los Angeles police officers, three of whom were white, were acquitted.

> Twenty-five years ago this week, four Los Angeles policemen—three of them white—were acquitted of the savage beating of Rodney King, an African-American man. Caught on camera by a bystander, graphic video of the attack was broadcast into homes across the nation and worldwide.
>
> Fury over the acquittal—stoked by years of racial and economic inequality in the city—spilled over into the streets, resulting in five days of rioting in Los Angeles. It ignited a national conversation about racial and economic disparity and police use of force that continues today." (npr.org - *When LA Erupted in Anger: A Look Back at Rodney King Riots*, 7/26/2017, Anjuli Sastry, Karen Grigsby Bates).

The riot took place in 1992, but the circumstances mirror the situation with George Floyd and so many other Black men over the years before and after Rodney King.

In March 1991, Rodney King led police on a high-speed chase. He was on parole for robbery. Later they charged him with driving under the influence.

> When police finally stopped him, King was ordered out of the car. Los Angeles Police Department officers then kicked him repeatedly and beat him with batons for a reported 15

93

minutes. The video showed that more than a dozen cops stood by, watching, and commenting on the beating.

King's injuries resulted in skull fractures, broken bones and teeth and permanent brain damage" (Ibid.).

The trial was moved from Los Angeles to Simi Valley, a suburb in Ventura County "where nine whites, one Latino, one biracial, one Asian," found the four officers not guilty (Ibid.).

According to NPR, the jury verdict of acquittal was announced and three hours later riots broke out in South-Central Los Angeles. The riots continued for three days. "On May 1, ... Rodney King himself attempted to publicly appeal to residents to stop fighting. He stood outside a Beverly Hills courthouse with his lawyer and asked, 'People, I just want to say, you know, can we all get along? Can we all get along?'" (Ibid.).

To quote the writers of this article, "That shocking, grainy video of his beating would be the first of a long line of police brutality videos to go viral" (Ibid.).

My notes from my Song of Creation class with Star Mother, in 1992 include, "Only about one million enlightened souls on the planet right now." We were approaching the 18 years preceding the precession of the equinoxes of December 12, 2012.

The purpose of Reed College's "Take Charge," of which I was a founding member, was to encourage at-risk students to go to college. It was the brainchild of an alumnus who had been head guidance counselor for Los Angeles Unified. He, along with his wife, also a guidance counselor, and son, all Reed graduates made an arrangement between Reed and Los Angeles Unified School District (LAUSD).

As an alumnus, I was drawn to the project and because Watts was the closest area to me geographically. I chose Markham Middle School as my place to volunteer. For three years, my co-volunteer Mark and I worked with about 24 students selected by Dr. Johnson, head counselor at Markham, in Reed College's Take Charge program. Each year, we took them on buses from all LAUSD schools involved to a different college.

The first year we took students in the program from all over the district to Occidental College. After a tour, we went to their stadium where we saw Bill Cosby receive an honorary doctorate. They had a gospel choir that sang the Star-Spangled Banner and Cosby noted that it was the best rendition he had ever heard of that song. I couldn't have agreed more. It was hot in the stands and the dark skin of our students magnified the heat—we covered up as best we could from the strong, hot rays of the sun.

The second year we took the student in "Take Charge" to California Institute of Technology or CalTech. The third year we took them from all over LAUSD to California State University Dominguez Hills (CSU Dominguez Hills). My oldest son Jesse was a 6th grader. He had been to Markham Middle School with me once and pleaded with me to take him on this field trip. I finally relented when he pointed out that we could drive in the carpool lane.

Jesse got along great with the boys. He saw there were only two entrances to Markham Middle School. We went through the one that led through the cafeteria and kitchen adjacent to the staff parking lot. The other entrance was a large gate with rods that ran perpendicular. A woman with a walkie-talkie stood sentry at the locked gate on the inside. I believe she was a volunteer.

We took the bus from Watts through Compton to CSU Dominguez Hills. Jesse had a great day, and the students enjoyed his boyish company.

In my notes from Star Mother, she states that "individuals aged 30–55 are the people that are here to change consciousness" (this would include those born between 1938 and 1960, at the time). If we don't raise consciousness as a group, those following us will cut off heads without guilt," and then she referenced Nancy Tappe. In this Star Mother is referring to the Indigo children. In other words, the Indigos,

Star Mother would remind us, are here to bring balance and harmony to the planet. She taught they will do whatever is necessary to accomplish their purpose, including cutting off heads which is a metaphor about their determination to bring about transformation.

Star Mother spoke about how most of humanity in 1992 used "Three and a half bands of the rainbow. We were still in the physical and mental parts of our chakra bodies. The majority of people do not use the spiritual bands of the rainbow, but the baby boomers do."

In reviewing my notes, I see similarities in Star Mother's teachings and those of Kryon. She describes the 5th ray. We, "have come into Earth plane with the knowledge of the past, present and future. We are strongly connected to the memory of all things. No matter what we do we are in the wisdom halls of Akashic records—the caves of humanity" (7/4/1992).

In Star Mother's teachings, each ray of light signifies something different. The indigo ray, which is the seventh ray in her tribe's teachings, is about "steadfastness, persistence, and drive. Indigos have enough fortitude to complete what we set out to do. The shadow side is holding on too long, the need to know when to let go—hard to know when to let go. This ray represents the Black brothers and sisters on the planet" (Ibid.).

This has always made sense to me since learning these teachings that the African Americans are here to bring about change. That was the campaign phrase for Barack Obama who is half African American in his 2008 and 2012 presidential runs.

These Indigo children are here to bring about radical change and the African American community is a significant catalyst to this change. These children, who we refer to as millennials, are here to bring about this change from the Piscean Age to the Aquarian Age and they won't stop until they achieve their purpose for coming to Earth Mother, with a focus on an equal voice for All.

In my notes I also see a reference to the "crystal people who are here to move the masses by being an example—to work with the energy"

(Ibid.). The crystals are those born after the millennials or Generation Y.

One thing I remember after the Rodney King riots was Representative Maxine Waters and her staff going through their purses and wallets and giving the money they had to their constituents in Nickerson Gardens, a public housing community in Watts. These public servants were on hand to help even if it just meant emptying their pockets.

In our studies with Star Mother, the women always wore skirts so we could better access the magnetics of the earth, enhancing our intuition and receiving feminine energy. The order of the colors of the rainbow is different for the Acjachemen in that the colors are red, orange, yellow, green, sky blue, violet, indigo and turquoise. Each color represents a higher vibration in consciousness.

When I took our children camping throughout the Southwestern United States in 1993, we camped at the North Rim of the Grand Canyon in the Kaibab National Forest where we saw multiple double and triple rainbows at an elevation of 8,000 feet, but we never saw the violet ray. If you have looked at a rainbow in the last 15 years or so, you can see the violet ray. At first it was just a sliver but now it is a full band.

In Star Mother's teachings, the red ray is dying out to make way for the higher vibrational frequencies to come in, such as the violet ray. So, when Star Mother said in 1992 that humanity was only operating under three and a half rays of the rainbow, she meant that we were operating under "red which represents communication, the heartbeat of Earth Mother. Its increase, or positive quality is passion, its decrease is anger. The second ray or orange which is about observation and the lessons of innocence, or the child within. Yellow, the third ray of the rainbow, represents the Creator and Co-Creator. In this ray we are able to call in energy from the outer realms and inner dimensions, to reshape and redesign the affairs in our lives. In the third and fourth spectrum, we need animals around us because they know how to filter. Animals know how to change weird energy. The decrease of the third ray is a tendency to be lazy. The increase is writing, animals, creativity, painting. This is where the fine arts come from" (7/4/1992).

In 1992, humanity was operating under the first three and a half rays of light, which means we were using part of our fourth color, green, which we all know represents the heart chakra. This is the chakra that bridges the lower senses and consciousness with the higher senses of consciousness above the heart. The fourth chakra and above represent Spirit, while the first three chakras represent the body, or material affairs.

"This green ray represents Earth Mother and emphasizes willingness as spiritual power. It is the lesson of manifesting for others, and the capacity to know others' abilities. It is the knowledge that points others to new thinking, attitudes and highest good" (7/25/1992).

This is where we were in 1992, with some consciousness of working to clean up our environment and respect and honor Earth Mother. As the ray of light of the heart, it suggests that, in 1992, humanity was not fully open in our hearts. We were halfway there, considering what we could do for others, rather than just ourselves. "The fifth ray is sky blue which represents honesty and sincerity and is the lesson of integrity" (Ibid.). This ray is about "being asked to focus energy on goodness and reflects the quality of genuineness in us and others. It is about fairness and being straightforward" (Ibid.).

Sky blue is about clarity. Seeing clearly. Because Star Mother is not here in her physical body I can only tap into her consciousness and ask where we are now. Current events would suggest that we are embracing the green ray of light as individuals are coming out around the world to march and protest for entire groups of individuals, who are not of their tribe. As white people around the globe march for Black Lives Matter, we are opening our hearts to All people.

Witnessing the blatant cruelty and corruption of the Trump administration in America is a test of consciousness. Are we ready to embrace integrity, or move into the sky-blue realm of clarity and honesty? This is the struggle and question of the day. The benefit of the Trump administration is that we see the contrast. It is not subtle.

America will reflect to us on November 3, 2020, in just a little over a month, where we are in consciousness. Have we fully embraced the green ray and the wisdom of manifesting for others, open to new ideas and paradigms—are we ready for the universe to reward us for taking on new ways of being? Are our hearts open and healthy? Do we see love as our guiding light? Do we know how to love ourselves? Do we love others unconditionally?

This election represents an embrace of the 5th ray, which matches with the 5th dimension of higher consciousness where integrity, honesty and sincerity are the model for a new paradigm, leaving corruption, greed, and selfishness in our rear-view window. This is the question of our time.

Because we passed the marker on December 12, 2012, it is destiny for us to move beyond the green ray and become the clear vessel for Spirit to move through with clarity, wiping away the dirt and grime from our perspectives to see the divinity in everything and everyone on this planet and beyond. While forces are attempting to unwrite history and human rights, they are out of sync with the precession of the equinoxes, the stars and creation's unceasing move towards higher levels of consciousness. The regressive forces are doomed and are doing what they are doing to thwart any progress, because, in fact, they know they are doomed.

In Star Mother's teachings, the red ray is dying out to make way for the higher vibrational frequencies to come in such as the violet ray. "Africa and Mexico are preparing for a redo—they are beginning to die back, so they can be reborn under a higher vibration of light" (7/18/1992).

According to the teachings of the indigo ray, everyone has an equal voice. This is compatible with the dawning of the Age of Aquarius where we recognize that "we are One," and we "transform, reshape, remodel and rebuild" our society to honor this truth. This is what is happening to us in the summer of 2020.

Turquoise is the color that follows Indigo and it represents "the path of the true will. Its increase is kindness, its decrease is cruelty" (Ibid.). We have a ways to go before we get to this ray, but many of us contain it as part of our Song of Creation. Notice that the American indigenous use turquoise often in their jewelry and ceremonies.

In another note, Star Mother says, "Those 12 and under are here to show us the future. They came here to change things without feeling guilty." Again, these are the Indigos. She also explains that "people born with the violet ray are here to get things into an enlightening phase," and she references Nancy Tappe. The Indigos were "sent to make sure the change happens as a safety measure for God—who will make the change anyway" (Ibid.).

Star Mother refers often to the magnetics of the Earth which parallels Kryon who describes himself as the "Magnetic Master."

The Indigos and Black brothers and sisters who are under the indigo ray are here to bring about dramatic and significant change. Based on Star Mother's teachings, they will stop at nothing to do so because it is their, and our, cosmic obligation and purpose.

The violet ray's appearance in the rainbow, 15–20 years ago, signifies that we are indeed raising consciousness as the higher levels of frequency and vibration raise humanity to a greater expression of freedom and light. At first it was just a sliver and as we approached the precession of the equinoxes, it got more broad and deeper in color in my observations. Today, it is as wide as the other rays. I get so excited every time I see the rainbow with the violet ray. When I see it, it shows me that we are evolving in consciousness, despite the appearance of chaos and confusion.

After my co-volunteer, Mark, and I went up to Markham Middle School following the riots, I, along with my friends in Cardiff, collected clothes and household items to donate to a community center in Watts that Dr. Johnson had taken Mark and myself to when we first met with him, and he had treated us to lunch.

I arranged through Dr. Johnson to drop these items off on a Sunday. We packed my Volvo station wagon full of goods including three dozen donuts donated by Cardiff's famous VG donuts. My friend, Chris Powell, drove up with me. As we drove through Watts, Chris was impressed by the fact that people lived in small bungalows with front yards. We drove by Nickerson Gardens, which I passed every time I went to Markham. It is a huge complex of public housing in the form of garden apartments, so it is nothing like the tenement buildings of some of our other cities, such as New York and Chicago.

There were always victory gardens and flowers planted in this complex. Jordan Downs was a similar public housing project. It was at Nickerson Gardens where Maxine Waters and her staff reached into their pockets and purses following the riots, to help their constituents. I don't know if we stopped to get gas on Imperial Highway when I was with Chris, but when I did stop to get gas on my trip to or from Markham, I was noticed by the other patrons who seemed to appreciate my lack of fear, and ease at just filling up in the 'hood. Men would nod at me, in a gesture of appreciation almost, that as a white woman I was unphased by the neighborhood.

Returning to Star Mother, the very first notes I have from 6/20/1992 begin with the directions I identified that I came in on, in this lifetime. I came from "Above: Great Mystery. Need to write. All of humanity. Spiritual Enlightened Souls. Beyond the Stars. Get the information from Stars and beyond to bring to Humanity." The other direction I identified (under my dream blanket where we were sent by Star Mother to retrieve information) is that I also came in from the "South: Community. Be beautiful, self within community—not to conform—to be myself." I look at these very first teachings and I see them reflected perfectly in this writing 28 years later.

During one of our Sacred Passages for Women gatherings, a huge, powerful Santa Ana swept down on us on a Sunday morning. A Santa

Ana is a weather pattern in Southern California where hot, dry winds come over our mountains from the deserts and wreak havoc. They are also called "the devil winds." Our tents tumbled down the hill in the strong gusts and our set-up was distributed throughout the coastal mountain sagebrush. As we cleaned up and trudged everything up the hill to safety from the powerful wind, I asked Star Mother as she was coming down the hill to retrieve more stuff, and I was carrying supplies up, "What is the meaning of this beyond a strong cleansing?" She said fourth rightly, "It means we have earned the right to do this inside."

From that point on, we worked in a room that had a wooden plaque that said, "Star Mother," over the doorway, where we had previously used the bathroom. Dan fixed it up for us and that's where we had our classes from then on. We continued doing weekend gatherings, later doing work with the stars.

Star Mother was an alumnus of Crawford High School, where I taught, as my teachings up the mountain began to wind down. This just created another beautiful connection as we are Crawford Colts! I had first become familiar with the neighborhood when Star Mother, her mother, Star Dancer, and I along with some others took Herbology for a year at Star Dancer's house. It was taught by John Finch, founder of Self-Heal School of Herbal Studies and Healing. John is also the partner of our star sister Jane, with whom I studied with Star Mother. Together they run the herbology school. Star Mother taught Jane how to train others in "The Song of Creation."

To get to Star Dancer's house in Southeast San Diego, we had to go the same way I drove to Crawford for twelve years, although Star Dancer's house was about 20 more blocks South. Fourteen years later this would become my commute and my daytime home.

Later, my star sisters, Lori and Aletha, and I took our children up the mountain to do "Song of Creation." There my children learned their power animals and plant totems. My power animal is a wolf. "This is our primal nature, our primal power source" (Ibid.). My notes on the wolf are: "Protective with young—equal power in the household. Able to teach instincts of survival to children. Frolicking, having fun—serious when the hunt is on. Playful. One mate for life—the animal of the wolf" (Ibid.). And I have been married to Jim Sadler for 46 years.

Star Mother passed away in 2015. Like many Native Americans, she had diabetes and had a kidney transplant to extend her life, for which we were all grateful! I was unable to attend her Hyan or burial ceremony because I had an obligation at Seaside Center related to just becoming a licensed spiritual practitioner. This was a hard decision for me, but I knew Star Mother supported my decision, putting Spirit first in my life. She is dearly missed, but all I have to do is think of her and she and Star Dancer are all around me, sharing wisdom and great fits of laughter. I have a photo of each of them over my desk to remind me of my beautiful Earth and Star teachers. In her passing Star Mother took on her Spirit name, Star Mother. I am so blessed to have received the Earth and Star teachings from the Atiatich of the Acjachemen people of Orange County, California.

The violet ray that began as a sliver in our visible rainbow, twenty or so years ago, is now a broad band. In Star Mother's teachings, violet is the sixth ray and represents a spiritually enlightened humanity. My notes say, "Spiritual enlightenment is an energy" (7/4/1992). In this frequency we "work with the energy behind the thought." Those born under the violet ray are the weavers of this cosmic energy emerging from the precession of the equinoxes in 2012.

One of my sons came in under the violet ray, and he, along with myself, learned to weave Torrey pine needle baskets. In fact, at one point, some of us learned basket weaving at Star Mother's, through a Native American who came monthly to teach us the ways of his people, using beautiful native grasses. Those under the violet ray know how to weave the energy around them to create peace and balance in their environment and in our world. Those who have the violet ray in their Song of Creation are here to weave peace, using the chaos and whatever is in the field, to bring about order.

Chapter 11

TIME Magazine

7/1/2020

I attempt to be cautious about media information. I try to avoid mainstream sources because to me they represent "dominant elite culture"—a term I learned in the Multiple Subject Credential program at Cal State San Marcos (CSUSM). Right now, dominant elite culture is being challenged from outside by minorities and inside by its own members who recognize, and acknowledge, white privilege.

But when TIME Magazine put Greta Thunberg on its cover as "Person of the Year," (Dec. 23/Dec 30, 2019) I had to pay the $6.99 price of the magazine on the display at a store. A friend of ours had expressed his irritation to my husband regarding my conviction that the millennials and those that follow will fix this mess that has unfolded before us, in these times of transition.

"She almost sounds like an evangelist," he whined to my husband. It made me aware that so many individuals still reside in a three-dimensional realm, physically, mentally, and spiritually. It also caused me to acknowledge that since I was 25-years old I have been exploring a multi-dimensional cosmos. As a result, I have been open to information, as you can see through these writings, that others discount, leaving them limited to a world of the senses. So, I have information that 3D folks do not because as Kryon says, "They are too smart to look." This is not a judgement. It is the duality that we live in today, with folks in the 3rd dimension, 4th dimension, and 5th dimension and beyond.

These dimensions are colliding. As Matt Kahn, a mystic and healer pointed out; "With this virus the whole world is now in the 4th Dimension, or the unknown." The chaos and confusion we feel is because our three-dimensional world of the known has been destroyed, and we are now on a collective journey through the dark night of the soul, as we see our humanity and inhumanity play out, particularly, on the American stage.

For those holding on to the 3-dimensional world of the known, the winds of change have literally and metaphorically cut us off without our consent, and all of the denial and anger and blame is just hot air.

We need to embrace the chaos because it is allowing something much greater to emerge for all of humanity, not just for dominant elite culture.

The cover of the TIME Magazine "Person of the Year," depicts Greta standing on a rock adjacent to the ocean with a solemn gaze into the unknown. Her name, *Greta Thunberg*, is followed by *The Power of Youth.* For me, this was a confirmation that my evangelism is right on target. Even corporate TIME Magazine is waking up to the power of these up-and-coming youth—to make a better world.

In the feature article titled, *The Choice,* by Edward Felsenthal, he writes:

> That Thunberg is the youngest individual ever named
> TIME's Person of the Year says as much about the moment
> as it does about her.... But in this moment when so many
> traditional institutions seem to be failing us, amid staggering
> inequality and social upheaval and political paralysis, we are
> seeing new kinds of influence take hold. It is wielded by
> people like Thunberg, leaders with a cause and a phone who
> don't fit the old rubrics but who connect with us in ways that
> institutions can't and perhaps never could (49).

Felsenthal sums up the challenges facing us. He continues:

> When she first heard about global warming as an 8-year-old,
> Thunberg says she thought, "That can't be happening, then

the politicians would be taking care of it." That they weren't is precisely what motivated her to act, as it has youth the world over who are forcing us to confront the peril of our own inaction, from student-led protests on the streets in Santiago, Chile, to the young democracy activists fighting for rights and representation in Hong Kong to the high schoolers from Parkland, Fla., whose march against gun violence Thunberg cites as an inspiration for her climate strikes (Ibid.).

So here are the Indigos, creating change, and being recognized for their power and influence.

I don't know what you were doing at eight years old, but these youths are coming in, being born, with a sense of compassion and an astuteness that we haven't seen on this planet. They came to remake, remodel and remold our world, and so they are. In another article celebrating Greta titled, *The Conscience,* by Charlotte Alter, Suyin Haynes and Justin Worland they write:

> It began as a solitary protest on August 20, 2018, in front of the Swedish Parliament, carrying her homemade sign, "SKOLSTREJK FÖR KLIMATET," calling for a school strike to demand climate action. She skipped school on this Friday and many Fridays that followed. This birthed a movement called "The Fridays for Future."
>
> By the end of 2018 tens of thousands of students across Europe began skipping school on Fridays to protest their own leader's inaction. In January, 35,000 school children protested in Belgium following Thunberg's example...
>
> By September 2019, the climate strikes had spread beyond Northern Europe. In New York City, 250,000 reportedly marched in Battery Park and outside City Hall. In London 100,000 swarmed the streets of Westminster Abbey, in the shadow of Big Ben. In Germany a total of 1.4 million people took to the streets, with thousands flooding the

Brandenburg Gate in Berlin and marching in nearly 600 other cities and towns across the country. From Antarctica to Papua New Guinea, from Kabul to Johannesburg, an estimated 4 million people of all ages showed up to protest.... Hundreds carried images of Thunberg or painted her quotes on poster boards, *MAKE THE WORLD GRETA AGAIN,* became a rallying cry" (59, Ibid).

Greta's simple act of civil disobedience by skipping school on a Friday to protest climate change became an international movement.

Edward Felsenthal of TIME Magazine wrote about their choice of her as their Person of the Year:

For sounding the alarm about humanity's predatory relationships with the only home we have, for bringing to a fragmented world a voice that transcends backgrounds and borders, for showing us all what it might look like when a new generation leads, Greta Thunberg is TIME's 2019 Person of the Year (49, Ibid.).

Greta is an international leader who exemplifies her words through her actions. She traveled by sailboat from Lisbon to New York in 2019 to attend the United Nations climate summit, abstaining from travel by jet that leaves contrails of pollution. During the U.N. General Assembly, she spoke simply and directly; "We are in the beginning of a mass extinction, and all you can talk about is money and fairy tales of eternal economic growth. How dare you!" (67, Ibid.).

Going back to our 26,000-year cycle, as planet Earth moves through our universe within our galaxy, we see the delineation of the marker of December 21, 2012, manifesting itself. We are coming from millennia of a consciousness of "separation," separation from Spirit in our organized belief systems, separation from one another in our political, social, and cultural structures, separation from Earth Mother in our notion of dominion and power over others including our planet.

But with the lead up to the marker and the eight years since we passed it, our whole world is shifting in consciousness to a world view, a cosmic view, founded on the Truth that we are ALL ONE, that we are "in this together," as the virus is showing us.

The resistance we see to acknowledging the power of this virus to damage and even kill us has been demonstrated by the same folks who politically deny climate changes or cycles. The result in America on July 3rd is that states that politically resist social and climate change are on fire with Covid-19. Believing they were the exception, they eschewed social distancing, wearing masks, and keeping their communities and businesses closed. The result is that Florida, Texas, and Arizona are experiencing an overflowing need for ICU beds that has these states in a red-alert medical melt down.

Politically in this country, the Republican Party has held firm to the Fourth World of Separation, denying climate change, denying the power of a pandemic, denying that we are in this together. They are a retroactive political force signified by Donald Trump's bizarre commitment to protecting Confederate statues by saying, "They're trying to take away our culture. They're trying to take away history," Trump said at a rally in Phoenix (*Trump on removing Confederate statues: 'They're trying to take away our culture,'* by Max Greenwood, August 22, *The Hill*). The Democrats are an imperfect political hodgepodge of various constituencies who recognize climate change and have acknowledged and embraced the science behind Covid-19. They also recognize the science behind climate change.

California, a solidly blue state (Democrat), on June 26, 2020, passed a landmark rule mandating electric commercial trucks starting in 2024.

In another first-in-the nation move to tackle climate change, California will require automakers to sell more electric trucks starting in 2024. The measure, approved unanimously Thursday by the California Air Resources Board, says that by 2045 all new trucks sold in the state should be zero emissions (NPR).

The climate change championed by Greta and global youth is finally being addressed in ways that are real and relevant.

Greta Thunberg leads School Strike for Climate protest.
(Copyright: Ale Mi/DepositPhoto.com)

At the age of 16, Greta became a global icon. But she is not alone. *The TIME Magazine* article on Greta noted that:

> Thunberg's lonely strike outside Sweden's parliament coincided with a surge of mass youth protests that have erupted around the world—all in different places, with different impacts, but fueled by a changing social climate and shifting economic pressures.
>
> The common thread is outrage over a central injustice: young people know they are inheriting a world that will not work nearly as well as it did for the aging adults who have been running it" (*The Conscience*, by Charlotte Alter, Suyin Haynes, Justin Worland, *TIME*, 64).

And yet their impact is formidable. In reading the April 2020 *O, the Oprah Magazine*, the make-up columnist, Gria Ways, wrote an article devoted to going green, regarding packaging for make-up. She writes regarding her own choices:

> I've been less Greta Thunberg and more Oscar the Grouch, surrounded by trash cans heaped with waste—not only discarded packaging but also sheet masks, face wipes, and cotton balls and swabs. And I feel bad about this (46).

She then expands upon ways to avoid this waste under the subheading, *Waste Not*, Way writes; "Another way to BMLG (be more like Greta)" (48), demonstrates the impact of this 16-year-old young woman from Sweden on popular culture. Wray's Ariel concludes; "If this beauty junkie can take baby steps in the right direction to BMLG, so can you" (Ibid.).

In the first channeling of the *Homeroom* Kryon Meeting in Newport Beach on December 8, 2019, Kryon spoke about this youth phenomenon. He begins by describing what an "Old Soul" is, which is his audience—those who tune into him. "Old souls have lived multiple lifetimes, so many, some are original, having lived thousands of lives. The purpose of those lives is for this time now."

He continues:

> There is no plan or contract when humanity has free choice; free to take light and dark into any direction. These last weeks something has begun to happen. The grids of the planet are starting to change.
>
> In 1987 when the Harmonic Convergence happened something flipped—a switch almost, that was consciousness driven that said we are staying; we did it. The dark or negative and light or positive are being worked on by other elements—always here—but waiting—this is what's making the difference.
>
> Young people here may say it's too soon to ask those questions—you have to be over 50—that's an old paradigm. This is what you do when you retire, you begin to think spiritually. That's not so anymore, that's an old attribute. There are those who like to put humans into a box and say this is what they think about at certain ages.
>
> Old Souls and young people are asking the questions:
> 'Who am I?'
> 'Why do I feel like I've been here before?'

> 'Why do I feel like I have some wisdom and
> nobody is listening to me?'

I'll tell you, we are all listening to you because the Old Souls have something to say.

How many recognize your grandchildren have something to say? Some of you have grandchildren that have mastery and you know it. This is the difference. It affects the energy of birth. They land on a planet that has more light than we did. The consciousness of the young has a wisdom factor that starts to flow much earlier than anything we had.

Ask psychologists. We had to be almost 26 before we were settled.

How about 15? That place where young people start to become difficult with adults. That's starting to change; not for everyone, but for the Old Souls because the 15-year-old is starting to ask:

> 'Am I here by accident?'
> 'What is it I feel?'
> 'Why are things the way they are?'
> 'Why is there so much dysfunction here?'

They are standing up and going to others of the same age and saying, 'What can we do?' The answer is not 'go on a rebellion march in the street,' but 'get together, talk, think.'

Later in the channel, Kryon states:

It's beautiful to think there's no one out there that's gonna take you by the hand and walk you through safe places. It's you—that your Soul was always designed as a pure piece of God, and that hand that's been outstretched that we've asked you to take so many times is not a mysterious angel. It's the rest of you. A wise you.

This is a new consciousness. It's being measured on the planet and Old Souls are receiving it first. That's who sits here today. That's who often listens to these messages.

Can't you feel it? There is something present, inviting, that says; there are changes happening. Why don't you come along? Free choice is just that. It's not a coercement, it's not a "do it or else," it's not a reward system Dear Ones. It's free choice. It happens because you're ready. It happens because you're ready. I'll be back. I'll be back. And so it is" (Dec 8, 2019, Newport Beach, CA).

Sitting in the audience of about 100 people in a hotel conference room, in the first row, of course, I knew this message was for me. "I know who is here," Kryon will often say and the "entourage" that accompanies him each time he channels is colored by the energy of those present at the meeting.

Having taught tenth grade for two years at San Diego High School, the first and oldest high school in San Diego Unified, and twelve years at Crawford, this hit me square in the forehead or third eye, or pineal gland. I have taught other grades at the same time, but "I was never going to get out of tenth grade until I retired," I like to say.

Tenth grade is crucial and as Kryon notes—this is the age when students become difficult with the adults. In California the High School Exit Exam was administered at the end of tenth grade until 2013. This is because students begin to disappear from school in eleventh and twelfth grades.

My students always outperformed students in other English classes, year after year. I would do whatever I could to ensure my students, especially the boys, could successfully navigate this tumultuous time in life, so that they could pass the class. Flunking classes in tenth grade threatens one's ability to graduate on time. Often, I felt the obligation to do my utmost to save them from their lower instincts and raise them just enough to make that C minus. I have given a few D's for what I considered to be good reasons, but generally we as a staff required a C minus or better to pass the class.

But having spent 14 years with 15-year-olds, I knew Kryon was right on. He also validated my belief system that the millennials and

Generation Y are here to "change the world, rearrange the world," because "It's dying to get better" (*Crosby, Stills and Nash*, 1971).

Here was an angelic entity and voice from the other side of the veil letting me know in person that help is on the way, and it is here in the form of our youth across the planet.

When he speaks about the mechanics of the planet, he is referring to Nodes and Nulls placed on Earth by the Pleiadian Star Mothers when they came to seed humanity and thus the planet with the divine spark of the Creator. There are 12 Nodes and 12 Nulls. Since December 21, 2012, Kryon, through his channeling, has identified where these 24 nodes and nulls are located around the Earth; many of which we recognize as "Sacred Places." On November 17 to 24, 2019 during the Kryon Bucket Trip; *Peru Shamanic Tour*, the last two Nodes and Nulls were matched, completing the identification, and matching of all 24 features.

This is the "mechanics" Kryon speaks of—that these 24 power centers are now fully activated.

Lee Carroll's partner and Kryon archivist Monika Muranyi writes in her book; *The Women of Lemuria: Ancient Wisdom for Modern Times,* published in 2018:

> The Pleiadians created the Nodes and Nulls approximately 200,000 years ago, at the same time that they created the conscious grids of Gaia. They put themselves into a quantum state, all over the planet in various areas, and specifically they created 12 pairs of energy points. These 12 energy points are found at 24 geographical locations—a total of 24 Nodes and Nulls, where they work as a polarized pair. Each polarized pair is a time capsule that has energy set in place. Should humanity ever reach a certain consciousness, these time capsules would release information for the individual Human Being, as well as for the whole (24).

Muranyi continues:

Since 2012, the Nodes and Nulls of the planet have been identified, opened, and activated. Slowly, multidimensional information is being broadcast to the Earth's grids, allowing for higher consciousness, invention, and Human DNA evolution. The Nodes and Nulls are "hooked" into the benevolent design of the Universe (25).

NODES	NULLS
1a) Maui, Hawaii	1b) Tibestii Mountains, Chad, Africa
2a) Lake Titicaca, Bolivia/Peru	2b) Mt. Kailash, Tibet
3a) Yucatán Peninsula, Mexico	3b) Mt. Kilimanjaro, Tanzania, Africa
4a) Mt. Shasta, California, USA	4b) Mt. Ararat, Turkey
5a) Uluru, Australia	5b) Mount Logan, Yukon Territories, Canada
6a) Mt. Ida and Hot Springs, Arkansas, USA	6b) Mt. Fitz Roy, Patagonia, Argentina
7a) Aoraki (Mount Cook) New Zealand	7b) Ural Mountains, Russia
8a) Mont Blanc, French Alps	8b) Mt. Aconcagua, Argentina
9a) Glastonbury, England	9b) Gunnbjorn Fjeld, Greenland
*10a) Rila Mountain, Bulgaria	*10b) Victory Peak, Tian Shan Mountains, Kyrgyzstan
*11a) Machu Picchu, Peru	*11b) Aneto, Pyrenees, Spain
*12a) Table Mountain, South Africa	*12b) Meili Snow Mountain, China

*[The last three Nodes and Nulls were not matched at the time of publication of this book but have been matched since and are included here.]

These Nodes and Nulls are now fully activated. The Nodes tasks are to clean up negative energy from the past millennia. The Nulls push dark energy to the Nodes to be cleansed, which then releases new inventions. This system just became fully active at the end of November 2019.

Can you feel it? Can you see it? Change is all around us and the dark underbelly of racism and classism are being exposed in America in deeply profound ways that have awakened the youth in a global response demanding social and economic justice for all people regardless of race (which is a human construct), religion, gender, culture, etc. This is not just an Earth change; this is a universal evolution of consciousness away from separation and division to one of unity and cooperation. This is the shift to the beginning of a new 26,000-year cycle. Welcome!

Chapter 12

More TIME Magazine

7/7/2020

As mentioned in the previous chapter, the final pairings of the Nodes and Nulls took place at the end of November 2019, in Machu Picchu, Peru, activating all 24. These mechanics are called time capsules because they open at the right time. For 200,000 years these power centers have been waiting for the consciousness of humanity to reach a high enough vibration to activate.

The prophecy was that we would destroy ourselves by the year 2000. However, we passed the marker of December 21, 2012. The Nodes and Nulls are here to assist us in moving back into unity consciousness, where we can experience the balance of the masculine and feminine once again. We are on our way towards a collective Heaven on Earth.

How do we get there? By releasing the dark. To do this, we must recognize and identify the dark. At the *Kryon Homeroom* meeting that I attended on December 8, 2019, Kryon informed us that our new spiritual leaders are 15 years old. At the end of December 2019, TIME Magazine selected Greta Thunberg, 16 years old, as its "Person of the Year."

On February 3, 2020, TIME Magazine had another feature focus that caused me to spend another $6.99 at the magazine stand. *YOUTH QUAKE, HOW THE WORLD WILL CHANGE WHEN A NEW GENERATION LEADS.* Much as Kryon stated in December 2019 that the youth would not necessarily be marching, events transpired that triggered the need for youth to express their opposition peacefully and responsibly to a masculine-heavy world of separation.

The subtitle of the article, *Youthquake,* by Charlotte Alter is, *American politics is still defined by values and priorities of the baby boomers. But not for long* (40).

The article opens:

> "LOVE'EM or hate 'em, this much is true: one day soon, millennials will rule America" (42). She defines, Millennials—born between 1981 and 1996—are already the largest living generation and the largest age group in the workforce... Their startups have revolutionized the economy, their tastes have shifted the culture, and their enormous appetite for social media has transformed human interaction. American politics is the next arena ripe for disruption (42).

She continues:

> When it occurs it may feel like a revolution, in part because their generation has different political views than those in power now. Millennials are more racially diverse, more tuned in to the power of networks and systems and more socially progressive than either Gen X or baby boomers on nearly every available metric. They tend to favor government-run health care, student debt relief, marijuana legalization and criminal-justice reform, and they demand urgent government action on climate change. The millennial wave is coming; the only questions are when and how fast it will arrive (42).

When George Floyd was murdered on May 25, 2020, Memorial Day in America, by a Minneapolis police officer, millennials from around the globe left the quarantined safety of their domiciles and marched for social justice for weeks, most of them donning masks.

The video recordings of these senseless and cruel killings of innocent Black men erupted into a global movement called Black Lives Matter that began three years ago.

The lid is off the top of the bottle and the genie is out. In addition to the global outpouring of protests for equality and social justice for all people, Aron Baker in her TIME Magazine article on *Youthquake; GLOBAL YOUTH IN REVOLT; A new generation of leaders; inspired by activist movements, is driving change*, shares:

> Over the past year, citizens in Africa, Asia, Europe, Latin
> America and the Middle East took to the streets to raise their
> voices against inequality, corruption, and bad governance.
> And while from Italy to Iraq and Venezuela to Zimbabwe
> they promoted wildly differing slogans, the subtext was
> always the same: the system is not working (48).

In addition, Baker points out that many countries have elected very young leaders.

> On Dec. 10, Finland's Sanna Marin, 34, became the world's
> youngest Prime Minister, only to be upstaged a few weeks
> later by the return of Austria's Sebastian Kurz, who was
> sworn in as Chancellor for a second term at the age of 33 on
> Jan. 7. Kurz and Marin are the latest in a wave of politicians
> in their 30's winning leadership roles, including New
> Zealand's Prime Minister Jacinda Arden (39), Ukraine's
> Prime Minister Oleksiy Honcharuk (35) and El Salvador's
> President Nayib Bukele (38), (p. 48).

Though we in America do not hear this on our news feeds and sources, the shift towards radical change brought about by the youth of the world is well underway.

Baker adds; "What unites these movements is a desire to tear down and rebuild structures built by past generations" (49). This is the frequency of the indigo ray, to remake, remodel, remold and rebuild based upon a higher level of consciousness.

119

The cover of the magazine, ironically, depicts exactly what is taking place on our globe in an esoteric way. With a white background, the image is of an old Earth, with darker hues, cracked open with a bright, clean new Earth ready to emerge as a chick from an egg.

That TIME Magazine, a huge corporate entity and tool for dominant elite culture, could see that we are on this 26,000-year cusp, is striking. Moving from an old worn out and tired Earth to a vibrant new planet and humanity reflects the shift we are undergoing in our now tumultuous lives.

And indeed, a new Earth and a new Human are emerging daily. The current systems are clearly inadequate for our time. We are observing and participating in their dissolution to make way for a greater expression for humanity and Earth Mother, our home, based upon compassion and love.

Chapter 13

Kryon and Our Shift to Compassion

7/8/2020

In *Kryon Book 14, The New Human, The Evolution of Humanity,* Kryon tell us about God:

> … God does not see things as you do. From God, there is no forgiveness needed. You are magnificent in the eyes of the Creator! This is far different from the spiritual systems on this planet who offer you the "rules of God," and the judgement and punishment of a dysfunctional Deity, who would torture his children forever, if they break man-made rules. Connect the dots and use some spiritual logic. God is not an extension of Human nature (46).

Kryon repeats this spiritual truth often. This is the children's version of God referred to in the beginning of this book. He likens it to the Santa Claus version where we are rewarded (presents) or punished (coal in your stocking) based upon our behavior the previous year. He continues:

> Love is the source—the only source. Everything is based around it. You are going to have to re-write who God is in your life, and finally see that there is a hand out to you—a metaphor that invites you to see "God inside" you. It is you. Do you feel it? Do you feel the shift and the change away from anger, hatred and frustration?
>
> Old Soul, you represent the Human who is finally coming out of the cave of survival… Love builds a vital and

energetic bridge from Human to Human, and compassion is
the result. Compassionate action [action by Humans based
on compassion and caring] is what will change basic Human
nature forever.

Who are you? You are part of the elegant system of
creation (46).

We have projected the qualities of humans onto what we call God,
creating in our cultures a model based upon a "bad Dad." Spirit is love,
joy, compassion, creativity, beauty. Kryon will often say; "God doesn't
care what you wear, eat, or how you pray." These are human constructs
that have been created to manage various cultures by leaders who
imposed rules and regulations around God. These constructs reflect the
consciousness of where humanity has been but have little to do with the
infinite all loving vibration of ALL THAT IS! Therefore, we will
rewrite "Who is God in *our* lives?" The shift is grand. As we say in
Science of Mind, "Change your thinking, Change your life!"

As we redefine God or Spirit, we create a new Earth based upon
compassion. At long last compassion replaces the fear that comes from
a judgemental and punishing God—and moves us to Love, based upon
an All-Loving God!

Kryon describes himself as "The Magnetic Master." He speaks
about the magnetics of Earth and how they have changed more since he
arrived in 1989 than in the previous 100 years. This is scientifically
confirmed. In *The New Human,* Kryon writes:

When you are eventually able to measure multidimensional
fields in a clearer way, you will be able to see the correlation
between the magnetic field of the Earth and Human
consciousness. Therefore, you might say, "As goes the grid
goes Human consciousness." Now you know why I'm called
"The Magnetic Master."

The Magnetic Grid and the Change Coming

What you should be aware of is that the grid hasn't moved much in Human history and has remained static through your many lifetimes. In 1987 it started to move a lot. The reason? It is moving so it can be positioned to receive something—something expected that is coming... The reposturing of the grid is for something coming that we are going to call "evolutionary energy" and its physical (78).

Kryon goes on to explain the physics of this:

Months ago and years before that, we told you that your planet is going into an area of space that it has never been in before. This is not esoteric. Ask an astronomer. *It is the solar system coming out of a protective bubble into a new kind of radiation or energy that you haven't seen before'* Is it possible that your solar system is losing a protective sheath that it always had because of where it was in space? (Ibid.)

He explains further, "for those who don't understand much about galactic movement and your solar system" (78).

All the stars in your galaxy are slowly moving around the center. Your solar system and its star [the Sun] has always been on the move as it rotates around the center of the galaxy. As your solar system rotates around the middle, you are always in a new period of time and space. It moves so slowly, however [millions of years to go around one time], that for all of humanity, it has basically been in one energy, like a protective bubble—and now it changes. Don't believe it? Do your research and ask an astronomer if something is different (78–79).

Kryon continues with his explanation of "The Role of the Sun."

As you move into this new energy, or what some have even called "radiation," you should know how it works, for it's very related to your Sun. Physically, it affects the magnetic

123

field of the Sun [the heliosphere], which then in turn is blasted to your own [Earth's] magnetic field via the solar wind. That's the physics of it, but dear ones, let me give you the esoterics of it. This has been the plan all along, that if you made it as a Human race past the 2012 marker you would pass into this area of space and the magnetics would shift, allowing Human consciousness to change. Dear ones, this was always here waiting for you to pass the marker! This is why I came 26 years ago and told you the magnetics would shift. This is an evolutionary energy that is going to affect your Sun—the heliosphere of your Sun—which will then pass to the magnetic field of the Earth, a field that has now been repostured for this new consciousness (79).

Kryon speaks about the indigenous and their foreknowledge of this shift in consciousness on Earth.

So now you can see the prophecy from the indigenous is also being fulfilled, for they told you about the changes coming after the precession of the equinoxes [December 2012]… These things are not new, and even the Ancients told you it was coming! They may not have known the specifics of science, but their prophecy is the same one I have: New consciousness is coming (79–80).

Kryon acknowledges the indigenous as holding the truth of where we have been and where we are going.

Unfortunately, much like African descendants, the indigenous have also been marginalized and discriminated against worldwide. Right now our Native American communities are being decimated by the Covid-19 virus, as they have been relegated to isolation and poverty on barren lands. This social injustice was addressed by Marianne Williamson in her campaign for the 2020 presidency. She proposed reparations, or lump sum payments for African Americans and Native Americans as a way to begin to repair the harm that dominant white American culture has perpetrated upon these two groups of people.

A byproduct of passing the marker according to Kryon is the improved functioning of our DNA. Kryon says our DNA currently operates at about 35 percent efficiency. This is the level of consciousness we are at as a global society. The masters of this Earth such as Jesus Christ, Buddha, Mohamed, Mother Mary, operated closer to 90 percent efficiency. They were pure love consciousness.

Kryon speaks about the changes taking place in our DNA to raise its efficiency and therefore improve our health and raise our consciousness to a higher frequency of love and compassion.

DNA Evolution is Coming

The DNA of the Human Being is ready to shift and change. You'll never see it in a microscope, because it's not chemical; it's physics...

This 90 percent of DNA is like trillions of antennas in your body, ready to receive information and then rewrite the manual via the changes in your grids. The DNA is going to receive information and shift. It's going to affect genetics. Mothers will receive it first and pass it to their children... Are you aware of the books of my partner [Lee Carroll] from more than 10 years ago about "The Indigo Children?" These children were precursors to the new energy. The kids are different! It started before 2012—way before—since the potentials were very high that you would make it, and you did (81–82).

He describes this ascension of the efficiency of our DNA.

Changes in the kids are First

Instinct is going to work better than it ever had... You're going to see children remembering how to walk and how to eat much earlier, without training. It will be faster than the old paradigm... It will be 'off the scale.'

Get ready for it; it's instinct. It's simple chemistry. It's DNA working better (82–83).

What Kryon says about how our DNA becomes stronger is not through an activation but via a release. He explains:

> Your DNA is crippled in this old energy, and it's your own free choice that created this. Your DNA, your lifespan [aging], your diseases are all where you wanted to take the energy of this planet, and your DNA cooperated. This is what you've lived with, and what is now changing. It's not DNA activation, it's DNA release. Release! (84).

And if this isn't enough to expand your view of how LIFE in capital letters works, Kryon reassures us that we are in this together as a universe. He explains:

> The profundity of it all: Do you realize the help that you have? Did you think for a moment that all of this was going to be just *you* doing those things? It involves the galaxy, the part of space you're in; the nodes and nulls, and the Creator of the Universe. It involves the Pleiadians; it involves your timeline, and it involves love. All of this is for you to sit in a new energy and release the bonds of your DNA. Now dear ones, old souls, there is something you ought to know. You don't have to wait to be reborn for this. The old soul has the equipment inside right now, just like the newborn (84).

Kryon likes to remind us that part of the shift is that we can change our consciousness without having to take on a new life. We change our vibration by raising our frequency towards a higher embrace of love and compassion, increasing the efficiency of our DNA. But we do this through the release of discrimination, hate, separation, war, domination, cruelty, etc.

I close this chapter on Kryon with a quote from the final paragraph of this chapter which I think explains what is happening to us right now on our planet.

> Very slowly there is going to be a split of consciousness on the planet, and we have talked to you about it before. There will be those who are compassionate and those who are not,

and it's going to be obvious, so obvious! Caring and uncaring. There is a dark army right now on this planet. What is its "compassionate factor"? Do you understand? It's a free choice state of mind, but that's the split to come. Don't worry about this, compassionate one. When you take the attributes of the master, light surrounds you. No more fortressing or protecting yourself from darkness. It will retreat from you automatically. No more catching the diseases of the day, they won't be able to touch you with compassion. It's physics; it's real, it's physical and it's happening now. Your society will reflect this sooner than you think. When you turn on your news and you think I'm crazy, just wait. There's some wild cards coming. Benevolence is a new energy.

I'm Kryon, in love with humanity

And so it is (86).

This book was published in 2017. Kryon identifies Donald Trump as a wildcard, someone/something unexpected that changes everything. The Covid-19 virus is a wildcard too, according to Kryon. We can see clearly the differentiation in 2020 between those with no compassion and those with compassion. The contrast is clear and obvious.

The # MeToo Movement for women's rights and the Black Lives Matter (BLM) movement are real; they are potent, and they are founded upon the principle of compassion. We get to decide where we want to be on this continuum. Compassion is winning, light is winning. All we must do is embrace them to raise our societies and our planet further into our ascension which is in its infancy. The choice is ours—given by the Creator to believe or not to believe, to choose light or dark, compassion or the total absence of it. It's up to us individually and collectively to choose to go forward in time, space, and consciousness to our destiny to fulfill the prophecy of Peace on Earth.

Chapter 14

More Astrology

7/11/2020

On January 12, 2020, transiting (moving) Saturn, the planet of business, responsibility, government, and the meaning and structure of our lives, conjuncted transiting Pluto at 22 degrees Capricorn. This means that if you looked up in the sky with a telescope or an app, both the planet Saturn and Pluto are in the same line at 22 degrees Capricorn. Saturn rules Capricorn which represents our professional, social and economic position in life. "In Roman mythology Saturn is the god of agriculture, founder of civilizations and social order and conformity" (Wikiquote). Saturn is ruled by Capricorn which is symbolized by the mountain goat. In Saturn we put one foot in front of the other to get to where we are going. There are no shortcuts.

I don't crack open my Ephemeris that often. I have my well-worn *The American Ephemeris for the 20th century 1900–1999 at Midnight,* coverless for decades and missing pages from many years of use. Created by a computer program by Neil F. Michelsen, with revisions by Rique Pottenger, this resource is an essential tool for astrologers.

An Ephemeris lists the location of each planet and other satellites, including the Sun and Moon, each day of the century. I have been looking more closely at the Ephemeris because Saturn, Pluto and then Jupiter were about to conjunct the ascendant in my astrological chart.

Pluto represents nuclear energy, it is atomic, it is about death and rebirth. It is the great revealer, but often there is a dark night before the rebirth. Pluto brings to mind purging,

129

exorcising, and releasing buried power or core truths. It's the planet of creative destruction, and transits can feel like extended ordeals (Liveabout.com, *Pluto's Meaning in Astrology*, 6/11/2018, Molly Hall).

Your ascendant is where your first house cusp is, or the beginning place of one's astrological chart. It is determined by the time we are born. In a 24-hour cycle, it changes every two hours into the next sign of the zodiac. It is determined by the sunrise. If the sun is in Capricorn, like it is from December 21st until January 20th, then the rising sign at sunrise will be Capricorn. It then moves into the other signs in the 24-hour day.

It takes Pluto 248 years to go around the Sun, or around the zodiac. As a result, Pluto only transits (moves through) a part of our astrological chart once in our lifetime. "Live About," 6/11/2018 describes Pluto:

> In the birth chart, Pluto shows the area of life where you'll personally face the intense power of creation and destruction…. The Ego holds to its defenses, but Pluto tries to urge you to let go, and surrender to become a new person.
> Pluto rules Scorpio with its province being death and rebirth.

So, having transiting Saturn and Pluto conjunction my rising sign is something I kept my eye on. In addition, Jupiter, the planet of expansion, spirituality and travel or international activities as well as the scales of justice, went into Capricorn on December 3, 2019. It would also be conjuncting my ascendant at 23 degrees Capricorn. One's ascendant is the beginning of a new cycle, where the first house is and the home of Aries, the first sign in the zodiac. So, for me, this triple conjunction signifies that I will be expanding spiritually (Jupiter), finding a new way to make money (Capricorn), and restructuring my life around these changes (Pluto), all in one year.

Though the triple conjunction would be of particular interest to me individually, the collective impact would be just as significant.

At a Kryon Virtual meeting in Los Angeles on May 30, 2020, Michelle Karen, a professional astrologer and a Quero Shaman, initiated in the Andes Mountains of Peru, shared her insights on the conjunction of Saturn and Pluto in Capricorn. The more recent conjunctions took place in 1914 (World War I), 1947 (following World War II), and 1982, a time of an economic crash and recession.

But our recent Saturn and Pluto conjunction in Capricorn occurred on January 12, 2020. On this day, Donald Trump was impeached by the U.S. House of Representatives. This is also the day that Prince Harry officially left the British monarchy. These are very significant political and social events. Capricorn represents political, social, and economic structures. Saturn, which is ruled by Capricorn conjuncting Pluto, which is an explosive energetic in Capricorn, suggests that the foundations of our societies are being transformed in ways we cannot even imagine.

The British monarchy has been dealing with its relevance for decades, and the patriarchal hierarchy's power model for America has been crumbling during the same decades. On the day that both Saturn and Pluto conjunction exactly, these events occurred. Throughout 2020 there is a dance between Saturn, Pluto and Jupiter in Capricorn as planets go retrograde or backwards (at least they appear to from Earth). In July and August, the three planets are within six degrees of one another—close enough to be considered a conjunction. In September and October, they are within 5 degrees of one another, with Pluto and Saturn having just three degrees separating them not only did two historical events take place in America and Britain—but on January 12, 2020, the world was becoming aware of a deadly and highly contagious virus in Wuhan, China that resulted in millions of people being ordered to lock down in this Chinese province.

As Pluto can represent death and rebirth, it also signifies viruses that move through the air. Jupiter suggests that the virus is global and will travel to all parts of the planet. It also represents a lot of expansion, which in the case of a virus is not ideal. And then we have Saturn, the taskmaster, the template holder for business, corporations and government shaking things up in these areas.

Our entire global community is united by the air we breathe. Aquarius, the age into which we are moving, is an air sign, and represents the unity of all humanity. Anna Karen reported that this satellite, or triple conjunction, occurs approximately every 4,000 years. The last time it occurred was 1894 B.C. In my research I discovered that the birthday of Jeff Bezos, the co-founder of Amazon is January 12th. Clearly, Amazon has already played a major role in our lives during this pandemic as retail stores have been shut and we are buying many of our goods online, including groceries for many.

What does this conjunction mean for us personally? Wherever these conjunction planets fall in our native astrological charts is an area in our lives where we are experiencing a breakdown and a rebirth—a contraction followed by an expansion. The disintegration of what many have known as the truth moves us to a deeper level of understanding of how our world truly operates.

The past 12,000–13,000 years where we experienced separation and duality are giving way. The disintegration of the Piscean world and the birth of Aquarian consciousness moves us forward into 12,0000–13,000 years of unity consciousness. Here we not only remember, but we know that we are One, that we have always been One. We will always be One.

The past 12,000–13,000 years where we experienced separation and duality are giving way to a new place in space in our solar system and galaxy. This is a 26,000-year cosmic shift and that's why it is so all encompassing. We are remembering the spiritual truth that we are One global Soul living on planet Earth that is also unified in consciousness with us. Earth Mother is here to support us in our mission of ascendancy, and she is leading the way. It is up to us to rise to the elevating consciousness and higher frequencies she is currently emitting, affecting humanity personally and collectively.

For much of humanity, this is difficult and challenging. For those of us who have gone through the dark night of the soul multiple times and are now comfortable in the 5th dimension, or multidimensional consciousness, we are finding solace and peace and the opportunity to be creative in this time of pandemic upheaval.

Yet many souls are struggling to comprehend the Plutonic, or life and death, nature of this wildcard pandemic. It has upended our structure, our habits, our routines, our perceptions, our sense of peace.

At the end of her presentation, Anna Karen showed a picture of a Hopi Prophecy Rock. It showed, in her interpretation, many individuals ascending upwards in a long line. These were those individuals who were not honoring Earth Mother and so they were moving into "oblivion." Those honoring Earth Mother were fewer, but they remained on the ground—and would be the survivors. She saw this process taking place between 2020 and 2022, "two humanities choosing two different routes." For the Hopi, this represents the end of the Fourth World of Separation.

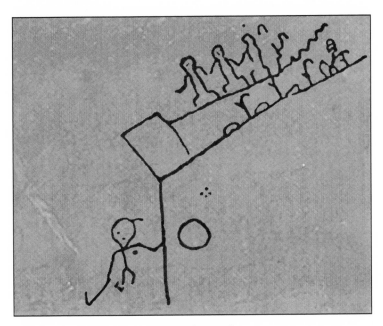

Hopi Prophecy Rock

Not only have we experienced the complete upheaval of the structures of our daily lives (Saturn conjunct Pluto), but we are in the midst of a social justice revolution that burst forth after the images of the murder of George Floyd on Memorial Day, May 25, 2020. What became the *BLM* movement, or *Black Lives Matter,* has engulfed the planet and continues to grow. This is the influence of Jupiter, the planet of philosophy, spirituality, higher education, international influence, and the expansion of consciousness. Jupiter also represents the scales of justice and the law.

During the weeks that followed George Floyd's death, the individuals marching around the globe averaged 34 years old. They came out in the rain, in a pandemic, largely with face masks on. Interestingly, there was no surge of the virus from these mostly peaceful demonstrations around the globe. Being outside helped, but so did their consciousness. Knowing they are taking a stand and doing something about the systematic social injustice on our planet increases one's immune system and protects it.

This triple conjunction of Saturn, Pluto and Jupiter facilitates remaking, remodeling, and rebuilding our global society from the ground up, which is an Indigo activity. This pandemic has exposed all the weaknesses in our society created by a world built on white male supremacy at the expense of other global citizens. The extreme poverty and disenfranchisement of a third of our U.S. citizens is a national disgrace that has been seemingly impenetrable.

But now, the light is exposing the dark and we see the inequities glaringly. The youth will not stand for it because not only are they more compassionate, but they have grown up in a much more diverse society than the baby boomers or silent generation.

We are to complete the revolution that began in 1776, only now we include all of humanity for the right to "Life, liberty and the pursuit of happiness," not just in the U.S. but globally.

In March of 2020, Saturn moved from Capricorn, the sign of its rulership to Aquarius, where it was on Memorial Day. Aquarius, as I have shared, encompasses all of humanity; it is the humanitarian sign of the zodiac in astrology. And so, it became an overnight explosion of global protests when the world saw the videos of the murder of George Floyd. Uranus rules Aquarius and represents modern technology and media as well as sudden and unexpected breakthroughs.

What people had been protesting—racial discrimination and the police brutality that accompanied and supported it—became exposed for all to see. A huge global shift occurred overnight. On July 2, 2020, Saturn turns retrograde (appears to be moving backwards from our perspective on Earth) to complete its cycle in this sign of Capricorn. Capricorn represents law and order as well as integrity in society's institutions.

Later in the year, in the first week of November 2020, Jupiter will conjunct Pluto exactly. This conjunction signifies that many people will come out and vote in America for social justice and that there is a rebirth taking place as signified by Pluto. This also suggests that the virus, which is ruled by Pluto, will expand globally as Jupiter represents expansion and is an international signifier.

That small, short experience and glimpse of what is coming as Saturn moves into Aquarius showed us what we need to release as race and global consciousness. But we now see we have a lot of work to do which is the provenance of Saturn in Capricorn to which Saturn has returned. On December 17, 2020, Saturn goes forward into Aquarius where our global Oneness will be acknowledged, and our solutions will emerge from this new consciousness of Oneness. On December 20, 2020, Jupiter moves into Aquarius as well.

When these two power planets, Saturn and Jupiter move into the Aquarius part of the zodiac, these two balancing planets of construction (Saturn) and expansion (Jupiter) in exact conjunction, will initiate us into a new Earth and a new Humanity. Here we will demand integrity, and social justice in all our institutions, corporations, and governments. The Aquarian Age will be upon us as technology and sudden inventions whisk us into the prophecy of ascension of consciousness across the globe. The young people will lead us to the promised land. We just have to be willing to go along for the ride.

Chapter 15

Moving From 3D to 5D

7/12/2020

*The key to growth is the introduction of higher
dimensions of consciousness into our awareness.*

—Lao Tzu

Dimensional reality is the physical realm. It is what we can confirm with our five senses. It is material. We can, for the most part, see and feel it. In the 3rd dimension, we perceive ourselves as separate from others as well as the universe.

The 4th Dimensional reality is the pathway to the 5th dimension which opens us up to all dimensions. It is when consciousness begins to awaken to the possibility that there is way more going on than we acknowledge in the 3rd Dimensional world we have been inhabiting. It is the dark night of the soul that occurs when our 3D world collapses around us and we are forced by circumstances to examine our stance, our viewpoints, our perceptions.

The doorway itself is the open heart (remember Star Mother said that much of humanity was only using half of the heart ray, or three and a half rays of the rainbow) and as "the light of consciousness begins to awaken within your belief system of 3rd Dimensional reality seems absurd" (fractalenlightenment.com). One's attention "has shifted from the pursuits of the material world into the pursuit of knowledge and understanding" (Ibid.).

Facing our shadow side in the despair and seeming dysfunction of the 4th Dimension we release much of race consciousness or race karma. We gradually move into the 5th dimension where reality is perceived as unity, as Oneness, rather than the separation perceived in 3D. We realize that the ALL is One, and the One is ALL. Separation is an illusion.

As our consciousness awakens, the ego drops away and judgements begin to fade. Rather than trying to change the world, the focus becomes self-healing. "The love that grows within begins to translate into compassion and understanding for the external world" (Ibid.). Through self-realization we move deeper into this new dimensional reality. Our heart must be open to enter this higher realm. And from this 5th Dimensional place other levels of consciousness begin to open up for us and become more available.

This Covid-19 is the 4th dimension, and we see, in particular, Americans' choice and free will operating on individual and regional levels based upon belief systems (B.S.) and consciousness. While many have surrendered to the dangers and mortality of the virus, many others are flouting it. These would be those in the 3rd Dimension who need to see, feel, and experience the virus to confirm its reality.

This is currently playing out in the states of Florida, Texas, and Arizona. Hospital ICUs are overrun because enough of the population in these states denied the potency and danger of an invisible microbe. They tested its talent and now they are experiencing the potency of its economic, social, physical, and global power.

Welcome to the 4th dimension. As a global family, we are all in the midst of change. This is the in-between part of the appearance of certainty and solidity in the 3rd dimension, in contrast with the limitlessness of the 5th dimension. We are in the unknown of the 4th dimension, striving to find our equilibrium in the middle of radical and permanent transformation. This is how we raise consciousness, by traveling through the unknown, the confusion and the chaos. This is where we are in 2020 individually and collectively.

Chapter 16

Kryon on Magnetics and Astrology

7/14/2020

In the Book, *The Gaia Effect; The remarkable system of collaboration between Gaia and Humanity,* by Kryon and Monika Muranyi, the archivist for Kryon, writes in depth about the grids of the Earth. According to the teachings of Kryon there is the magnetic grid, the Gaia grid and the crystalline grid. These are what Monika describes as the *Energy Grids of Earth.*

In Monika's explanation of Kryon as the Magnetic Master who "arrived as part of a grid changing entourage," (Ibid. 80) she shares his message that:

> ... the magnetic grid of the planet would move more in the next 10 years than it had in the previous 100 years. By 2002 that is exactly what happened, and it is measurable even with a simple compass. The changing of the Magnetic Grid was a direct result of humanity's intent to create a new reality. The collective consciousness of humans raised the vibration of the planet and the magnetics changed (80).

Muranyi explains that the magnetic grid is the "grid of communication" (80).

> For many years, the magnetic grid remained the same, because humanity never gave the intent to claim the power of what lies within our DNA. That is, until recently, when humanity decided it wanted to change its reality (80).

She further explains that:

The Magnetic Grid is also like the planet's antenna to the Universe. It communicates with the magnetics of the Solar System. In order for the entanglement to occur, you have to have magnetics. Entanglement is a quantum energy, and so the magnetic field becomes part of the engine of entanglement between us and the center of the Universe (82).

Entanglement is what unifies the universe. Vera Rubin, PhD, an astrophysicist, discovered that beyond our galaxies the stars and galaxies rotate as one, like a unified field, because they *are* a unified field.

In the 1970s, Rubin showed that the speed at which stars orbit around the centers of spiral galaxies remains high even at the outskirts. This contradicts the Newtonian theory of gravitation, which predicts that the speeds of distant stars should fall off as the pull of gravity declines, just as the farthest planets in the Solar System orbit more slowly around the Sun than do closer ones. This discrepancy is striking—if Jupiter moved at the same rate as Earth, for instance, it would orbit the Sun every 5 years, rather than every 12.

The only plausible explanation for the galactic 'flat rotation curves' (named for their shape on a graph) was that the mass of the galaxies must extend invisibly beyond the most distant stars and gas clouds. That excess mass is known as dark matter. Its existence was first suggested in 1933 by astronomer Fritz Zwicky, who saw that galaxies in clusters moved more quickly than would be predicted from observable mass. (Nature.com, Vera Rubin (1928–2016) *Observational astronomer who confirmed the existence of black matter,* Neta A. Bahcall, February 2, 2017).

Kryon is fond of mentioning Vera Rubin because he speaks about entanglement in our universe. An article titled, *Ancient Quasars*

Provide Incredible Evidence for Quantum Entanglement, by Chelsea Gohd (space.com) highlights this phenomenon:

> Using two ancient galactic cores called quasars, researchers have taken a massive step forward toward confirming quantum entanglement—a concept that says that the properties of particles can be linked no matter how far apart in the universe they may be.
>
> If quantum entanglement is laid, then a pair of entangled particles can exist billions of light years apart from one another and actions affecting the properties of one particle will affect the properties of the other. Albert Einstein described this correlation between particles as "spooky action at a distance." Last year, physicists from MIT, the University of Vienna and other institutions provided strong evidence for quantum entanglement, and now, this same team of scientists has gone even further to confirm quantum entanglement.
>
> Scientists looking to prove quantum entanglement have to show that measured correlations between particles cannot be explained by classical physics, according to a statement from MIT describing the new work. In the 1960s physicist John Bell calculated a theoretical limit, past which correlations between particles must have a quantum, not a classical, explanation. [Time Crystals to Tetraquarks: Quantum Physics in 2017].
>
> … So, with these findings, it is "implausible" that the measured correlations have a classical explanation, the researchers said. This is strong evidence that quantum mechanics caused this correlation and that quantum entanglement is valid, they say.

Science is validating the oldest spiritual belief system on our planet, the Buddhist notion that the universe is One, bringing spirituality and science together in what we are learning is the unified quantum field. Vera Rubin was born in 1928 and passed away on December 25, 2016. She is described by Bahcall as: "a pioneering astronomer, an admired role model and a passionate champion of female scientists." Had she been born a male, Kryon and current scientists agree that she would have won the Nobel Prize for astrophysics.

Regarding the actual magnetics of the Earth, *Popular Mechanics,* in an article by Jennifer Leman (May 15, 2020), describes the measurable shifts that have taken place recently in the Magnetic Grid:

> While poles have drifted and even swapped places numerous times over the course of Earth's long history, what's different about this recent shift is how quickly it's happening. From 1999 to 2005, Earth's magnetic North Pole went from shifting 9 miles, at most, each year to as much as 37 miles in a year (Ibid.).

This is exactly what Kryon addresses in his channeling through Lee Carroll.

Kryon often tells us, reminds us, that the magnetics have shifted so much since he arrived in 1989 that the runway numbers have been altered at airports around the globe noting the changes of due North. Leman explains:

> In 2017, the magnetic North Pole fell within 240 miles of the geographic North Pole. The movement was so rapid that the British Geological Survey and U.S. National Geophysical Data Center, which updates the World's Magnetic Model, had to accelerate their process in order to keep up (Ibid.).

She explains the consequences of those dramatic changes:

> These shifts have major consequences for global navigation systems. Anything or anyone that uses a compass—from ships at sea to the smart phones in our pockets—is impacted by this magnetic game of tug-of-war (Ibid.).

Kryon stated when he arrived that the Magnetic grids would change and indeed the self-described "Magnetic Master," was correct.

In *The Gaia Effect,* Muranyi includes information from Kryon readings about the magnetics of the solar system, by first providing some background.

> In 1989, Kryon's message was that the magnetic field of the Earth was critical to our consciousness. Magnetics is a quantum energy. So is gravity, and so is light. So, we are surrounded by a quantum field, and that is the magnetic field of Earth. The potential was that, if Human consciousness changed, then the magnetics would change. It did. The magnetics have moved greatly since 1989. However, there has to be more. Our solar system is the engine of the magnetic change for the planet. If the magnetics of the Earth have changed, what is happening with our solar system? (212).

But it is even greater than this because Earth Mother as a consciousness is involved as well. Monika explains:

> There is another thing that is related and still yet to be understood by science. There are other sets of instructions to Gaia that come from the center of the galaxy. With all these changes, there is an invitation to reawaken our relationship with Mother Nature, the Gaia. If we are able to do that, we will understand that we are in control of all of it…. The Ancient indigenous knew it. They could make rain where none was in the forecast. They could grow crops in places where they shouldn't grow. They honored the land and gave thanks and received from it (213).

She then includes a Kryon channeling from January 27, 2012, called; *Recalibration of the Universe,* given during a Kryon Patagonia cruise.

> … The magnetics of our solar system itself are changing. So here's the challenge. Go find the facts. You'll see it, literally, as your solar system moves through space. It intersects certain attributes of space and this is changing some of the magnetics, which then become different from

the way they ever were before. This, then, changes the sun. Do you see the cycle? One enhances the other in a fractal of circular reality. Your movement around the center changes your solar system. The solar system's new position changes the sun's attributes. The sun's attributes are sent to the planet via the heliosphere, and this affects your DNA…

… You are changing the past by changing the future. You are rearranging the energy of your solar system and also something else…

… The change of consciousness on this planet has changed the center of the galaxy. This is because what happens here, dear ones, is 'known' by the center…

Kryon goes on to explain why this is unknown to our scientists.

"Let me tell you something about physics. Yet, again, I'll make it simple. Everything your scientists have seen in physics happens in pairs. At the moment, there are four laws of physics in your three-dimensional paradigm. They represent two pairs of energy types. Eventually, there will be six. At the center of your galaxy is what you call a black hole, but it is not a single thing. It is duality. There is no such thing as singularity. You might say, it's one energy with two parts—a weak and a strong quantum force. And the strangest thing is it knows who you are. It is the Creator engine. It's different in other galaxies than this one. It's unique."

He concludes his channeling with the following:

The very physics of your galaxy is postured by what you do here. The astronomers can look into the cosmos and they will discover different physics in different galaxies. Could it be that there's something going on in the other galaxies like this one? (213–214).

Kryon is telling us that our consciousness on Earth affects the magnetics, not just of our planet but of our solar system. As the

144

indigenous controlled the elements, so can we. In fact, our consciousness affects the galaxy. This is how powerful we are. The impact of raising our consciousness to a higher vibrational frequency elevates the efficiency of our DNA. This improves our health and extends our lives. By aligning ourselves with love and compassion, we not only improve our lives but radiate a higher frequency out into our galaxy.

We are not small. We have a very important role to play in raising the vibration of our planet through the passion of our ability to love all and have compassion for all. Right now, we are cracking through the eggshell of resistance into the full embrace of a love and kindness-filled existence that supports all life. We do this in communion with our home, Earth Mother.

Those not aligned with celebration of our individual and collective magnificence and our desire to create and manifest a world that works for everyone will be going up to oblivion as the Hopi Prophecy Rock illustrated.

Monika goes on to write about what Kryon says about astrology in *The Gaia Effect*, published in 2015. She shares from the Kryon message from January 27, 2012:

Human DNA is sensitive to magnetics, since it is a magnetic engine itself. At birth, when the child is separated from the parent, there is a signal sent to the brain of the infant that says, "Your system is now active on its own, apart from your mother." During that first breath of independent and unique life, the child's DNA receives the pattern from the magnetics of the Earth grid, and takes on what you have come to call "astrological attributes."

Different places on the planet will carry the basic pattern, plus or minus what Earth's magnetic field has contributed, due to geographic location. This explains why world-class astrology must take into consideration the location of birth...

Astrology is the oldest science on the planet, and can be proven to be accurate. In addition, "generic" astrology is also a significant influence in Humanism, from the cycles of the female's system, to the profound changes in human behavior when the moon is full. You can't separate yourself from it, and those who don't believe in it might as well not believe in breathing, because it's that much of an influence on your life.

The new energy on the planet invites you to change your DNA. This is the teaching of Kryon. When you change your DNA, you're working with the very core of the pattern you had at birth, and so you're able to then work on some of the attributes of your astrological blueprint, and actually change it—even neutralize it. We told you about this in 1989. Masters did this, and you're now coming into a time where your abilities are those of the masters. Look into your life and eliminate the things that are challenges and keep the attributes that support you. This is the true balanced Human Being" (219).

Kryon continues to discuss what we should do to become balanced Human beings:

Meanwhile, plant the seeds of understanding, of peacefulness, of appreciation and of love. Become slow to anger, slow to create drama. Take on the attributes of the masters, and that is what your abilities are changing to right now. Soften in all things. Look at each other differently.

There'll come a time when there's no war…" (220).

He concludes:

Blessed is the Human Being who has understood this message as personal for themselves, not about the cosmos. It's about the inner being and the journey of the soul—and the Universe within" (Kryon live channeling, *The*

Recalibration of the Universe, given in Patagonia (Bottom of South America) - January 27, 2012, 220).

We all know that the moon regulates the female cycle and that the full moon does bring out the lunatics. Ask any first responder, EMT, police officer, emergency room doctors and nurses as well as teachers. As a teacher working in an urban high school, I would see that the moon grows larger and more round in the night sky and I would plan accordingly. I would create lessons on the full moon where students could work collaboratively in small groups, often with large sheets of chart paper and colored markers because they were going to be up and talking anyway, so I needed to channel the energy.

I recall substitute teaching for a middle school science teacher several times. Her classes were well behaved and easy to manage. One time I substituted and there was more energy, talking and commotion in the class. "Oh, I know what's going on." I stated. "It's the full moon. That's why you are more active." I then explained about the full moon and its effect on people and explained about the word lunatic in answer to their questions derived from Luna or moon.

When I returned to substitute another time in this same class, the students told me that they shared my observation with their science teacher. She didn't believe the full moon had an effect on us as people. I probably brought up the cycle of the tides on the planet which the moon clearly influences, moving the oceans twice daily from high tide to low tide and back again, and that we are mostly water and therefore, also under the influence of the moon. Keep in mind that this was a science teacher insisting our moon has no influence on us.

Our scientists for the most part still cling to a Newtonian model where matter and energy are separate, and so Spirit and Science are separate. The truth is we live in a multi-dimensional quantum field that is infinite in its size and infinite in possibilities. It is also a unified field, it is One. Science is still trying to fit new discoveries such as the entanglement Vera Rubin documented—which they want to interpret as dark matter—squishing her theory into a 3D model. Her observation is that the stars and the planets out in the wider universe move together—that they move at the same rate showing that the universe is interconnected and yes, multidimensional, and quantum. Our scientists have yet to catch up.

However, the Spiritual community that follows the work of Kryon knows there is so much more than we are told by our supposed experts. Kryon addresses this in *The Gaia Effect."*

> Oh, there'll come a day, dear one, in science, where the scientists will be able to apply what I call a quantum filter to alter what they see. This will be a filter developed for telescopes that involves a supercooling of the filter itself. Astronomers will be able to look out into the cosmos and, for the first time, see quantum attributes.
>
> The first thing they'll notice is two things in the center of the galaxy, not one. The next thing will be the colors around the human beings. And science will start a whole new section called "The Study of Human Auric Energy" (220).

These truths have been known by the indigenous on our planet. Star Mother taught us to read auras. It was a prerequisite class to joining the Council, which met monthly for many years of Earth and Astro studies.

Soon we will have the technology to verify the quantum field and quantum energy that is life and the universe, and we will see that it is all unified. We are all connected, not just on this planet but within our galaxy and universe. The notion of separation is an illusion we have lived under for the past 13,000 years. It is time to release the illusion and embrace our Oneness with All That Is, the Creative Source, Universal Intelligence, energy, The Force, call it what you want.

Chapter 17

Kryon on the Pleiades

7/17/2020

Continuing in Kryon and Monika Muranyi's book, *The Gaia Effect, the remarkable system of collaboration between Gaia and Humanity,* they include a channel called "Your Story," referring to planet Earth. It describes how the Pleiadian mothers seeded our planet. Get ready…

Several hundred thousand years ago, humans began to form into the Human that you recognize today. That's just yesterday. Don't confuse this with human development. You have had that going on for a very long time. But the DNA that is within your body is not the DNA that developed naturally on your planet. Yours is outside of the system of Earth-based evolutionary processes, and the scientists are starting to see this. The "missing link" that they speak of is not Human. [that'll send some over the edge!]

So again, we tell you that the ones who came to help seed you approximately 100,000 to 200,000 Earth years ago were the Pleiadians, who had gone into graduate status and who had changed consciousness. They had become quantum with free choice, and you have part of their DNA within you (235).

And in a parenthetical note at the bottom of the page Monika includes a selection from a channeling given on September 29, 2012, in Toronto, Canada called *The Bridge of* Swords. She writes:

Kryon has told us that not only did the Pleiadians create an ascended planet, but also those from Orion did it, and the Arcturians also did it. These are the parents of the planetary systems, and someday humans will be the planetary parents of another civilization within our galaxy (235).

Clearly, our story is much greater than we have been told.

The Kryon channel continues about the Pleiadians and how they starseeded humanity:

New information for you: the seeding process was not a one-time event. This is why we give you these large sections of time where the Pleiadians worked with you. It was done over time and in many places. It was not all simultaneous, and this was for reasons that will remain unknown to you for now, but we will later explain why you will find other human types that now are extinct. Now you have only one Human type, and that is counterintuitive to all mammal development on the planet. This was a design, and it took more than 100,000 years to create this for humanity, as you know it (236).

And here Kryon makes me chuckle because he refers to our "children's version" of the creation story of our planet.

It's your human bias that has the creation story of the knowledge of light and dark being given to humans in one day, in a garden involving a talking snake and other mythologies. Spiritual logic should tell you that these stories are simply metaphors of a real truth, that indeed there was a major shift of consciousness, but over a longer period of time and not instantly. The same mythology has the Earth created in seven days. However, this only represents a numerological truth [7 in the number of divinity], meaning that there was a divine design in the creation of the planet. It's time to start using spiritual logic within the teachings you have about spiritual history, for the revelations will be wonderful and lead to fuller understanding (236).

Our creation story is metaphoric. It is not literal as so many organized spiritual systems believe. Again, it is way bigger than we have been told—our creation story, that is. Kryon continues:

> Now, what really is in your DNA? It's the Pleiadians' code, and it's the ones before them. You can't remember it, for that is not the set-up. The system is that your Akashic Record is only from Earth, but your "divine remembrance" will take you back to the beginning, where system after system after system created that which you see as the divinity within the galaxy and the Universe.
>
> Who are they? They're your "divine" parents. They're the seed divinity in you and they visit here. They're not all Pleiadians, did you know that? Instead, they're from all over the galaxy. You see, they all represent the seeds of the Pleiadians, and they keep you safe. You wouldn't have it any other way, would you? 'Safe from what?' You might ask (236).

This is where Lee Carroll and Monika Muranyi would say we get to some "eye-rolling" information. This comes under the heading of *"The Bubble of Safety."*

> Your universe is teeming with life. Only a relatively few planets over millions of years have made it to a place where they have "Creator DNA" in their corporeal bodies. Some were seeded and never made it. Some are now dead. Some are technically advanced, but have no spark of divinity at all. So while a planet is "deciding," it is kept safe from other life that might interfere.
>
> You're surrounded by divine beings that keep you safe, and will continue to while this only planet of free choice— the only one at the moment—makes its decision. You're turning the corner of consciousness and they all know it, for

151

they've all been through it and they remember it. Oh dear ones, consciousness is volatile! You've seen it change so slowly, but it's about to change faster. It's not going to take generations and generations as in the past. Instead, you're going to see real-time changes. Humans won't have to wait to have children for them to grow up and have children (237).

Keeping you safe is done quantumly and at a 3D distance (Kryon live channeling *"The Big Picture,"* given during the Patagonia Cruise, February 3, 2012).

Through channeling we receive extra-planetary and galactic information that we cannot access in our 3D world. Kryon and other entities like him are assisting humanity to discover a larger spiritual truth about our origins and our greater galactic and universal environment that goes well beyond our contemporary science and spiritual systems that are organized. Seeing this "big picture" is exhilarating and resonates with our DNA.

Chapter 18

Death and the Reboot

7/18/2020

People are dying from Covid-19 virus in numbers that are mind-numbing (written 7/18/2020). We first heard about this virus which broke out in Wuhan, China in early January 2020. Within a month it had spread to Iran and then to Italy. Shortly after that it brought Spain to its knees as well.

The virus hit New York City with a wallop where over 20,000 people died in a few short months. The United States has had no positive national response from the leadership, so state governors and mayors have had to take the virus on independently. Southern states that rejected the reality of the invisible microbe as real are now reeling from the effects in July 2020, with hospitals and ICUs overrun with sick people.

The first channel I read was the *Seth* books channeled by Jane Roberts. *Seth Speaks* is still one of the most humorous books I have ever read. I read all the Seth material I could get my hands on in the 1980s. I gave away all but one of my books because that is how I manage my personal library—give away the good ones.

On a YouTube channel, a gentleman read out of a book called *The Individual and the Nature of Mass Events,* a Seth book channeled by Jane Roberts, which is not available in print anymore. I took notes from his readings of this Seth book because they directly relate to the pandemic taking place in 2020.

Seth says that pandemics are a "mass global protest by those dying—it is a biological outrage and mass statement." He maintains that "the quality of life must be at a certain level" and when it is not, a biological protest takes place.

According to Seth, "All epidemics are mass statements both biologically and psychically." He states that there is a "mass belief that has brought about certain conditions that are abhorrent at all levels—such as war." He continues, "Whenever the quality of life is threatened there will be a mass statement" in the form of an epidemic.

Seth states that, "Beliefs that foster despair are biologically destructive and cause the physical system to break down." He even says that those who may be preparing to die will choose the epidemic disease as a way to leave their body, thereby giving their death added purpose by joining the protest.

"Everybody chooses when they die," according to Seth. Those who have "psychologically decided on death will die." In epidemics, "Whole groups of individuals make mass statements—as a form of protest." He adds, "All involved want death to serve a purpose beyond their private needs. It is a despair of the conditions," these people face.

This despair lowers defenses and "initiates disease conditions where the first outbreak occurs due to ineffective political or social action—hopeless, wartime." He states this low "mental state brings about activation of a virus that is passive that touches those in the same state. It is an acceleration of something that can be done in group action. Death becomes death of mass social protest."

The result of these Seth notes is: "Various elements of social life are disturbed and rearranged, which can include the overthrow of governments and a return to the love of nature. Despair and apathy are biological enemies" (Ibid.). Epidemics, Seth maintains, are statements that "certain conditions will not be tolerated" (Ibid.). (*Mind Over Body*, reality revolution.com, Brian Scott.)

The first demographic group in America affected by the virus included individuals living in group homes or assisted living, who died in large numbers suggesting that warehousing old, infirm people in one place is not quality of life. The second and third demographic groups most impacted by mortality have been the African Americans and Latinos—both groups who live in poverty across our sorrowful nation.

According to Seth's perspective of pandemics, these groups of individuals do not have a quality of life that makes life worth living—and so their despair has led to what Seth describes as a mass protest for their unsustainable living conditions. This is a wake-up call to all Americans. As Seth reminds us, "Suffering is not good for the soul" (Ibid.).

Seth asserts that "everybody chooses when they die" (Ibid.). This is accepted knowledge in esoteric or spiritual circles. Kryon reminds us all the time that "there is no sting in death." The "sting" is with those left behind, mourning the physical loss of a loved one. Seth states that "an active desire for death is a positive healing for survival." He describes death as a "slowing of the body processes, a sudden natural stopping of the body processes. The body follows the wishes of the self." In the Virtual Kryon meeting in Los Angeles on May 30 and 31st, 2020, Adironnda, a council of light channeled by Marilyn Harper, described those who died as "volunteers," in this pandemic.

She also described George Floyd as a "volunteer." When I read that George Floyd's elementary teacher shared with the press that his dream as a young boy was to become a Supreme Court Justice, it made so much sense to me in an instant. George Floyd came to this planet to be an icon for social justice. Within a week of the images of his murder a movement named "Black Lives Matter," reemerged on a global level and is now referred to as "BLM."

George Floyd had three funerals; one in Minneapolis, his new hometown, at the North-Central University of Minneapolis where civil rights leader Al Sharpton delivered the eulogy; one in Raeford, North Carolina where Floyd was born. A third funeral took place in Houston where former Vice President Joe Biden, the leading nominee for the

Democratic Party for president, at the time, met with the family and provided a video message for the service.

Former boxing champion Floyd Mayweather offered to pay for Floyd's memorial and funeral services and the family accepted. George Floyd's first two services were broadcast on major television stations. George Floyd was buried like a Chief Justice of the Supreme Court who had made dramatic social advances for humanity. His destiny to be a global leader in social justice was fulfilled in the best way he could, as a black man in a racist twenty first century America.

More people came out to protest George Floyd's murder by a cop around the world than any other event in history. George Floyd's destiny is fulfilled not as he perceived it as a hopeful youth, but in the context of a racist and divided America that came together to say enough is enough on his behalf.

What about the survivors of an epidemic? According to Seth, "They see themselves in a different light—they see themselves as effective and performing with bravery. They have new ideas about sociological, political and economic changes for public problems." Seth even speaks to vaccines stating, "inoculations work well for those who believe it. It is the belief that makes it work." He goes on to say, "You cannot be inoculated with the desire to live."

In case there is any doubt, Seth reiterates; "No man or woman has died who did not want to die." This is very hard for most of us to grasp from a human point of view, but it is a spiritual truth. Kryon likes to remind us that when polled, approximately 80 percent of the world's population believes in some kind of afterlife. As Kryon points out, most of us have a sense we came from somewhere, and that we will return to that somewhere.

Seth states that "diseases have meaning." This makes me think of my spiritual teacher and mentor Louise Hay who self-published, *You Can Heal Your Life,* in 1984, which became a worldwide best-selling book.

In this book she includes what was originally called, *The Little Blue Book,* which lists many physical ailments and their meaning in consciousness along with an affirmation to heal the disorder. I discovered this work shortly after it was published.

When my sister Judy, one year and seventeen days my junior, died of bladder cancer in 1986, my entire family got a copy of *You Can Heal Your Life for* Christmas. I remember my Aunt Judy saying it made a lot of sense, but she questioned that "we pick our parents."

I began attending Seaside Center for Spiritual Living beginning in the fall of 2010. Many months later I was referring to *You can Heal Your Life,* our family bible for the past 35 years, when I read on the back cover that Louise Hay was a Religious Science minister. It was no wonder going to Seaside felt like coming home. I had been practicing Religious Science which we also call Science of Mind, for decades without knowing it.

We love to say: "Change your thinking; Change your life." In fact, Seth states, "Thoughts have shapes and form. Mental patterns form temporal weather patterns, which is a physical version of man's emotional states." He continues: "Behind all realities there are mental states. Ideas or thoughts form general patterns bringing forth material organization. This can be political patterns, invisible mental patterns. Each person's thoughts create earth's psychic sphere" (Ibid.).

Seth goes on to state unequivocally; "We are never victims of natural disasters—we are creatively participating in our planet's atmosphere" (Ibid.). The events such a hurricane or a pandemic occur

"...to right a condition, adjustments are made: The victims choose to participate—they might otherwise die of extended illnesses. They can connect in dreams, they are finished with their challenges. This death can be a face-saving device. Some want to die in the middle of the drama—a group death experience so they can all embark to another level of reality at the same time. Each is aware of this unconsciously and could choose to avoid the encounter [with death] at the last minute" (Ibid.).

Seth reminds us that "Our natural state of life is one of joy and we have the power to act."

Quality of life is important to make survival worthwhile. The vote is in; quality of life in America is not worth living for many of our citizens. Kryon says that the pandemic is a "reboot" for humanity. In fact, he says, the virus "stopped a future." While life has come to a slow down at the very least, we can decide to choose another way, based upon compassion for all, especially for those that this virus has called out who are suffering the most.

Chapter 19

Hope and Heroes

7/20/2020

The mass protests regarding the absence of quality of life for so many of our American family members exposes the despair, the lack of access, the discrimination, the police brutality, the cruelties of our political system. Despite the Emancipation Proclamation issued by Abraham Lincoln on January 1, 1863, which declared the end to slavery and discrimination based upon skin color, our progress has been glacial in speed. However, there is always hope and there are always heroes.

On July 18, 2020, Congressman John Lewis passed away at the age of 80. The July 19th San Diego Union Tribune's heading was: "REMEMBERING JOHN LEWIS, CONGRESSMAN'S COMMITMENT TO RACIAL JUSTICE LAUDED." The article is a compendium of quotes by notable politicians of the day across the political abyss. Under the headline, "Civil rights icon called 'conscience of our nation,'" an article by Colby Itkowitz begins:

> The tributes to John Lewis poured in Saturday morning, as leaders from across the political spectrum expressed gratitude and reverence for the civil rights icon's commitment to racial justice, even at great personal cost. The Georgia Democratic congressman, who died Friday at 80, spoke at the March on Washington in 1963. He led the march for voting rights across the Edmund Pettus Bridge in Selma in 1965 with Rev. Martin Luther King Jr. in what became known as "Bloody Sunday." Lewis suffered a brutal

beating by police who violently confronted the demonstrators with bullwhips and nightsticks. It was appropriate then that his final act was to visit the newly named Black Lives Matter Plaza on a street leading to the White House—a symbol of the progress the country had made on issues of racial justice and the work that needed to be done.

D.C. Mayor Muriel Bowser, a Democrat, who accompanied Lewis on that visit, described him as "the conscience of Congress ... the conscience of our nation."

"John Lewis had faith in our nation and in the next generation," she wrote on Twitter. "He warned us not to get lost in despair. So, in this moment of grief, we are hopeful— we are hopeful that, collectively, we can live up to his legacy."

Former Vice President Joe Biden, the presumptive Democratic nominee for president, released a stirring statement on behalf of himself and his wife, Jill.

"We are made in the image of God, and then there is John Lewis," Biden began. "How could someone in flesh and blood be so courageous, so full of hope and love in the face of so much hate, violence and vengeance?"

"He was truly a one-of-a-kind, a moral compass who always knew where to point us and which direction to march," Biden wrote.

"I first met John when I was in law school, and I told him then that he was one of my heroes. Years later, when I was elected a U.S. senator, I told him that I stood on his shoulders," former President Barack Obama wrote in a eulogy on Medium. "When I was elected President of the United States, I hugged him on the inauguration stand before I was sworn in and I told him I was only there because of the sacrifices he made." ...

The Rev. Al Sharpton: "My friend, role model, and activist extraordinaire has passed. Congressman John Lewis taught us how to be an activist. He changed the world without hate, rancor or arrogance. A rare and great man. Rest in Power and may God finally give you peace." ...
(Itkowitz writes for the Washington Post, New York Times.)

This is a man, a spirit, a soul, who chose the light in the midst of the dark, who reached for that extended hand that reaches out to all of us to provide help and support from a power greater than us, and it was given. Through despair and hopelessness rises the phoenix of renewal, hope, beauty and humanity.

Congressman John Lewis at One Book,
One San Diego, 2018

Rep. John Lewis' graphic novel, *March: Book One,* depicting the Selma-to-Montgomery march, was chosen as the 2018 One San Diego book.

Congressman John Lewis paved the way for a more perfect nation. To see the video feeds on television of him standing just two weeks ago at Black Lives Matter Plaza, a street leading to the White House, is a symbol of the progress we are making now at warp speed. As the Confederate leaders' statues come crashing down and the Confederate flag is removed from the state of Mississippi's official flag and banned from NASCAR as well as all U.S. Armed forces, we see the shift in action. Congressman Lewis got to see the fruits of his labors. This is a sweet thought—that he could cross over to the other side knowing that his good work, which he referred to as "good trouble," was now blossoming in a new generation capable and courageous enough to pick up his bright torch. Born the son of sharecroppers in Troy, Alabama on February 21, 1940, Lewis left Alabama in 1957 to attend the American Baptist Theological Seminary in Nashville, Tennessee. It was at the seminary that Lewis learned about nonviolent protest. It is also where he began to organize sit-ins at segregated lunch counters. This upset his mother but established his commitment to the civil rights movement.

The future congressman went on to become a Freedom Rider in 1961 and in 1963 he helped plan the March on Washington where he stated in his speech, "We all recognize the fact that if any radical social, political and economic changes are to take place in our society, the people, the masses, must bring them about" (biography.com). Later, Lewis graduated from Fisk University, a historically black university in Nashville, Tennessee, where he received a degree in Religion and Philosophy. This is also where he met Rev. Dr. Martin Luther King, Jr.

Lewis led the demonstration that became known as "Bloody Sunday" following a march from Selma to Montgomery, Alabama on March 7, 1965. After marching across the Edmund Pettus Bridge, he and his fellow peaceful marchers were attacked by state troopers. Lewis received a fractured skull from the state's violence. Lewis recalled:

"They came forward beating us with nightsticks, trampling us with horses, releasing tear gas. I was hit in the head by a state trooper and a nightstick. My legs went from under me. I thought I was going to die" (NPR). This was one of the events that increased the urgency of the 1965 Voting rights Act.

Lewis was elected to Congress in 1986 in Georgia and received the Presidential Medal of Freedom in 2011. There is discussion upon his passing of renaming the Edmund Pettus Bridge, the John Lewis Bridge. John Lewis talked about the "good trouble" he got in. He was arrested 43 or 44 times during his lifetime. Lewis made a surprise appearance at a reenactment of the bridge crossing in Selma in March 2020.

"I'm not giving up," he said. "I'm not going to give in."
Surrounded by a crowd of marchers Lewis urged younger generations to take up the mantle to "help redeem the soul of America." "Keep the faith," he said. "Keep our eyes on the prize. We must go out and vote like we've never ever voted before" (NPR. Obituaries - *Civil Rights Leader John Lewis Never Gave Up or Gave In,* July 19, 2020).

In this time of great transition towards integrity and social justice, Representative John Lewis literally and figuratively represents hope. Despite the power struggle between the dark that is clinging to power for power's sake, and the light that is brightening and expanding around our globe, we continue to see grave injustices.

There are heroes everywhere. Our media doesn't focus much on them. The San Diego Union Tribune and the Women's Museum of California partnered to celebrate "a century of female achievement in San Diego to mark the 100th year of women's suffrage in America," in the Sunday, June 28, 2020, edition.

In a separate section of the newspaper three local women were highlighted. The title was, *Advocates & Empowerers, SAN DIEGANS WHO HAVE CREATED CHANGE AND INSPIRED OTHERS,* with beautiful illustrations of Dr. Shirley Weber, Rachel Ortiz and Geneviève. The top of the page says **PHENOMENAL MARKING THE**

100TH ANNIVERSARY OF THE 19TH AMENDMENT **WOMEN.** The fourth page of the section features 20 other women who "have improved the lives of others through their advocacy" (2).

Dr. Shirley Weber is a force to be reckoned with. She is the best friend of my former colleague Debra Maxie, who I had the joy and good fun to work with during my 12 years at Crawford High School. Debra was the counselor of the small school I was hired to teach at, The School of Law and Business. Later when our high school reunited (small schools was a Gates Foundation initiative that was largely abandoned after much expense and fanfare) she became a vice-principal. Debra and Shirley met when their oldest children began kindergarten at Encanto Elementary School. They were the only African American students in all—day seminar Kinder class. Their children were then in class together through high school. They go way back.

Dr. Shirley Weber is a trailblazer in many areas of social justice as well as a role model for what is possible. In the feature article on Dr. Weber by Charles T. Clark, he writes: "The 71-year-old is known to take up fights that many shy away from, ranging from education reform and accountability to police use of force and affirmative action" (2).

Like Bill Clinton, Dr. Shirley Weber was born in Hope, Arkansas in 1948 but she and her family "were forced to flee in 1951, after a lynch mob threatened to kill her Black sharecropper father over a dispute with a white farmer" (Ibid.). The family found its way to South Los Angeles where Shirley, her parents and seven siblings lived.

Dr. Weber's parents valued community service. In fact, "When she was a little girl, Weber's mother volunteered her to help people in the neighborhood write obituaries of their deceased loved ones, which Weber said taught her about people, their challenges, victories and failures" (Ibid.). This also highlights that Dr. Weber was a good writer and had literary skills to share with her community as a young girl.

In fact, the article makes clear the emphasis on education in Weber's household. Her father, who was educated through the sixth grade, "also put a high priority on education and rejoiced at his children's graduations, which Weber delivered plenty of" (Ibid.).

Weber attended UCLA at an early age. By the time she was 26, she had a master's degree and a PhD in Communications from UCLA. Wow! She became a professor at the age of 23, where she taught for four decades at San Diego State (SDSU) and helped to launch its Department of Africana Studies. She also taught at California State University at Los Angeles and Los Angeles City College before coming to SDSU (Dr. Shirley N. Weber, Biography).

> "This was really an ideal career for me." Weber said. "I could basically do my stuff, do my writing, do my work and at the same time go out and serve on the Board of NAACP, or Urban League, and tie what I did at the university to community action" (San Diego Union Tribune, 2).

Dr. Weber also served on the San Diego Unified School District school board starting in 1988, for eight years, including as president where "she became known for her advocacy for closing the achievement gap and a higher standard of excellence for children " (Dr. Shirley N. Weber, Biography). She then returned to SDSU where she worked to build an international program that took students to South Africa and Ghana.

Debra Maxie would accompany Dr. Weber on these trips to Africa, along with her students. Debra always took a few students from Crawford each year, spending much of the school year fundraising. Debra had a school club at Crawford, which served the African and African American students and others who chose to join.

On staff development afternoons, Dr. Weber would come to Debra's counseling office which was a classroom she shared with another counselor, and she would teach the students from Debra's club, Africana Studies. Dr. Weber was also the President of the Association of African American Educators or "Triple "A" "E," for short, for several years. I attended their annual conferences almost every year that I taught at Crawford.

San Diego Unified School District has a more diverse teaching staff than any other school district in San Diego County. The "Triple A E" conference was an opportunity to be reminded, as Dr. Joe Johnson so poetically urged us year after year; that "we have to do better." He would quote his grandmother from the deep South, who would pore over this PhD dissertation and ask him, "Where can you do better?"

In November 2012, Dr. Weber was elected to represent California's 79th Assembly District, which includes areas of South San Diego. One of Dr. Weber's greatest achievements as Assemblywoman was the passage of AB 391, a bill that she wrote to establish one of the highest standards in the nation for when police can use deadly force. The bill passed 34 - 3 in the California Senate and 68 - 0 in the Assembly. By the time of the vote law enforcement in a surprising move, withdrew their opposition to the bill.

Lark writes in the feature article:

> "Weber didn't take a victory lap or settle old scores, though. Instead she spoke about how the bill was the product of a 400-year challenge of African Americans, how the Black community has lived in fear that their lives could be taken with little hope of justice" (Ibid.).

Her deep knowledge and life experiences have made Weber a catalyst for change not only for racial justice but also for education accountability, calling out powerful unions representing law enforcement and teachers. She spars with members of the Democratic Party and has "butted heads with governors, notably Gov. Jerry Brown—with whom Weber and her late husband were friends" (Ibid.). Her husband, Judge Daniel Weber died in 2002. She is the mother of two adult children and referred to her two grandsons when AB392 passed. She said of her grandsons, Kadir, 7, and Jalil, 5, at the time:

> "'Their lives are idyllic,' Weber said of her grandsons.
> "They have great friends of all colors. They enjoy life, and they believe at this point that they have just as much right

and respect as any child in this nation—and that should never change" (Ibid.).

Weber shared that she did not want to ever have the conversation Black parents and grandparents have, particularly with their sons and grandsons about how to handle interactions with police and *avoid getting killed* [my italics].

Currently Weber is championing "a bill that would create a task force to study slavery and reparations, and a constitutional amendment known as ACA5 that will put a repeal of California's 1996 affirmative action ban on the ballot in November" (Ibid.). The article concludes:

> Weber says she's taken on contentious issues because she has seen what real fear looks like, from people who ran from the Ku Klux Klan. She also doesn't want to fail her community and her parents, she said.
>
> "Once you decide, you can take the mountain," Weber said.

She has and continues to do so. Debra Maxie was named as a Commissioner of the California Department of Education and traveled to Sacramento on official business during her last years as a vice-principal at Crawford. Debra retired in 2017 after 40 years in education. I retired at the same time. We were offered a golden handshake by our district, as an incentive to retire.

Debra's story is inspiring as well. She grew up in Chicago public housing, raised along with her sister by a single mother. When I first met Debra, she was constantly on a plane going to or coming from Chicago to help take care of her aging mother. Debra always calls Chicago, "home."

There was a woman in Debra's community who observed her intelligence and tenacity and became a mentor to her. This woman connected Debra with Lincoln University, a historically Black college. She helped Debra apply to the university and drove her to Jefferson, Missouri where she graduated four years later. Every fall, Debra would take time off from school to return to Lincoln University for a reunion with her sorority sisters.

There are countless Dr. Weber's and Debra Maxie's helping to pull up others across our planet. In 2019, Dr. Shirley Weber was "The Union Tribune San Diegan of the Year." I am grateful to have known these powerful and beautiful soul sisters in peace and equality. Their stories open my heart and make me weep right here, right now.

"Shirley Nash Weber, Ph.D. was nominated to serve as Secretary of State by Governor Gavin Newsom on December 22, 2020 and sworn into office on January 29, 2021. She is California's first Black Secretary of State and only the fifth African American to serve as a state constitutional officer in California's 170-year history" (sos.ca.gov).

Dr. Weber's daughter Dr. Akilah Weber ran for Dr. Weber's District 79 seat to replace her, and won in a special election in April 2021 (a79.asmdc.org and drakilahweber.com).

Chapter 20

Change is Upon Us

7/24/2020

The San Diego Union Tribune, Thursday, July 23, 2020, front page, bottom half, has two articles that reflect the impact of the Black Lives Matter movement on education. The headline on the left is: *CSU TO REQUIRE ETHNIC STUDIES COURSE*. The other headline, center page in bold is: ***S.D. UNIFIED ADOPTS RACIAL-EQUITY REFORMS***.

We know the impact of education on politics. Polls measure college-educated voters as well as voters without a college education, and currently these groups make different electoral choices. In the CSU article by Nina Agraval, Los Angeles, she opens the piece by sharing:

> "In the first major change to general education across its
> system in decades, all 430,000 undergraduates attending
> California State universities must take an ethnic studies or
> social justice class course, a requirement approved by CSU
> Trustees Wednesday…
>
> The Board of Trustees voted in favor of the requirement,
> which will take effect starting in 2023 in the nation's largest
> four-year university system" (A1).

Ironically, many of those who opposed the measure "prefer a bill sponsored by Assemblywoman Shirley Weber, D-San Diego" (A8), but "The Cal State systemwide Academic Senate opposes Weber's bill (AB1460), arguing that state legislators are improperly interfering in matters of higher education curriculum, setting a dangerous precedent… 'If we were in a different state, we would be scared out of our wits by the idea that the Legislature would be telling us what we should be teaching,' trustee Rebecca Eisen said. 'This is our responsibility'" (A8).

For the largest university system in America to require a three-unit lower-division course on Ethnic Studies or Social Justice raises consciousness, as education is intended to do. It reflects the need for all of us to better understand one another. It has long been a requirement in California Teaching Credential programs to take a multicultural course as a prerequisite to entering the teaching program. All teachers in California public schools have demonstrated proficiency in this area to maintain our teaching credentials.

The subtitle for the San Diego Unified article is: "De-escalation policy for school police, banning some suspensions OK'd." In the article by Kristen Taketa, she outlines agreed upon changes by the Board of Education in an online workshop on racial equality. These include "Ban future 'skillful defiance' suspensions for all middle school students," and "The district will discuss banning such suspensions for high school students in the future." Other initiatives include:

"Write a new de-escalation policy and require de-escalation training for school police by the end of next month.

Train all educators on anti-bias and cultural responsiveness starting next month.

Increase the number of diverse candidates chosen for positions."

And my favorite:

"Change grading policies to give students chances to correct their work and improve their grades" (Ibid.).

Too often the third-dimension model of punishment and authoritarian control on the part of educators is still part of school culture. Students should be given EVERY opportunity to succeed and have the teacher on their side. Though this may seem obvious, it is too easy for teachers to just "blame the kid," or "the parents" for a student's seeming intransigence—when in fact, the student needs an ally.

As Board Trustee Richard Barrera stated at the close of the workshop: "We've had this conversation so many times before ... these are not new issues and these are frankly not new strategies and those are certainly not new data points" (A9). City Schools (SDUSD) has been focused on equity for some time.

To highlight the quality of the work done at City Schools in the area of equity, the district has made ethnic studies a graduation requirement by next school year. Wendy Ranck-Buhr, PhD, the instructional support officer for the district, shared that the district has "rewritten its history courses to include perspectives of historically marginalized groups" (A9). She states:

"In order for us to become an anti-racist and socially just

system, we must also work to humanize and de-colonize

both our curriculum and our instructional practices" (Ibid.).

Dr. Wendy, as I called her, is passionate about student equity, particularly for students with challenges to learning.

In a training she mentioned she had read Bryan Stevenson's *Just Mercy,* which was published in 2015. I put that book on my reading list and finally got to it in retirement. It is the story of heroes in our culture, particularly Bryan Stevenson who also played a major role in freeing many innocent Black men, in particular, on death row. His advocacy goes to keeping children out of prison and not having children tried as adults. He has argued and won several times before the Supreme Court on these critical issues.

It is happening. The shift is here. We are in the midst of it. As change transforms our institutions into more open and accepting paradigms that support all people in a way that is equal, humane, and compassionate, life improves for all of humanity.

While the news shows our old paradigms crumbling before our eyes, great work is being done behind the scenes in all areas of life laying the foundation for a much more just and healthy humanity that leads us to the collective 5th Dimension and World Peace.

Chapter 21

The Dispensation of Compassion

7/25/2020

In Kryon *Book 14, The New Human and Evolution of Humanity,* published in 2017, Kryon shares much about the shift occurring at the precession of the equinoxes that took place December 21, 2012. In the words of Kryon who is melded with Lee Carroll, who channels him, we are reminded, once again:

> The teaching of the ancient and current indigenous of the planet, as well as that of Kryon, is that the precession of the equinoxes marked a demarcation point to all of humanity. It represents a point of change—one that the planet has never seen before. Human nature was going to start growing up and evolving. Wisdom would begin to be more common. Solutions to hatred would start to occur that you never thought possible. These are not just Kryon's words. These come from the indigenous of the planet, those who have been around for thousands of years before Abraham. That is original prophecy. Here is the overall prophecy of the Ancients. If humanity would make it past 2012, there would be an exodus of old energy. The exodus would be from an old prophecy to a new future, and a new prophecy.
>
> It represents another kind of slavery… coming out of an old land of slavery of thought, where war seemed to be the only way" (198–199).

I find it ironic that the issue of slavery in American history is forefront in our collective consciousness in July 2020. But even greater than this, we have a president who has unleashed unmarked/unidentifiable federal armed forces in Portland, Oregon against a mostly white, middle-class community. The excuse is to protect a federal building against people who have been protesting peacefully since the Earth-shattering murder of George Floyd, a Black man, by a Minneapolis policeman.

In addition, we have a Republican led Senate that left Washington, D.C. for the weekend without presenting a plan for contending with the end of supplemental unemployment. This program is keeping Americans and our states afloat. It ends tomorrow, July 26th.

So right now, the president and the U.S. Senate are allowing all of us to see the truth; that in the eyes of this government, or at least the presidency and the Senate, we are all part of a system of slavery. We are to get "back to work" in the middle of a global pandemic where our country's leadership has been so intentionally absent that we have the greatest number of Covid-19 cases in the world.

As of July 25th, over 140,000 Americans have died with many more deaths to come. This is due to overrun hospitals in states like Florida and Texas where doctors are practicing triage because of the lack of beds in ICU's. The president's response is to unleash federally initiated confrontation and violence on the citizens in "liberal democratic" cities.

Last night our daughter Ada called from her home in Portland, Oregon to let us know that after careful consideration, research, and planning, she and her housemates were joining the protest last night. When she called and I saw her name on the TV Screen [isn't technology awesome] I had just been thinking of her.

I answered the phone and I said, "I was just thinking about you!" And what I was thinking was how she would contribute to bringing about peace and calm in Portland. Ada is what Kryon calls a "tree hugger." She hiked the Pacific Crest Trail from Tuolumne Valley in

Yosemite National Park to the Oregon, Washington border, at the Bridge of the Gods as her way to move to Portland.

She and her housemates have been sheltering since March. They have an agreement to stay safe at all times so as not to endanger anyone's health. Ada has a lot of camping gear from working for REI and then an outdoor gear company called Sea to Summit, from which she, like many Americans, was laid off.

Ada and her housemates have been going camping as their outlet, to beautiful places in Oregon. They are holding the energy of peace and calm for P-Town when they are communing with nature. One of the most wonderful features of Portland is that 20 miles out of town you are in wilderness areas that are absolutely beautiful. Portlanders are very close to nature. The city also has Washington Park with its arboretums and miles of hiking trails.

My husband's immediate reaction was "That's great." He later advised her that Vaseline on your lips and around your eyes will help lessen the sting of tear gas or pepper gas, recalling his experiences marching on Washington, D.C., to protest the Vietnam War.

Ada assured us they wouldn't be heading to the front line and that they would be staying together. I added, "That's really important. Every time I go to a protest march, I go with several people, and we stay together." We wished her well, knowing they were informed, they would be masked and would be showing solidarity with their hometown under siege from government thugs. If it was a riot, as Trump insisted, it was a riot of white people who have come out in a very white state to say, "No More!"

And our government's message? "Get back to work!" We aren't giving you any aid. If you don't agree with our politics, we are sending hostile troops to spray you with tear gas and beat you with batons. This is exactly what everyone is protesting against.

So, it is not just Black slavery. It is slavery of the working class, the middle class, the upper class who are being called back to work. Even our children are being ordered back to school while people are getting sick and dying all around us. The fact is, in order to save our lives, we need to shelter in place—with work and school be damned until we get this virus under control. It isn't just the Blacks, the Latinos, the immigrants. It's over 60 percent of us who are being attacked in the U.S. by our government because we are stepping up to a form of institutional slavery which has kept us on a hamster wheel of productivity creating billionaires, and looming poverty for most of us.

I awoke to a text, "Home safe and sound, 2:31 am."

And what do I as a mother do when my daughter is heading into a protest march in a volatile situation? I put the light around her in my mind, like a bubble. I also imagined another light bubble around her and her housemates. I have also been opening my heart chakra and sending light to Portland as well as across our nation, and to Washington D.C.

As a licensed spiritual practitioner of Religious Science or Science of Mind, I work directly with Spirit to set the intention for the outcome I choose. This includes peace, prosperity, new medicines, vaccines, and healing for humanity. I also claim the intention that Trump and his administration, his family and the entire GOP return to the nothingness from where they came to be replaced with transparency, integrity and compassion. This is what prayer looks like for me. Earnest Holmes, the founder of Religious Science, teaches that: "There is a power for good greater than us, and we can use it." The truth is we all use it. But most people use this infinite power unconsciously, not aware that our thoughts, feelings, words, and actions create our lives. Our lives are the out-picturing of these mental processes and actions. This is why we always say in Science of Mind: "Change your thinking, Change your life."

Ernest Holmes recommends that when we are feeling challenged or stressed, we go to the opposite feeling, thought, emotion. If you are feeling anxiety, shift to a happy thought—something that makes you feel good. We call this work, because it requires us to be conscious at all times of our thoughts, feelings, words, and actions.

As Dr. Joe Dispenza teaches, based upon his vast research and data collection, changing your thinking changes your neural pathways. Shift your thought to happiness and the neural pathways of anxiety and worry get pruned from the absence of use. It is up to us in this shift to consciously manage, direct, and redirect our thoughts to what we "want" and take off from "what we don't want." As the song says, "Don't worry! Be happy!" It is that simple, but it requires awareness, vigilance, and self-patience to consciously change our thoughts from negative to positive as a way to change our lives for the better.

Kryon reminds us, "You are slowly moving into the Promised Land of new thought" (*The Gaia Effect*, 199). He completes this channel by stating:

> For this place will slowly lose its energy of doom. It will not be the end of anything. It will dissipate eventually, but dear ones, there is something going on that is bigger than any kind of prophecy. If you understand what I'm really telling you in this place you will call it cognizant. You'll believe it, and every cell in your body can stand tall and say, *Now I know why I was born at this time!* You are Masters, all. You have the wisdom of love, and the solution. The Second Exodus.
>
> ... Say goodbye to the Armageddon as you leave.
>
> And so it is (199).

Kryon goes on to say, "I will show you that this planet is actually designed to shift consciousness. It has happened before, dear ones. You are not the first" (200).

Kryon describes the Laws of Dispensation, and our shift in human nature towards compassion taking place on this planet now.

> ... There are those of you who feel that Human nature never changes, and yet it has. It has changed in history so profoundly that you restarted your clock! The prophets that you have studied so far, mostly belong to what we have called the God of Law. In fact, the biblical scholars would

call it the Old Testament of humanity — "The Dispensation of Law."

Then two thousand years ago, right in this land, was brought the Jewish prophet, Christ. He gave you a new concept. He was here with an Akash, yes an Akash (since he was Human), and he was Jewish! Right time, right place— and he changed so much for the entire planet. He changed the perception of the relationship to God. Scripture became new scripture—The New Testament—the new humanity. The One God became the One Loving God. It was an evolvement of thought. Then it became what biblical scholars call the "Dispensation of Love."

Muhammad continued this, and, being the most recent prophet, if you look at that which was spoken so many times, he refers to the love of God, constantly.... You passed from Law to Love and all the prophets felt it (*The New Human,* 200).

We see that it was Moses in the Old Testament who brought the 10 Commandments down from Mt. Sinai, laying a foundation for the laws or what Kryon refers to as "The 10 Suggestions," for humanity to live by. Then Jesus, the Christ, came and taught that this one God was a loving God, which Mohammed "in expression after expression, after expression, describing the infinite love of God.

Kryon shows us that shifts of consciousness have taken place on our planet in the past and they have been recognized by humanity at the times of the consciousness shift. He continues to clarify:

Now in the process of the shift, it was so profound, that you now actually measure time differently! Before Christ (B.C.), and After Death (A.D). Do you see what you have done? There was a recognition of a consciousness shift! It was so profoundly new, that you had to restart the clock, and the entire planet now measures history with this system. Now, did God change? No. So what changed in this story?

Humans did! You did! All of your Akashic records and all
your past lives tell of a Human perception shift from a God
of Law, to a God of Love The Letter "C" represents the
"DISPENSATION OF COMPASSION" (200–201).

Here Kryon is giving teachings based upon the letters of the word
"compassion."

This is what we are seeing in the Black Lives Matter movement that
has become the largest global protest movement in modern history.

In Portland, Oregon a city block of mothers dressed in yellow
showed their compassion for Black Lives and continue to do so night
after night. As they face Trump's secret armed forces, they come armed
with bicycle helmets and umbrellas as well as their "mother" status. The
dads have united by wearing orange and many are armed with leaf
blowers to disburse any tear gas unleashed upon them.

The white folks from the suburbs, which Portland really is, are rising
up and saying, "No More!"

Kryon explains about the calendar and how it may be reset once
again.

The Maya (and others) created a calendar, a long one of over
5,000. years, but the calendar stopped in 2012. A new
calendar was created years ago to start up, if humanity
passed December 2012 (at the start of a new cycle of the
Precession of the Equinoxes). According to the Maya
calendar prophecy, if humanity would make it past that point
without destroying itself, there would be no Armageddon.
You would also have to reset the clock again. The clock is
one of Human consciousness (201).

Kryon talks about how we will look back at the years before 2012
as the "Barbaric Period," because all we did was go to war against one
another which is not productive or creative in a positive way.
Dr. Christian Sorensen, the Spiritual Leader of Seaside Center for
Spiritual Living, once said at Christmas time in a Sunday talk: "It is not

about the birth of a baby! It is about the birth of consciousness!" By this he means the Christ consciousness of infinite love.

Kryon concludes:

> The Dispensation of Compassion is now upon you. It represents compassion for one another. It's a wisdom that has not really been seen yet... I want you to look at the Ancients and what they did with their clocks. This is now new. ... It represents the wisdom of Human ancestors who have reset their clocks when consciousness changed on the planet. It is a precedent!" (201).

Humanity has reset our calendar to match our evolution in consciousness.

Kryon elaborates:

> Get ready for new thought. It's more now than just love. It's a mature love that creates compassion for life and humanity. Before I finish, many will ask *Who is the next prophet?* Humans are starting to become mature and wise. What if I told you in this new energy, the prophet is now within you. Your Higher-Self knows it all! This is the prophet you are now following. This is the new wisdom—the compassion of the Higher-Self (202).

Here we are on July 26, 2020, and Kryon said we would see the demarcation of those with compassion and those without compassion. This is the evolution of human consciousness taking us to a higher level of Dispensation from love to compassion for all. Politically, we have a party arguing for economic support for Americans as we move through this pandemic, and we have a political party that does not want to spend our taxpayer dollars supporting the taxpayers through this unprecedented time. This is what the absence of compassion looks like.

Higher consciousness, which is unconditional love, infinite love, peace, beauty, compassion, and joy, is our birthright and it is our destiny as New Humans. Many of us are already there. Those in resistance may follow the line of the Hopi Prophecy to oblivion, by choosing freely, as is their God-given right, to shun the compassion and denigrate peaceful and loving action on behalf of ourselves and others.

What is low consciousness? It is hate, violence, and the absence of empathy or compassion. It is a belief in "not enough to go around," when the truth is we live in an infinitely prosperous and opulent universe. Just look out your window. Paradise is right there teeming with an infinite variety of life that cycles itself to reproduce again and again without any assistance or input from us.

In America we are seeing the struggle between the dark and the light. In the new energy of the feminine and unity side of our 26,000-year cycle, the light, in the words of Kryon, "is winning." This is why we can see the corruption that has always been taking place—but before it was hidden from us. Today, in America, the dark energy is in our face, and we are not pleased, especially the women.

On July 27, 2020, the San Diego Union Tribune *Tweet of the Week: Goes to TIME Magazine (@TIME).*

> We human beings have these marvelous, brilliant minds. But we are also the biggest troublemakers on the planet. Now we should utilize our brains with compassion, and a sense of concern" writes the @DalaiLama (726/2020, SDUT).

Chapter 22

More About the Wobble
& the Archetypes

7/27/2020

In the Book, *The Gaia Effect, The remarkable system of collaboration between Gaia and Humanity,* by Kryon and Monika Muranyi, the archivist of the Kryon channeling, Monika writes about the shift of the Kundalini of the planet from India in the Northern Hemisphere to South America in the Southern Hemisphere.

Spiritually, the Northern Hemisphere represents the masculine archetype while the Southern Hemisphere represents the feminine archetype. As we passed the marker on December 12, 2012, we moved back into a feminine generated energy marked by an era of unity and light that we are moving into. We are leaving the past 13,000-year cycle where masculine energy dominated.

Just as we are changing as humans with this shift, so too is Earth Mother.

Kryon describes what the Kundalini means during the *Kryon Patagonia cruise* at the start of 2012.

> The Kundalini is coiled at the bottom of the spine of the
> body. It only uncoils when the male and female are
> balanced. It wraps around three energies of the body, three
> and a half times, and it wraps around what is called the
> lingam [Hinduism: a symbol of divine generative energy,
> especially a phallus or phallic object worshipped as a symbol

of Shiva (Definitions from Oxford Languages)]. Three wraps represent easy unwrapping parts of energy, but the final half wrap represents the most difficult part, which is the divine enlightenment of balance. When the Kundalini unwraps and stays that way, you have a balanced Human Being, if not even enlightened. This is a metaphor of the planet and this is beginning to happen (140).

In describing the timing of the kundalini energy movement, Kryon once again refers to the completion of the 26,000-year galactic cycle that is in a new beginning, a new epoch. The channel is called *The Movement of the Kundalini,* given during the *Patagonia Kryon Cruise* - January 28, 2012.

The 26,000-year alignment of the equinoxes of your planet is a grand alignment, and it has been known in astronomy as the Galactic Alignment. It is called that because the start and stop point of the wobble of your Earth on its axis aligns through your sun to the center of the galaxy. This alignment only happens every 26,000 years.

In order for the equinoxes to proceed through the equatorial plane of your galaxy [the Milky Way strip in the sky] and work themselves through the end of this cycle and beginning of the next one, it will take 36 years. This final stage began approximately 18 years ago, and 2012 is now the center, or the beginning of the last half of the last cycle. You have 18 years left of this energetic event, which actually represents the end of one thing and the beginning of another.

… Even the ancients who watched the stars knew of this alignment. It corresponded to the potentials of consciousness shift, since it also represented a decision point or time fractal in the pattern of potentials that has been the core of ancient astronomical prophecy for eons. So all of this was expected and is not a surprise. But it carries with it profound change, and this is what we all saw 20 years ago when I arrived to begin my messages. Humanity has these opportunities about every half cycle of the 26,000-year alignment. The last one was 13,000 years ago and humanity was not ready. Now you are (140–141).

This is the clearest explanation I have found on the Galactic Alignment. When Kryon states: "The stop point of the wobble of your Earth on its axis aligns through your sun to the center of the galaxy," this is a physical alignment of Earth and our Sun to the center of our galaxy. Kryon also explains in very simple terms that currently Earth is moving through the milky part of our Milky Way galaxy. The transit of Earth through the milky part of the Milky Way takes 36 years. In 2020 we have another 10 years crossing this light filled part of our galaxy, making the transition from the previous 26,000-year cycle to a new 26,000-year cycle.

We cross this part of the Milky Way galaxy, our home, every 13,000 years, or twice in a 26,000-year revolution of our sun and solar system around the star Alcyone in the Pleiadian star system. These are significant transits for humanity reflecting the dramatic changes we are experiencing in 2020. The last time we transited this part of the Milky Way was during the Age of Leo, where humanity began to see itself as individuals.

Chapter 23

The Astrological Ages

7/29/2020

The website *astrolada.com* describes each astrological age from the Age of Leo forward. Kryon, during the 2019 Egypt bucket list trip, stated in a channel that the bottom of the Sphinx was 13,000 years old. He said the top or head was a lot more recent and was the head of a pharaoh. This is why I love Kryon so much. He provides information that is other-worldly or beyond our 4-dimensional perception of our world, awakening us to higher frequencies and higher dimensions.

The lion shape of bottom of the Sphinx, which dates from 10,000 to 8,000 B.C., or 12,000 years ago, represents the Golden Age of Leo. This astrological sign is ruled by the Sun, which is the center of our galaxy. As a result, Leos are very dramatic and like to be the center of attention. According to *Astrolada.com:*

> This was when individuality started appearing for the first time. Humans gradually started to think as separate beings with unique qualities. The desire to lead and organize the primitive social structures, and have superior power over others, brought on the horizon the first kings/priests/rulers/shamans of human origin… All these qualities of individuality, superiority and leadership are common features for people with Leo in their horoscopes nowadays (Ibid.).

Leo represents royalty and kings, so it is a sign of leadership. This was considered the Golden Age for humanity "because the consciousness of connection with God and the Higher invisible worlds and their inhabitants, was still a living reality for every human, and they were not afraid of death as they experienced the multidimensional levels of the Universe" (Ibid.). Humanity was still connected consciously with the unseen realm. This site states that "back then, we could not think clearly for ourselves as individuals—the reasoning and logical abilities of humans were rudimentary then (Ibid.). But the influence of the Age of Leo awakened the individual and established the notion of leaders ruling the populace.

During the Age of Cancer which spans 8,000 to 6,000 B.C., or 8 to 10 thousand years ago, "Humans started to settle down, build houses, and settlements, do agriculture and farming" (Ibid.). Cancer signifies home and family. It is ruled by the Moon which is feminine and regulates feminine cycles on Earth. "The Mother and her nurturing skills were exalted and worshipped—women had power and it was a matriarchal society! ... Figurines of voluptuous Mother Goddesses are found all over the world from this period (Ibid.).

According to this website:

> Humans were still highly intuitive and were connected to the
> "invisible worlds." The average human from the Age of
> Cancer would receive [picture images directly] such that
> there was no need for organized religion yet, because
> everyone would experience the Divine directly... (Ibid.).

Though they organized themselves as a Goddess oriented agrarian society, those living in the Age of Cancer maintained their connection with the Divine energies of the Universe, revealing the consciousness of humanity before organized religion.

The Age of Gemini spans the years of 6,000 until 4,000 B.C., or 6,000 to 8,000 years ago. *Astrolada* states:

> This was the time the first settlements started turning into
> cities and trade between different people of the world started
> appearing. As you know, Gemini is a sign of trade,
> exchange, communications, connections. Infrastructures

between different cultures based on exchange of trade and information appeared (or shall we say—reappeared after the downfall of Atlantis)... Humans discovered the written word again and "reinvented" writing. At first it was rudimentary glyphs but then it became more and more complicated. The first written records date from then (Ibid.).

We see that writing and cross-cultural communication and exchange was developed during the Age of Gemini.

According to this website, "People started developing and using more skills, crafts, arts," but even more significant:

The reasoning, practical and logical abilities of humans were become (ing) more pronounced [as Gemini rules the mind and thinking], but with the need for use of the left rational brain, the right intuitive one started to loose (sic) its power— telepathic and psychic abilities started to be substituted with practical ones. ... It was the descending age—from Spirit into Matter, we had to lose contact with the Higher Worlds in order to develop our individual thinking processes and not just be like the instinctual animals, which follow the dictates of their Group Soul Spirit (Ibid.).

Reason, which is a feature of mental Gemini, an air sign, began to dominate the human mind as we moved in consciousness from Spirit to be closer to Matter or our physical three-dimensional world.

The Age of the Bull or the Age of Taurus took place 6,000 to 4,000 years ago or from 4,000 to 2,000 B.C. Humans continued to establish a more settled life as well as to improve farming and agriculture methods. *Astrolada* describes *The Astrological Ages:*

Massive and sturdy building(s) were being constructed around the globe, reflecting the sturdy and lasting nature of Taurus. Knowledge of the material realm and Nature increased. We became more and more merged and identified with the physical, the practical, the 5 senses, and the last vestiges of direct perception of the Higher Worlds were disappearing. We were sinking into matter fast! But we needed this in order to get to know the Natural World. ... Many cultures who were at its height worshipped the Bull/the Cow: The Egyptians, the Indians, the Thracian. The beautiful and plentiful feminine forms ruled by Taurus— were worshipped and women had much more power in society than we believe (Ibid.).

Taurus is the most stable sign in the zodiac. It is an Earth sign which makes it very grounded, and it is a fixed sign which makes it very stable. It is ruled by the planet Venus, so it is about beauty and feminine principle frequency. It was at the end of this age that Moses climbed Mt. Sinai and returned to the bottom of the mountain with the 10 tablets of the Ten Commandments where he found the Jewish people he was leading, worshipping a golden calf. He admonished his people not to worship false Gods, as humanity was moving out of the Age of Taurus into the Age of Aries.

The age of Aries was 2,000 to 4,000 years ago or from 2,000 B.C. to 0 B.C. *Astrolada* says (maybe up to 500 A.D.). Aries is the first sign of the zodiac, so it represents beginnings. It is also ruled by Mars, so it is masculine and aggressive in its nature. *Astrolada* explains:

This is the time of Great military cultures: Egyptians and Persians, the Jewish, the Trojans, the Greeks, the Spartans, the Romans! Aries being a martial and masculine signs (sic), put into power cultures which worshipped the perfect Male body and Male power and trampled on the Female—the role of the stronger over the weaker! History from this age has left us the myths of mighty male heroes and warriors; Moses, Hercules, Spartacus, Alexander the Great. The law of "tooth for tooth, eye for an eye" became a mantra! Metallurgy developed, so did engineering, mathematics and logic—all under Aries. Many of these above-mentioned cultures worshipped the Ram—the Jews, the Egyptians, the Romans (Ibid.).

Through the twelve ages of the zodiac, we and our Earth physically and esoterically pass through the 26,000-year cycle of the Precession of the Equinoxes. Through this, history becomes History, with a capital "H." We see the powerful influence of these astrological eras on our known and unknown history. Our history is not just myth. It is real and builds upon itself one astrological sign, or 2,100-year period, at a time. This breakdown of the succession of astrological ages puts myth and history into a more broad and meaningful story. It connects and makes sense over large swaths of time providing a continuity that is missing in our contemporary view of history and religion.

We can see the development of humanity from nomads to agrarians, to builders, to warriors. *Astrolada* identifies the Age of Pisces as going from 0 to 1900 A.D. Not surprisingly, it states, "The Age of Pisces was the age of Christianity," and so it is. *Astrolada* continues:

It is not by chance that the symbol of the Christians is the Fish. (Early Christian catacombs were covered in these). Jesus' disciples were fishermen and he was the Lamb that was sacrificed [the lamb was from the Aries Age, like Moses' ram was from the Age of Taurus—or the previous age before his time, indicating the symbolic end of the preceding age of Aries and the coming of the New Age of Pisces]. Christianity (Buddhism in the East) and the age of Pisces introduced the feeling of compassion, turning the other cheek, kindness and sacrifice for an idea or others. Before that, charity, forgiveness and empathy were rare qualities—it took 2000 years for these impulses to become more natural to humans. Mind you, we still have so much to strive towards the ideal love of Christ, but at least the seed was planted. The age of Pisces was full of bloody and barbaric moments/throwback to the vicious Aries age (the old age usually continues parallel for most of the new one) but amongst these higher manifestations of Pisces also were born: amazing and refined pieces of musical and artistic genius, soaked with mystical inspiration" (Ibid.).

Pisces is ruled by Neptune which represents spirituality. Venus is exalted in Pisces which means it operates very easily in this sign. Thus, the flourishing of the arts and music during this Age. Spiritual houses of worship in many different forms were built and maintained during this age.

According to *Astrolada*:

Humans had to learn to believe in a Higher being, without the ability to feel or experience God directly (in contrast to the previous ages when humanity still had an inner knowing of the Higher worlds)—so faith and hope were also developed. This was the age of the Maya, illusions, lies, suffering, victimization of innocents and martyrdom, another Pisces manifestation, but this softened the hardened materialistic souls of humans and created a new impulse towards something perfect, the Divine merging with the Higher. Out of this the most exquisite pieces of art were born and the soul became compassionate, gentler. All this is a painful but needed process for our incarnating souls, in order to prepare us for the age of Aquarius—the age of brotherhood which is gradually starting and will come in full power within the next 2000 years (Ibid.).

Faith and hope are the anchors of this age. Somehow, we moved past the places where we could feel Spirit directly and so we developed these two qualities. Humanity became more gentle and compassionate. Music and art reflected the influence of Venus being exalted in Pisces. It's rulership in Neptune allows humanity to have spiritual experiences through the spiritual systems created during this Age—yet a mystery surrounds what occurs in the unseen realm.

As we move deeper into the Age of Aquarius, the spiritual systems developed and relied upon by humanity during the Age of Pisces are buckling under the gravity of this new age pushing back on the institutions of this previous age.

Ironically, one of the greatest challenges facing organized religion in July/August 2020 is the Covid-19 virus. People are unable to safely gather in groups of any size. The result is that here in America most churches, synagogues, mosques, and other spiritual gatherings have moved on-line to live-streaming, a very Aquarian activity.

There is a lot of political pushback from some organizations who have gone ahead and gathered, often without social distancing or wearing masks because of their beliefs in some kind of freedom. The result has been that many people have gotten the virus, and some have died because they gathered with fellow parishioners.

When I watched the Tour de France in the summer of 2019 on television, one of my favorite sporting events of the year, I wondered out loud, "What is going to become of all the churches in the small, medium and large villages and towns. How will they be repurposed?"

During the Piscean Age, spiritual leaders were the agreed upon conduit between Spirit and humanity. Spiritual acknowledgement and ceremonies were done in a building led by an intermediary, such as a priest or minister. This individual was the connection for the people to God—someone who guided the populace and provided the link to the unseen power of Spirit.

As we move deeper into the Age of Aquarius, we are finding that we can commune with Spirit on our own, through meditation, contemplation, being in nature, gathering with like minds. You can literally see the unraveling of the Piscean way as traditional religious activities decline.

Astrological Ages Through a Platonic Year (26,000 yrs.)

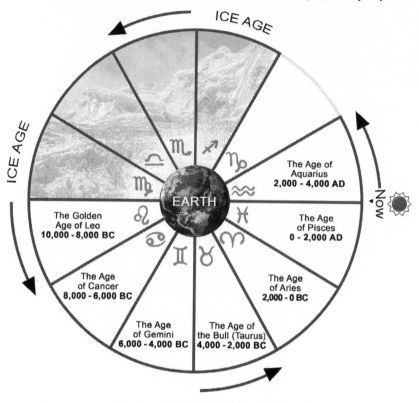

This is no longer a one-day-a-week event supported by prayer throughout the week. Spirit moves in, through and as us at all times, and we become the holy repository of Spirit's greatest good 24/7. And yes, the power of gathering in community to celebrate the beauty and love of Spirit, is powerful, uplifting, and inspiring, and so it will continue in new and unexpected forms and venues.

But this virus is challenging us to go within—to find our own true compass of wholeness, joy, and love. Spiritual leaders who risk the lives of their parishioners by asking them to gather in the middle of a pandemic, in my perspective, are not walking the path of wholeness. Yet, we all have the choice and free will to put our lives at risk by not following the science and recommendations of health officials and experts around the globe.

Astrological Ages - Attributes

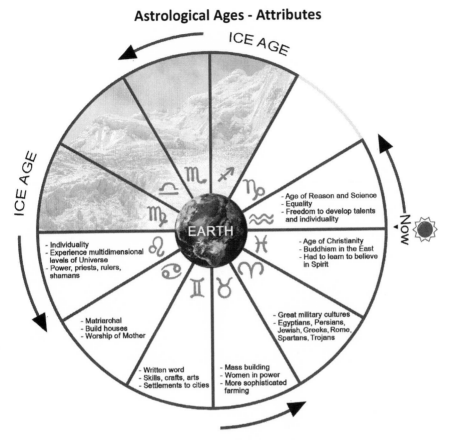

Note: The Ice Age preceded the Golden Age of Leo, so the top part is the Ice Age, with the exception of the Aquarian Age, which is now.

We exercise this God-given gift of choice and free will every moment of our lives. Spirit is always there for the asking, but for those who choose to not believe, nothing is taken away. It is the metaphor of the story of the Prodigal Son. The son who repudiated his family and left for years wandering the land was greeted with open arms and received by his father, just as the son who stayed home and followed the cultural norms.

So, in America right now there are many making the choice that the virus is a "hoax," as they have been told by our president; that it is just the flu. So, wearing or not wearing a mask has become a political hot potato. As one side chooses Science, the other side embraces a nihilistic attitude towards what they can't see, touch, and feel—until they contract the virus, should that happen. The states in America led by Republican Governors have downplayed the virus and rejected medically recommended safety precautions such as mandating the wearing of masks, not allowing gatherings of more than 6–10 people, socially distancing and washing hands frequently.

Their reasoning for rejecting the advice of experts is what Kryon refers to as "B.S." or a "Belief System." Some even say, "If it is God's will I die from this, so be it."

The Republican Party has taken on the mantle of fighting for the Piscean past while the Democratic Party is embracing the science, facts and inventions of the Aquarian Age. Our politics in America in 2020 are between the religious domination of the Piscean Age and the scientific discoveries of the Aquarian Age.

One political party is backward looking and backward longing. The other is forward-looking and forward longing. This is just a reflection of what happens when a 26,000-year cycle ends, and then begins a new 26,000-year cycle. We are experiencing the clash of these ages and the powerful transition that takes place every 26,000 years in our galaxy.

We all stood in line to incarnate and be here for this time of cataclysmic and seismic change in humanity. The Earth supports us, and the galaxy and universe hold us as precious and powerful and significant—which we haven't even been taught about. We are each here to be a part of this universal shift of consciousness from fear to love, from destruction to creation, from war to peace and each one of us has a part to play, or we would not be in these bodies right now.

The Aquarian Age goes from our present day to 4,000 C.E. This is the age of reason and Science. Aquarius is an air sign, so it is mental, like Gemini and Libra. According to *Astrolada:*

> Since the Constellation of Aquarius started approaching the
> Vernal Equinox for the past 200 years, we became
> industrialized, mechanized and now a highly technological

civilization! No wonder, since Aquarius rules Science. The higher octave of Aquarius is Science which is liberating for Humanity—which gives us freedom to develop our true individuality and talents rather than having to just toil for survival.

The Lower octave of Aquarius is Science used destructively (atomic bomb, pollution). ... Also totalitarian dictatorships, fascism, communism, corporations list (etc). But thankfully the further we progress into the Age of Aquarius the more its higher manifestation will come into being—discovering inexhaustible sources of free energy (even the sign of Aquarius depicts an electrical current), working with Nature, not against it, technology providing the spiritual nature of Reality and the higher dimension and technology helping raise the vibration of human consciousness so we can connect directly to these, telepathy (Aquarius rules telepathy and clairvoyance) and, of course, brotherhood, freedom, justice and equality.

What we are witnessing in the protests for justice and equality around the world by the youth is literally the dawning of the Age of Aquarius.

Llewelyn George, in his seminal book, *A to Z Horoscope Maker and Delineator,* first published in 1910 describes the attributes of Aquarius as:

Leader, truthseeker, scientist, sincere, earnest, defined, humane, co-operative, sociable, service, considerate, unbiased, patient, steady, inventive, philosophical, intuitive, pleasant, progressive, cosmopolitan (656).

He also lists the words that describe what Star Mother would call the shadow side of Aquarius. George lists these as: "Words describing characteristics for correction: radical, scattered, irrational, skeptical, anxious, agnostic, sentimental, gullible, easily imposed with 'hard luck stories'" (Ibid.).

We can see these attributes playing out in our Covid-19 world with those embracing science to manage the virus. In contrast, there are those who deny the science, often based on religious beliefs. The same dynamic is playing out on the planet regarding climate cycles that are changing our weather patterns drastically.

Just like the 26,000-year cycle of the progression of human consciousness repeats itself in an ever-evolving spiral over time, our Earth's climate cycles are also dynamic and operate to keep our planet balanced and healthy. The signs of Leo and Aquarius mark the cardinal points of this cycle where change is most dramatic (Leo) and transformative (Aquarius).

We have waited and incarnated for these 26,000 years to reach this apex point of total and complete transformation and planetary renewal. We are not living in an ordinary time, if such a thing exists. This time, right now, is a radical and seminal shift in planetary dynamics that sets up the energy for the next 26,000 years. This physical revolution of our sun around the star of Alcyone in the Pleiades star system, begins a new Platonic cycle. The galaxy, and the universe that holds it in place, are supporting our transition as what happens here affects everything because we are all connected by the quantum field in which we dwell. We learned from astrophysicist Vera Rubin that our galaxy is entangled, connecting us all in a unified field.

We are ascending as a planet and as a people. The prophecy is here and now. Peace is our focus along with harmony and unity consciousness. While it appears in America that "we are at each other's throats," the fact is that we are moving toward consensus on many issues including wearing masks, valuing our health over the economy, and coming together around social justice and equality as issues that must be addressed and solved. The youth, the Indigos, and the crystals, came for this transformational time to ensure that the changes take place. These changes are established as a new foundation for our crumbling and obsolete institutions that no longer serve us. We now have emerging models of cooperation, equality, and justice for all of humanity and Earth Mother herself.

We are putting the endless cycle of war and greed behind us for once and for all. We are moving to a higher frequency built upon universal love and honoring for ourselves, our fellow humans, the plants, the animals, the air, the soil, the Earth, renewing the Paradise that is the promise of this grand galactic cycle of life.

Astrolada, The Astrological Ages, provides a glimpse of where we are going as a planet and as humanity.

> Aquarius is the most global sign of all—it rules interconnected networks and friendships based upon mutual vision—blood connections will no longer be as important— what will matter is that we are all connected, we are all brothers and sisters in spirit and we are heading in the same direction. Each country will reach out a helping hand to the smaller ones rather than prey on them. Social justice and equal, free access to resources will be available for everyone. "Divide and rule" will no longer be applied—it just will not work, as people will be seeing through it more and more. The internet is one of the most powerful connecting tools at the start of the Age of Aquarius—and it is helping us see and spread truth and awareness about the state of humans—we are being misled by some Elite trying to divide and rule us, but we will realize we are all the same—with the same fears, hopes, trepidations in the heart. Soon wars will become extinct, mind you it might take another hundred years first. ... Aquarius rules the Cosmic Mind and connectedness to it. By the end of the Age of Aquarius, most humans will have developed a direct connection and interaction with the "Central Intelligence" of the Universe and will have finally understood the mystery of the Cosmos. We will be Citizens of the United Cosmos! (Astrolada.com)

We can literally see the beginning of this dramatic and significant shift in humanity through the events unfolding in our world, both individually and collectively.

The internet is proof that we are in the Age of Aquarius, uniting the youth in a platform that enables us to connect instantly, globally. The description of the Elite using divide and conquer to have power over us is crumbling before our very eyes, a Piscean tool that is no longer effective in the Aquarian Age. As we find connection with others outside of our families, finding those of like mind, we form new families that are not just tied to bloodlines.

Large countries are assisting smaller countries, sharing resources and information across cultures and nations in the search for medical treatments for Covid-19. Our connection to the cosmos is awakening through the practice of meditation and mindfulness around the globe as we open ourselves to receive Cosmic input consciously.

We also witness those cleaving to the Piscean Age, resisting the sudden changes taking place. Uranus rules Aquarius and this planet represents sudden and unexpected changes. This virus brought our world to its knees in one month and, despite the denial of many, we are not returning to the world we lived in pre-Covid-19, pre-2020. That world is gone! In the U.S. we see a lot of juvenile behaviors on the part of some of our leaders across the country, and the citizens that follow their example. In my mind, these would be the young souls on the planet, the newbies.

The old souls have been through many pandemics over multiple lifetimes, and we recognize this in our Akashic—or soul memory of our lifetimes. We settle in and embrace the silence, the quiet, the solitude, the opportunity to rest our nervous systems, to heal our bodies and minds, to be the love and the light in the midst of darkness playing out its last role. Old souls know to shelter at home, see the importance of wearing masks and socially distancing because, on some level, we remember what we must do to survive in a plague.

This is when Shakespeare wrote *King Lear,* and Newton discovered gravity, during a plague. This is not new. Yet, as Kryon points out, it is a benevolent way to bring us to our knees versus a war. When we get the virus managed our infrastructure will still be intact. We won't have to start all over from scratch.

The final aspect to note is that Aquarius is ruled by Uranus which represents "astral science" according to Llewelyn George who describes Uranus as:

> It precipitates sudden, unexpected events. It denotes
> astrologers, inventors, eccentric persons and has rule over
> astrology, metaphysics, psychical research, telepathy and
> occult subjects. It has rulership over electricity and electrical
> appliances, telegraphy, telephony, radio and electronic
> devices, airships, airplanes and aeronautics, vehicles,
> dynamos, phonographs, etc. (45).

Hence, we see the shift from religious organizations and systems to more spiritual endeavors without rules, regulations, a standard text or even a leader. We will also continue to experience sudden and unexpected shifts, such as Covid-19. This virus rearranged the way we live, work, and socialize in a matter of a month. The political landscape in America has shifted just as radically. Uranus is an important planetary force because it can shift energy almost instantaneously so that structures, such as institutional racism, fall in a short period of time. This is what happened with the fall of the Soviet Union and the Berlin Wall.

We should continue to expect to see other antiquated systems or businesses disappear before our very eyes to be replaced with higher systems and structures based upon equality, empathy, and compassion not just for some, or a privileged group, but for ALL of humanity. We are becoming a global family, and much that no longer serves us is dropping away or disappearing at lightning speed. So be it! Great technical inventions are being born now to facilitate the coming together of humanity as One Soul Family.

Chapter 24

Simultaneity and Synchronicity

8/3/2020

On the day of Congressman John Robert Lewis's funeral, an op-ed piece he wrote was published in the New York Times, our newspaper of record in the United States. Entitled, *Together, You Can Redeem the Soul of Our Nation,* with the subtitle, *Though I am gone I urge you to answer the highest calling of your heart and stand up for what you truly believe.* This is the congressman's final call to action. It is direct, clear, concise and speaks to the mind, soul, and heart—a trifecta of infinite power.

Three of our former presidents spoke at Representative Lewis' funeral at Atlanta's Georgia's Ebenezer Baptist Church where Dr. Martin Luther King, Jr. was baptized as a child and later preached. This church was also the spiritual home for John Lewis and his wife Lillian and son, John Miles. It is registered as an Historic Structure by the National Park Service. In addition to the remarks by former President George W. Bush and Bill Clinton, former president Barack Obama gave the eulogy. But before that, the presiding Rev. Raphael Warnock read a brief, heartfelt note from former president Jimmy Carter and his wife Rosalyn. Not bad for "the boy from Troy," as the Rev. Dr. Martin Luther King, Jr. referred to him.

Prior to his funeral Lewis's body was placed on a horse-drawn caisson and crossed the Edmund Pettus Bridge in Selma, Alabama where, fifty-five years earlier, Alabama state troopers beat John Lewis and hundreds of peaceful protesters as they crossed the bridge marching peacefully for civil rights. "Rep. Terri A. Sewell (D-Ala.) [noted], "It is poetic justice that this time Alabama state troopers will see John to his safety" (*Washington Post,* 7/26, 2020. Eric Velasco).

On that day of March 7, 1965, Lewis, at the age of 25, was "chairman of the Student Nonviolent Coordinating Committee" and "suffered a cracked skull on what became known as Bloody Sunday" (Ibid.).

If Seth is right that we choose our time of birth and death, Congressman John Lewis understood irony and synchronicity. Just as the media kept showing the photographs of Alabama state troopers beating John Lewis and his fellow marchers with batons on the Edmund Pettus Bridge in Selma in 1965, we are witnessing similar images on our news feeds now. We are witnessing secret police, as some have called them, sent by President Trump to attack peaceful Back Lives Matter protesters in Portland, Oregon with tear gas, and rubber bullets. In addition, we saw these forces sweep people off the streets and put them in unmarked vans in which they were whisked away to who knows where.

The past and the present have an eerie synchronicity. Except in the case of Portland, Oregon, it is mostly white people who have been demonstrating peacefully on behalf of Black Lives Matter. For showing solidarity with their Black neighbors and friends, these citizens were tear gassed, pepper sprayed, shot at with rubber bullets and whisked away, just like in 1965. In fact, our daughter, Ada, shared with us after joining the protest in Portland that she and her housemates were also tear gassed and sprayed with pepper gas. This is the ongoing price Portlanders have been paying for their commitment to fairness and social justice. The irony of sending in federal law enforcement to stop white people from protesting for equal rights for Black people could not be missed by even the most dense of consciousnesses.

Trump refers to these protesters as "anarchists and agitators." So now, white people marching on behalf of equal rights for Black people are our new civic threat. Fortunately, Americans did not perceive this to be so, and the Trump administration withdrew its federal troops. The result was the sudden absence of the violence that had been triggered by their intrusive and destructive presence.

In the 1960s, John and Robert Kennedy sent federal troops to the South to desegregate universities and schools. In 2020, Trump sent federal troops to a predominantly white suburban city to incite violence for the purpose of his campaign for re-election. Americans saw through it and overwhelmingly disapproved of this order that is counter to the direction in which this nation has been moving for 55 years. Taking on "Moms," "Dads," and lines of "Veterans" separating the peace protesters from the violence of the federal troops is not exactly a call to Law and Order that resonates with those who live in the suburbs.

Congressman Lewis begins his final message by acknowledging the power and consciousness of the youth, not just in this country, but around the world, to bring about permanent and lasting change for equal rights for all citizens of the Earth.

> While my time here has now come to an end, I want you to know that in the last days and hours of my life you inspired me. You filled me with hope about the next chapter of the great American story when you used your power to make a difference in our society. Millions of people, motivated simply by human compassion, laid down the burdens of division. Around the country and the world you set aside race, class, age, language and nationality to demand respect for human dignity.

> That is why I had to visit Black Lives Matter Plaza in Washington, though I was admitted to the hospital the following day. I just had to see and feel it for myself that, after many years of silent witness, the truth is still marching on.

> Emmett Till was my George Floyd. He was my Rayshard Brooks, Sandra Bland, and Breonna Taylor. He was 14 when he was killed, and I was only 15 years old at the time. I will

never ever forget the moment when it became so clear that he could easily have been me. In those days, fear constrained us like an imaginary prison, and troubling thoughts of potential brutality committed for no understandable reason were the bars" (*NYT*, July 30, 2020).

In these words you can hear the preacher from the American Baptist College, where Congressman Lewis received a BA (Bachelor of Arts). He received this degree before graduating from Fisk University, a historically black university in Nashville, Tennessee.

In specifically addressing the youth of the globe, he shares his views about nonviolent civil disobedience. Lewis continues in his op-ed piece:

Like so many young people today, I was searching for a way out, or some might say a way in, and then I heard the voice of Dr. Martin Luther King, Jr. on my old radio. He was talking about the philosophy and discipline of nonviolence. He said we are all complicit when we tolerate injustice. He said it is not enough to say it will get better by and by. He said each of us has a moral obligation to stand up, speak up and speak out. When you see something that is not right, you must say something. Democracy is not a state. It is an act, and each generation must do its part to help build what we call the Beloved Community, a nation and a world society at peace with itself (Ibid.).

And then he returns to his call to action and the lessons of Congressman Lewis himself.

Ordinary people with extraordinary vision can redeem the soul of America by getting in what I call good trouble, necessary trouble. Voting and participating in the democratic process are key. The vote is the most powerful nonviolent change agent you have in a democratic society. You must use it because it is not guaranteed. You can lose it (Ibid.).

He reminds us that there is such a thing as "good trouble," and we should embrace it as he did, particularly when it comes to the right to vote. Congressman Lewis concludes his final communication with us while still in his body temple:

> Though I may not be here with you, I urge you to answer the highest calling of our heart and stand up for what you truly believe in. In my life I have done all I can to demonstrate that the way of peace, the way of love and nonviolence, is the more excellent way. Now it is your turn to let freedom ring.
>
> … So I say to you, walk with the wind, brothers and sisters, and let the spirit of peace, and power of everlasting love be your guide (Ibid.).

What a magnificent, beautiful and heartfelt call to action to our Indigos who came for this reason at this time. Dr. Martin Luther King Jr.'s *Letter from Birmingham Jail* is in most high school textbooks. I believe this final letter to humanity by Congressman Lewis will be read in the same way as Dr. Martin Luther King's call to action, for many years to come. The eloquence, the heart, the simplicity of the message takes us deeper into the Aquarian Age where "peace finally triumphed over violence, aggression and war."

That Congressman Lewis survived to the age of 80 is destiny. So many times, he thought he was going to die because of the situations he placed himself in, over and over. Congressman Lewis' life is a miracle. He came to teach peace and he fulfilled his destiny heroically and inspirationally. Humanity's vibration is raised by this magnificent life, so well lived in the spirit of good trouble. Two steps forward. Thank you!

Chapter 25

The Great Shift

8/5/2020

Just in time for the shift created by Covid-19, upending our lives individually and collectively, Matt Kahn published a book with the title; *The Universe Always Has a Plan: The 10 Golden Rules of Letting Go.* The movement of the planets and stars in our universe is part of this plan and we are in the midst of sudden and dramatic change which is the Uranian energy of moving into the Aquarian Age. We are experiencing sudden and unexpected changes that literally and metaphorically catapult us to a higher vibrational frequency of love and peace as we move into the fifth dimension of peace.

In the book, *The Women of Lemuria; Ancient Wisdom for Modern Times,* by Kryon and Monika Muranyi, with Dr. Amber Wolf, Muranyi describes the astronomy of what she calls, "The Great Shift."

> Regardless of what prophecy you heard, you should know that the 2012 event is completely based on astronomy. Let's discuss the 2012 galactic alignment. The galactic alignment is a precise astronomical term that occurs as a result of the precession of the equinoxes. This alignment is caused by a 26,000-year wobble of the planet that starts and ends when our sun perfectly lines up (as we look at it from Earth) with the center of our galaxy. All over the planet, a few days on or after December 21, 2012, was the alignment of the solstice point with the Galactic equator—this was the 2012 galactic alignment (202).

She continues her explanation to further clarify this 26,000-year cycle we have been studying throughout this book.

> I want you to visualize the true shape of the Earth—an oblate spheroid with an "equatorial bulge." The Earth is also tilted and it rotates (wobbles) around an axis that is inclined with respect to the orbital plane (the flat space in which Earth orbits the sun). The tilt creates the four seasons on Earth, while the axis wobble is responsible for the precession of the equinoxes. This wobble (rotation) of the Earth's axis is extremely slow and takes a period of 26,000 years. The start and stop point of the 26,000-year cycle is known as the center of the galactic alignment (202).

And for those who would like a little more in-depth science about how this works, Muranyi provides a more detailed explanation.

> Now let's take a look at the precession of the equinoxes. The precession refers to the apparent motion of the equinoxes along the plane of Earth's orbit caused by the Earth wobbling very slowly on its axis. The position of the equinoxes and solstices shifts one degree every 71.5 years. Because the sun is one-half of a degree wide, it will take the December solstice sun 36 years to process through the galactic equator. This means that the 2012 experience wasn't something that happened on December 21, but was a part of a 36-year event. It began in 1994 and will finish in 2030 (202–203).

This passage reiterates that we are in a 36-year cosmic shift from the ending of a 26,000-year inner galactic cycle, and the beginning of a new 26,000-year inner galactic cycle. The shift is real, it is cosmic, and it is happening right now—we are the participants and witnesses of the greatest shift that takes place on planet Earth. Hence, the changes, the chaos, the confusion that is surrounding us as we individually and collectively seek new balance out of the decay, disintegration and disorder that is engulfing us on a planetary level.

And this shift was known by the ancients. It was prophesied and every soul on this planet is an important and significant participant in raising consciousness to a place it hasn't been on Earth, since perhaps the last galactic alignment. Muranyi reminds us:

> Modern astronomers are all aware of the galactic alignment,
> but how is it that ancient cultures knew about this?
> Civilizations such as the ancient Egyptians, Aztecs, Druids,
> and Incas studied the stars. They knew about the movement
> of the sun, the moon, the equinoxes, and they noticed that
> the Earth wobbled. They didn't need telescopes as they used
> observatories, and in some instances, they used this
> knowledge to create calendars. The most well-studied and
> known calendar was from the Mayans (203).

This time in which we live was anticipated. It is not random; it is a part of what Matt Kahn declares in the title of his newest book, *The Universe Always Has a Plan*. Those of us here now chose to be here at this time to assist with The Great Shift—we applied to be here, and our application was accepted.

Muranyi goes on to explain some of the mechanics of life and of "The Great Shift" that are not known to most of humanity. These mechanics were put in place 100,000 years ago by the Pleiadian Star Mothers to assist in "The Great Shift," if we made it past 2012. This is information that has been given by Kryon over the last three decades and, as the archivist of the Kryon channeling over this time, Muranyi has a deep and inherent understanding of the teachings.

Muranyi addresses what she names in a subtitle in this chapter, *The Great Shift, The Re-emergence of Ancient Wisdom*. What she shares is what she and Lee Carroll describe as "eye rolling" [smile]. It also answers primal questions we all have about this experience we are having on planet Earth that we call "life."

> The Old Souls, who have incarnated thousands of lifetimes
> on this planet have an Akash rich in experiences. The
> Human Akash represents all the energy of your past, present,

and future expressions of life on Earth. Your personal Akash is stored in several places, the most profound being your own DNA. Each time you are born and die on this planet your essence (soul) comes and goes from the Cave of Creation. This cave is a real place that Kryon says will never be found. The Cave of Creation connects and unites the physical with the spiritual and multidimensional with the dimensional. Within the multidimensional part of the cave it holds an esoteric crystalline object for every soul that has ever been on the planet and every soul to come. Each crystal holds the Akashic Record of each specific soul (211).

If you ever wondered how LIFE works, and we all do at the soul level, this information is empowering. It is also, in our time, available to all those who are open to receiving the answers to questions that run through our DNA, our minds, and our spirits as we walk this Earth. You can also readily identify why Muranyi, and Carroll call this information "eye rolling."

Muranyi continues to explain the dynamics of how our planet operates in concert with humanity.

The Cave of Creation interfaces with Gaia through the Crystalline Grid with your consciousness and actions, it then alters the Cave of Creation. The Crystalline Grid is a multidimensional spiritual grid that lays over the planet's surface and remembers everything that Humans do and where they do it. The energy of humanity affects the vibrational level of the planet in actual time. The Crystalline Grid "responds" to Human consciousness, but it goes both ways: it receives and gives. As humanity passed the marker of 2012, both the Crystalline Grid and Cave of Creation have been recalibrating to a new vibrational level (211).

What we are experiencing in 2020 is this recalibration of our planet to a higher vibration of consciousness. This is unsettling to much of

212

humanity, yet, by being here now, each one of us is an essential actor in the transformation into what Kryon calls, the "New Human."

Muranyi moves deeper into the explanation of what is taking place on our planet because we passed the marker of 2012 without blowing ourselves up:

> The biggest change of this recalibration is that the
> Crystalline Grid is no longer going to remember in a linear
> way. This changes the *importance* of certain energies, so that
> the energy of war, hatred, and drama from the past are
> *reduced* in importance. This recalibration means that the
> Crystalline Grid is now responding to light and dark
> differently. The old energy of the past, no matter how dark,
> will not have the effect it did before. This is why light is
> winning over dark (211–212).

Kryon is constantly reminding us that light is now winning over the dark and that the dark has always been here, but now we can see it because it is being illuminated by the light.

Muranyi includes a Kryon channeling from August/September 2007 entitled *The History of Humanity,* given in Western Mediterranean Sea—8th Annual Kryon Cruise (215). This contains startling (eye rolling) information.

> Looking at the lineage of the planet, we have information. It
> wasn't until the year 1900 that the actual new enlightenment
> process started on the planet. Indeed, there was not much
> before then. It then took 87 more years to bring the vibration
> of the planet up to a point of decisions—decisions about
> vibration and the future. Whereas all the prophets said that
> you would have a termination at approximately the
> millennium shift, instead, you changed the vibration of this
> planet to a rate where that did not have to happen. Make no
> mistake, there was no plan of God's to terminate this planet.
> It was the vibration of the test that you had created over the
> eons. Humans create your own prophecy. It is the

consciousness of the planet that does it. You, therefore, created a different future than any of the prophets had seen, and now, almost all of the prophecy before 1987 is moot.

You are on a completely different track (212).

In 1987 we had what we called the "Harmonic Convergence," which Kryon says is when we shifted the energy of the planet and made the decision to shift consciousness and remain on the planet.

What comes next in the channeling is profound. It ties in directly with the Indigos and the crystal children born most recently on this planet.

Now let me tell you something that you may love to hear. Between 1987 and 2007, something amazing happened. Due to the new energy, the crystals awakened in the Cave of Creation that had Lemurians names. They whispered, *Time to come back!* Three hundred fifty million of them. Listen to this, listen—all of the Lemurians who ever lived on this planet are alive again in Human bodies right now and are back! They are spread all over the globe. Listen. ... You wonder why there's an alliance with your cellular structure and Kryon? It's because you're a Lemurian, an old soul in a new energy (212–213).

This perfectly aligns with the outpouring of the youth and young adults around the world coming out en masse in a pandemic and protesting peacefully for social justice for all. This is not a phase; this my friends is "The Great Shift."

Near the end of Barack Obama's eulogy for Congressman John Lewis, Obama states:

He was a good and kind and gentle man. And he believed in us. And it's fitting that the last time John and I shared a public forum was on Zoom. And I'm pretty sure neither he nor I set up the Zoom call because we don't know how to work it. It was a virtual town hall with a gathering of young activists, who had been helping to lead this summers' demonstrations in the wake of Georg Floyd's death. And afterward, I spoke to John privately. And he could not have been prouder to see this generation of activists standing up for freedom and equality. A new generation that was intent on voting and protecting the right to vote. In some cases, a new generation is running for political office. And I told him all those young people, John, of every race and every religion, from every background and gender and sexual orientation—John, those are your children (Theatlanic.com).

Welcome to the Age of Aquarius, and "The Great Shift" led by those largely under 40 years of age. What a time to be alive!

And since we are in "eye-rolling" territory, in the Kryon channel entitled *The History of Humanity,* we learn about our tests as Humanity on planet Earth. Kryon explains how statistically, not that many of us need to awaken to put our planet on the path of ascension towards world peace and beyond.

Listen to what I've been telling you for years: Less than one-half of one percent of this planet has to awaken to make a difference in the vibration for all. You will move into 2012 with a new vibration. Less than one-half of one percent of seven billion people have to awaken. It's not that many. In fact, it's only 10% of the 350 million Lemurians who are alive today—a very reasonable percentage (213).

When I visualized the planet in my mind at the beginning of this pandemic, I saw triangles of bright light spread around the surface of the planet, signifying enlightened beings or light workers. When I looked again, after the young people began protesting globally, what I saw was a white glow or ring around the earth filled with millions of dots of light represented by the youth uprising. I interpret these lights and these youth as Earth Angels. This is where the healing of Earth Mother and Humanity will arise and flourish, in these young Lemurians, here to help us right our path, straighten out our crooked ways. I see these Earth Angels literally raising the vibration and frequency of humanity and the Earth in my ongoing visions!

But Kryon even lays out the future and tells us what is potentially ahead of us. The passage is illuminating in that it assists us to see what lies ahead.

Where are you in this puzzle? How long is civilization supposed to last? I will tell you. The answer is your future, and you will decide that. You are totally in control of it, so it can go as long as you wish. But I will tell you how long the test was designed for. Some of you will laugh. There are many kinds of popular numbers that float around a culture that have become doctrine and mythology. But quite often, there is core truth to their importance. One of them, which appears many times, as many things, is 144,000. It's intuitive and you all know it. It represents the length of the test in years—144,000 years.

You sit at the 200,000 mark (measured from when Pleiadians came). You see, there's plenty of time left if you don't destroy yourselves, and Lemurians can change that. They already have. You have a time coming up that is going to be what we call cooperative or commensurate with this entire growth. And the Mayans prophesied it. The energy of Gaia itself will start beginning to shift in 2012. A Cycle that will last longer than 1,000 years will occur, one that is more friendly to your spiritual growth than the energy you were born in (213–214).

And if this isn't enough of a stretch of your imagination, take in this information as Kryon continues in the channel.

The question has been asked, *So when are we going to meet our brothers? When will the Pleiadians return to the planet?* Oh, I don't think it's a mystery to any of you. They visit regularly. Some see them, some don't. There's no sinister plan, dear ones. When they watch you, they watch in love to see how the garden is growing. Should you last through the 144,000 years, at the end of the test you will be just like them—a planet that is enlightened, one with the attributes of the Great Central Sun [Kryon smile].

And I'll tell you something that many of you don't want to hear. If you're a Lemurian in the room, you're going to be there! That's how many lifetimes you've got left. That's how much you love the Earth....

You're all coming back! It's what you do. You can hardly wait. 'Tired' is Human talk. There's no tired on the other side of the veil, only compassion. This test you're in, it's all about compassion (214).

Compassion, compassion, compassion, compassion, compassion, compassion. This is the shift we are in and the questions we need to ask ourselves about every thought, feeling, word and action is: Is it compassionate? This is the work of all of us, and clearly, we have a ways to go!

Chapter 26

Human by Design

8/8/2020

In 2017, Gregg Braden published a book called *Human by Design: From Evolution by Chance to Transformation by Choice.* When I ordered this book in 2020, it had a new title: *The Science of Self-Empowerment; awakening the new human story.* What happened? Hay House, created and built up by Louise Hay starting with her seminal book, *You Can Heal Your Life,* apparently felt the original title was too controversial. This happened despite the fact that Hay House is the premiere publisher of new thought books, CDs and cards.

Gregg Branden is very well known and respected in the new thought community where spirituality and science are perceived as one whole and complete expression of how life works. The back jacket of this newly retitled book also highlights some of the contents of the book. The first is:

> **Our Origin**—Modern humans appeared suddenly on earth
> approximately 200,000 years ago, with the advanced brain,
> nervous system, and capabilities that set them apart from all
> other known forms of life *already developed,* rather than
> having developed slowly and gradually over a long periods
> (sic) of time (Ibid.).

Gregg Braden and Lee Carroll do a Science and Spirituality Conference every year attended by presenter Bruce Lipton, PhD, who wrote *The Biology of Belief,* and is the father of epigenetics. Sometimes referred to as *The Three Amigos,* Gregg Braden, Dr. Bruce Lipton, and

Dr. Joe Dispenza do their own conferences on the new science and what Kryon calls the New Human. Clearly, the work of Kryon complements the studies of Braden, Lipton and Dispenza.

The next bulletin on the back jacket of the book continues with information that matches the teachings of Kryon.

> **A rare DNA fusion**—Advanced genome analysis reveals that the DNA that sets us apart from other primates, including in our advanced brain and nervous system, is the result of an ancient and precise fusion of genes occurring in a way that suggests something *beyond* evolution made our humanness possible (Ibid.).

Again, this aligns with the information we have received from Kryon over the past 30 years.

The third bullet on the back of the book is also the teaching of Kryon:

> **Our extraordinary abilities**—We are born with the capacity to self heal, to self regulate longevity, to activate an enhanced immune response, and to experience deep intuition, sympathy, empathy, and, ultimately, compassion— and to do each of these on demand (Ibid.).

This bullet reveals how sacred spiritual truth is being grounded to our planet, replacing the children's story that Kryon describes as our cultural creation story. Kryon ascribes our creation story to our linear thinking. We have superpowers that have been dormant that are awakening now, through the chaos and destruction we are experiencing and witnessing. We are not small. We are *magnificent!*

In a *Kryon Worldwide Channeling* event held virtually in April 2020, Kryon once again encourages and reminds us to follow "common spiritual sense." He says, based upon my notes, that our linearity where we expect a beginning and an end is practical, but it gets in the way of even bigger things such as "God, Spirit and Angels." He then speaks about the Big Bang and our linear view of it. We are told that "nothing became everything." This makes no sense. There had to be something there. Kryon tells us the Big Bang was not a beginning; rather it's a continuation of multi-verses that collide and membranes that cross over to start new universes. Was there a first one? No. The universe is eternal in both directions" (notes).

Kryon says it is our linear perspective that gets in the way "of something incredibly beautiful." He then states that our soul has no beginning or end. He says we are taught that when we are born, we "take a breath and our soul enters our body." When we die or "the ending of the soul, there are judges to take us to hell where we are burned alive every day. This is the linearity—the children's story of humanity and God." He continues:

> What if we are eternal in both directions? What if we always were? Our Name is known. All the billions; known by God personally, intimately. We have the free choice to know it and use it. We are part of the Creator. There is nothing else that is eternal in both directions except God. We are a creature of God. Trillions of pieces and parts meld together; love and compassion. We are all part of the whole. This is the truth. The soul always was, it is always a part of Creative Source. When life is over, it returns. There is a bigger plan. Way bigger.
>
> There is a magnificence because God knows us as God. What else would we be if we had a soul? It's the beauty and compassion of All That Is. Take my hand [God's]—with free choice to see—raise the vibration. We are an ascended being. There is so much good to see, find and be; extended life, health, peace…. It's next to you if you would simply relax with it (notes).

Notice how the end of this message from Kryon matches the third bullet on the back jacket of Gregg Braden's book, *The Science of Self-Empowerment, awakening the new human story.* We have "extraordinary abilities" to repair our bodies, extend our lives and live in peace.

Below the three bullet points on the back jacket of Braden's book is, "Beyond any reasonable doubt, *The Science of Self Empowerment* reveals that we're not what we've been told, and much more than we ever imagined."

Before we even open *The Science of Self Empowerment: awakening the new human story*, we already have "eye-rolling" information about our origin which began suddenly 200,000 years ago. In addition is a reference to a rare DNA fusion that took place in these new humans, who we are, suggesting that our humanness *is* "by design." We are not the result of random selection. We are not the product of chance. Braden tells us that we have "extraordinary abilities" as a result of our origin and a DNA fusion. Sounds a lot like Kryon, yet Gregg Braden is approaching this from the perspective of science.

In the introduction of the book under a subtitle; *NEW DISCOVERIES MEAN A NEW STORY,* Braden writes:

> The undeniable fact is that something happened 200,000 years ago to make our existence possible. And whatever that something was, it left us with the extraordinary abilities of intuition, compassion, empathy, love, self-healing and more (xvii–xviii).

Beyond the astonishing message that there has been an intelligent intervention in our biology that occurred 200,000 years ago that gave us our current biology and physiology, it also gave us the human emotions of love, intuition, compassion, empathy and more.

This is how Braden concludes his introduction; with the impact of this new information about our origins, based upon science which acknowledges the 200,000-year timeline of when we became the form of human we are. We became one single human species 200,000 years ago. This is unlike the natural world where, for instance, there are many forms of primates, cats in the wild, bears, as well as all the animals in the animal kingdom which have many varieties.

Braden's thesis is that when we embrace our true origin, what Kryon would call the adult story, we can transform our lives and our world into a model much closer to what humans are marching for all over the world. In the wake of the murder of George Floyd, many are seeking a world of mutual respect, compassion, empathy, and peace.

In, *The Twelve Layers of DNA (An Esoteric Study of the Mastery Within) Kryon Book Twelve,* by Kryon and Lee Carroll published in 2010, Kryon/Carroll writes:

Enter the Pleiadian...

By design, a very advanced race of spiritual beings began to work with humanity. They had been on earth many times, waiting for the right moment to begin their work. They remained, in their own way, and made certain that the DNA they were changing within humanity was correct.

They were here by divine plan (156).

He explains:

The Pleiadians represent the graduate life forms of the Universe as you know it. They were the original "only planet of free choice" and had a spiritual influence on the energy of the very creation of your solar system. Their civilization is older than yours. Not by much in Universal terms, but enough so that they developed and went through their wars and tribulations and graduated with a task—to continue the work by giving their vibration to the next generation of Humanoid forms. They did this by passing on the quantum [interdimensional] portion of their DNA, right to the mammal called Human on the planet Earth. It was time. Earth was ready. It was approximately 100,000 Earth years ago—not too long ago really, compared to how long it took for Earth to get to the place where it was possible.

... They did their work at a perfect time, ordained by the creator energy to be correct and proper for the next evolutionary step of Earth—the seeding of the creator energy within the Human DNA (157).

It is not a coincidence that Kryon can explain the how's and when's of Braden's theory about the origin of Humans as we recognize ourselves today.

For a little more eye-rolling information, Kryon continues:

> The Pleiadians have quantum [interdimensional] technology and they understand the additional two rules of physics that you have yet to discover. This gives them the ability to entangle themselves with the quantum state of the Universe and travel to you almost instantly (157).

This is what I love about listening to Kryon. He tells us we have discovered four of the six laws of physics that govern our galaxy, missing the final two. This gives us humans an incomplete picture of our worlds and how they operate.

He also explains how the DNA from the Pleiadians became that of humans.

> Your Pleiadian brothers and sisters were not DNA alteration experts. They didn't reconstruct human DNA or add to it... Instead, they did what you think they did, and through a process of integration of birth attributes, slowly created a hybrid of themselves. The result was a Human Being with their spiritual DNA attributes—something that was completely missing on the earth. Also in the process, humanity became part Pleiadian. You have their DNA attributes, the spiritual ones that they gave you through the normal birth process of biological inheritance. Does it occur to you that they did this without startling anyone? Indeed, they did, for they "fit in" to the Human Society. This also should tell you that they look just like you" (159).

Kryon is telling us the Pleiadians mixed with the humanity that was on earth as one of us, and through the regular process of procreation, their DNA became infused in the DNA of modern Humans.

Kryon says:

How would you do this if you were them? It was done with tremendous integrity and love. They lived with you. They spent years and years, even beyond their own life spans (which is considerable), continuing the process for dozens of Human generations. Then when it was finished they left (159).

He shares that when we do meet the Pleiadians, "... you will laugh! For they look just like you! A bit taller, perhaps, but they will shock you for it will be so obvious who they are—your starseed parents, and a loving group they remain" (159).

Kryon provides more insight regarding this DNA infusion or fusion.

Slowly the quantum proportions of your DNA received what the Pleiadians wanted you to have—a system they had that includes the creator energy, the Akashic Record and all the other attributes that you today call spiritual (159–160).

And for those of us in the midst of the consciousness of Black Lives Matter, Kryon has a little joke.

We learn that this new expression of spiritual human flourished in one particular location.

Although the Pleiadian seeds were given worldwide, there was one large civilization that gained incredible understanding and strength... As described many times, the greatest society was in the middle of the current Pacific Ocean, which later became the Hawaiian Islands. Therefore you might say that the Polynesians were the first kinds of Humans to gain the full knowledge of what the Pleiadians did, and you would be right. Note, for those interested, that the first kind of fully realized Spiritual Human was one of color [Kryon wink] (160).

He continues after informing us that the first spiritual Humans were people of color by stating: "Lemuria, is, therefore the first divination of the planet with Humans like you" (160).

Hawaii is the place where the Pleiadians helped to build our first civilization with our spiritual DNA that gives us what we consider our Human qualities today. Kryon lets us know that this was new on the planet.

> Before the Pleiadians did their work with you all over this planet, there was no divinity inside, and the system of your divine coming and going [reincarnation - my note] did not exist (161).

And hold on to your seat as you read what Kryon has to say next!

> You were the same as much of the other life in the Universe, for there is an assumption by Humans that all life is the same. It isn't. There is only a fraction of life in the Universe that is "allied with the divinity of the creator, and you are one of them" (161).

Kryon describes how this came to be:

> The Pleiadians were following the intuition and synchronicity of Spirit to come to Earth and seed one kind of Human with their spiritual quantum DNA attribute. You simply did not have it before they got here (162).

Humans were seeded by the Pleiadians between 200,000 and 100,000 years ago. They came and lived among us and through sex they shared their DNA which included the quantum attribute of the creator of all life, giving us each what Kryon calls; "a piece of divinity, a piece of the creator inside." This is the adult story; that we are unique in the universe, that we have "God inside"' unlike almost all life in the Universe.

We were not born dirty; we are not sinners. Rather we are magnificent expressions of divine consciousness, here to bring in more light, love, and compassion. When we activate all the potential of our DNA, we become ascended masters just as Buddha, Christ and Mohammed demonstrated to us.

Kryon likes to say, "An all-loving God did not give us choice and free will and then turn around and judge us for it and sentence us and our children and grandchildren to a life in purgatory." Humanity has projected our lower consciousness onto an all-loving God and turned this energy into a vengeful, authoritarian father, or what I call, "a bad Dad." This story needs to be retired and replaced with the spiritual truth that we are all Spirit expressing and as such we are magnificent!

The scientific paradigms/models of our culture are not accurate, Braden tells us. We are taught we are just a random, chance product of biology, and as such we are just another piece of life. Our creation story reinforces our relative insignificance and, in many traditions, emphasizes that we are born flawed.

Braden explains an update of what he was taught in school regarding the names of our ancestors. Many of us learned as did Braden that our ancestors were called Cro-Magnons.

The new name used to identify the beings once known as Cro-Magnons is *anatomically modern humans,* or AMH's.

Scientists generally agree that AMH's first appear in the fossil record approximately 200,000 years ago and mark the beginning of the subspecies *Homo Spain's sapient*—the term used to describe the people living on earth today (43).

Braden continues to illuminate us on the discoveries that; "Scientists now believe that the AMHs are us, and we are they. Any differences between contemporary bodies and those of the AMHs of the past are so slight that they don't justify a separate grouping" (44).

Braden says there must have been some intervention that occurred 200,000 years ago that changed the human genome to what we have and are today, genetically. The science fossil records are the same story that Kryon tells us with more specificity; that the Pleiadian Star Mothers came to our planet 200,000 years ago and mixed with the existing humans. Over time, those other existing humans became extinct while those starseeded by the Pleiadians remained, and this is who and what we are!

Kryon reminds us that scientists will never find the missing link in their tree of life. The theory of evolution may work or describe the development of nature, but it does not describe human beings. We are the product of divine intelligence, and as Matt Kahn likes to remind us: *The Universe Always Has a Plan.* The DNA of the Star Mothers merged with that of the existing humans and changed the genetic codes.

One example of this is the development of language. We know from genetic mapping that chimpanzees share over 98 percent of the same DNA as we humans have. In a 2009 study published in the journal *Nature,* we get a clue about the gene expression that gives humans speech.

> According to these scientists, the mutation happened "rapidly around the same time that language emerged in humans." This was a pivotal discovery because for the first time a specific set of mutations in FOXP2 was scientifically linked to our capacity to create complex language (Braden 46).

Braden goes on to explain an "unexpected twist" in our DNA story, a twist that Kryon refers to often. While Braden does not state what he believes the intervention to be, he assembles the science that demonstrates, biologically, that we are the product of some kind of outside intervention. This goes beyond any explanation that the theory of evolution, as it exists today, can explain. The unexpected twist is that; "Our nearest primate relatives, the chimpanzees, have more chromosomes than we do, with a total of 48 in their overall genome. Ironically, humans only have 46 (47).

The question Braden asks is, "Where did the 2 missing chromosomes go?" He then explains:

> New research reveals that the second largest chromosome in the human body, forming 8 percent of the total DNA in cells, *human chromosome 2* (HC2, actually contains the smaller "missing" chromosomes found in the chimp genome (47).

Braden adds that new technology has revealed what happened to craft HC2. He provides the explanation from the *Proceedings of the*

National Academy of Sciences which he then translates into layman's language as:

It appears that long ago two separate chromosomes from chimpanzees (chimp chromosomes 2A and B) *merged* or fused into the single, larger chromosome 2—which is one of the key chromosomes that give us our humanness (48).

Braden explains that "Many of the characteristics that make us uniquely human arise from the DNA fusion that resulted in human chromosome 2" (48). He continues:

"From this small sampling, it's clear that human chromosome 2 plays a significant role in contributing to who, and what, we are" (49).

This information challenges current scientific theory that we are just a random result of chance and good luck as perceived through the theory of evolution.

The same time frame offered by Kryon of the Pleiadians starseeding humanity is supported by science as it exists today—stuck, in Braden's perception, in the unproven theory of evolution that seems not to apply to modern humans who appeared on Earth 200,000 years ago.

In very similar language to Kryon, Braden concludes:

If this is true, the chromosome 2 fusion happened to us, and only us, and it happened *after* we had already split from the other primates. They kept their 48 chromosomes and we experienced the fusion that gives us our 46 (51–52).

Kryon tells us we do in fact have 48 chromosomes. However, the last two chromosomes are multidimensional. As science advances, we will be able to confirm this with new instruments and inventions. The Pleiadians chose to seed our planet as part of their planetary evolution and according to Kryon we on Earth will be doing the same for another planet of choice in about 144,000 years (smile).

This is a new story for a new human. We are extraordinary, each and every one of us. Our myths and metaphors do not reflect the grandness of who we are and where we came from. As Braden illuminates, both science and our religions reinforce that we are small and insignificant. This is not at all the truth of our story and our glory.

This new 26,000-year cycle we have just stepped into offers the opportunity to acknowledge the physical and spiritual truth that 200,000 years ago there was an intervention from the Pleiadians. They planted a piece of the Creative Source into our DNA that makes us the humans we are today.

These are the scientific, political, and social challenges we are experiencing in 2020; the struggle between the establishment, which is the culmination of our last 26,000-year cycle, and the new cycle before us. In this new cycle of the precession of the equinoxes, the light overwhelms the dark. The feminine rises to meet and complement the masculine. We literally move from separation consciousness to unity consciousness as described in the Platonic Year diagram.

The old institutions are crumbling because something greater is emerging. We can see it on our streets, and in our news and in this pandemic, which is uprooting old paradigms in government, education and even science.

Welcome to The Shift!

Chapter 27

Kryon and Human DNA

8/13/2020

In Kryon Book Twelve, titled; *The Twelve Layers of DNA (An Esoteric Study of the Mastery Within),* by Lee Carroll, we learn the dynamics of how we are human by design, not by chance as our science tells us. Carroll shares:

> Kryon tells us that there is a system: When birth occurs, we have the following things imbued in our DNA.

Lee Carroll translates this for us:

(1) The heredity of our parents' biology.
… This is 3D chemistry in the double helix and represents the parts that carry over attributes from our parents and their parents.

(2) Karmic Imprint.
… It's a continuation of the last life. Do I have to mention guilt? It seems to be an attribute of certain cultures in all their children. This is Karmic, not chemical. That means its *information,* not chemistry.

(3) Astrological imprint. [My favorite]
This is obvious. It's a snapshot of the pattern of the solar system at birth. Astrology is the oldest science on the planet and is probably very related to gravitational and magnetic imprints, which are a multidimensional patterning of the sun. The incredible push and pull of the planets creates this pattern at the sun's core. This pattern gets transmuted to the

earth every moment through inductance with the solar wind (heliosphere). You can see the place where the inductance actually happens through the observation of the aurora borealis, where the heliosphere overlaps the earth's magnetic field (you actually get sparks!). This places the sun's quantum imprint onto the magnetic grid of the planet. This magnetic grid, which overlaps the magnetics of your DNA, then patterns a portion of your DNA at birth (again through inductance). [And my favorite comment...] And if you didn't follow this discussion, don't worry. It's not important to the book. But for those who did, it is the only place you will ever have seen the potential scientific explanation of astrology in a book [Deb Sadler smile].

... It's the force of planetary objects and their effects on Humans...

(4) The entire Akashic Record of all your lifetimes on this planet...

Kryon continues to teach that the attributes of these "past" lives are available today, and that's why they are there at all. He encourages us to "mine" the Akash—that is, to discover what we have within our own DNA's history and use it.

(5) The sacredness of God as represented by your Higher-Self—an energy given by the Pleiadians approximately 100,000 years ago (52–54).

This is Lee Carroll's analysis for the system that Kryon has taught for the past 30 years.

Lee Carroll shares a channel by Kryon that tells us some more about the quantum qualities of Human DNA. I made a note when I read this that it reminded me of the teachings of Seth that I read in the 1980s. Before I share this passage, Kryon provides us with an explanation about the significance of the DNA shared with us by the Pleiadians through normal procreation, here on Earth.

Let me take you to the interior of DNA itself and reveal to you the esoterica and love that this process has within it. Far more than chemistry, this *DNA event* defines the core of sacred life, the love of God within the Universe, mixed with dimensional confluences and the joy of creation. DNA is the crossroads of God and man, the mixture of quantum and non-quantum, and it vibrates with the essence of the truth of the Universe. If you could sit within the double helix and observe all the vibrations as I can, you would be in awe. For within that 3D structure surges the history of the Universe, of mankind, of the seed race and their love for you, and your relationship to the ages and to the earth. The multidimensional light show is grander than any Human can conceive, for this is the kind of light that is not seen, but felt. It sings a sonata of melding energies that soothes the soul, and the strains are similar to those you "hear" when you are on my side of the veil. For DNA contains the creator energy, your energy, the Human transformation energy and that of all your lifetimes.

Your angelic name is sung on top of it all... It's a place where physics meets spirituality and a place where complete peace and solace of consciousness are achieved. The bridge to the creator's reality is there, and in each DNA molecule there is a mini-portal that leads to a multidimensional Universe" (101–102).

Perhaps it is this portal we go through when we take psychedelics such as LSD and psilocybin mushrooms—where we feel and know the oneness of All.

The Kryon material provides information that matches up with the prophecies of the ancients and indigenous as well as spiritual teachings from the past. This next passage by Kryon parallels what Seth, channeled by Jane Roberts, said many decades ago.

This thing you call the double helix is sacred, unique, and is that way only for the Human. For the DNA of other life does not have the creator inside, but rather it is designed to *see* other DNA that has creator attributes. Simply said, it means that anything with DNA on this planet *knows* about the Human creator DNA, and bows appropriately to it. Even a vegetable *knows* who you are and lives to nourish the life around it and you. At the basic DNA level, animals are also aware of why they are here, and how the Human carries the creator energy on earth, and that they are here to support it and the planet (102).

Seth said the same thing; that nature, including the plants and animals, are here to support our lives; this is their purpose, and they know or are conscious of it.

Because this made sense to me, I have always had a different perspective on eating as a vegetarian. For many, that's a humane or compassionate statement. Yet, according to Seth, it is the animal's purpose and joy to provide for our human sustenance. I have always honored the perspective of others but when someone says it hurts their heart that a turkey will be killed/sacrificed for a Thanksgiving dinner, I always think of what Seth said; that it is their pleasure and mission to provide Thanksgiving dinner. Not all animals, of course, are here for us to eat, but they are here for us to enjoy.

Just as we project our humanness based on what we think God is, as a culture, we project ourselves onto our environment, including nature, feeling empathy for animals whose purpose is to feed us. But Kryon reveals the deeper relationships; that Spirit is all loving and that nature, Earth Mother, is here to support and provide for humanity. It is a beautiful model of giving and receiving—of life itself.

To show the depth of the world we really, truly live in, Kryon states:

The atomic structure of the Universe also sings with creation, but it represents the building blocks of everything, made up of multidimensional parts that Humans can only see a portion of, since Humans are in their own dimensional reality [3D] (review), for the rest just look like space and emptiness to them. But in the space between the nucleus and the electron haze is the "soup" of creation; the multidimensional glue that sets the rules for the way complete physics works. Also, in that glue is a natural nature bias, for it is designed to create life, over and over.

At the atomic level, the smallest of the small, there is a master plan, and it is not random. For it will configure itself over and over to let life start everywhere! This means that life itself is sacred, just as you might imagine, and as your intuition tells you (102–103).

This is the message of Matt Kahn's newest book, *The Universe Always Has a Plan,* and the work of Gregg Braden who recognizes that we are not a random result of evolution as our entire scientific community tells and teaches us. The truth is that we are a very significant and important part of a universal master plan biased towards life.

Kryon continues:

Now you can see that the DNA molecule is the result of this design, and is not random at all. Perhaps it's time to give it the respect that only a quantum thinker can? Can you imagine what it carries with it in order for it to create that mastery that is available to you? (103).

It recalls the teaching of Jesus that "this and even greater you too can do." Kryon will tell you Jesus Christ did not come to be a Savior. There is nothing for us to be "saved" from. We are not "born dirty." We are "born magnificent!" This was the message of Jesus; we can perform miracles just as he did. What is the difference between the consciousness of Christ and us? The efficiency of our DNA is reflected by our consciousness. The higher our consciousness is, the more efficient our DNA.

Humanity has had low consciousness for a long time; our DNA operates at the 30–33 percent level according to Kryon's teachings. The Masters, including Christ, Buddha, Muhammad, Confucius, and others, DNA operated at 90 percent. This is because their consciousness was pure love, beauty, integrity, empathy, and compassion. We can see clearly in our headlines that we are missing these uplifting qualities as a driving force in our culture. Yet, our DNA is awakening, and we can see and feel the awakening too, through other headlines such as the youth marching for social justice en masse!

Our DNA has a piece of the creator inside it. We are a part of the creator and the creative soup of the universe. The myths and metaphors from our science and our spiritual systems are outdated and outmoded. They do not begin to acknowledge the magnificence of each one of us, and as a result we have not recognized our own magnificence individually and collectively.

The vision for the Centers for Spiritual Living, based in Golden, Colorado with centers all over the world, is "Awakening humanity to our magnificence, and create a world that works for everyone." As Rev. Christina says after she tells people this at Seaside Center for Spiritual Living, in Encinitas, California; "If this resonates with you then you are in the right place."

Our new paradigm is being birthed right now. Knowing our magnificence and honoring that of every other human on this planet changes everything. We move from the fourth World of Separation to the Fifth World of Peace, just as the indigenous prophesied. We have long lived with the "10 Suggestions," as Kryon calls them, or the Laws between humans introduced by Moses. Upon that knowledge came the message of Jesus the Christ, to love and honor each other unconditionally. We are now moving toward an era of compassion for all. Here we recognize the principles of respect and honoring one another. The infinite power of love to create truth, beauty and compassion reflects the multidimensional qualities of life. We have graduated from *Laws,* to *Love,* to *Compassion* as our consciousness has evolved throughout the last three astrological ages of Aries, Pisces and now Aquarius.

We can look at the news and the grim headlines and see where we are coming from, and it is dire and depressing. But we can also see in our news and headlines a new paradigm emerging from the darkness and separation into unity and light. This gives us hope.

Ironically, the CBS Evening News reflects these dynamics. The first minute to dramatic music tells us about all the horrible events happening that day, often with a dramatic inflection by the broadcaster, with a hint of a good story at the end of the broadcast. The first ten minutes are brutal, but the content softens about halfway through the commercial filled half-hour. At the end, the dessert, the cherry on top of the cake, the reward for watching all of the dying paradigm is a story that almost each night causes me to get up and walk over to my box of Kleenex because it pulls on my heart and my soul—about the triumph of the human spirit.

It is clear that the conscious goal of the producers is to stimulate and awaken compassion in each viewer toward a stranger they do not even know. This is part of their programming formula. Personally, I believe they should sandwich the drama in the middle, beginning with inspiration (in spirit) and concluding with compassion. Baby steps.

Chapter 28

Girl Power

8/16/2020

On August 11th, Joe Biden, former vice-president for Barack Obama, and presumed Democratic Party nominee for the 2020 U.S. presidential race announced Kamala Harris as his choice for vice-president. When I heard the news, I wept.

I was surprised that I felt so much emotion. I attempt to practice non-attachment, and I had originally wanted Kamala Harris to be our candidate, a year ago. But Marianne Williamson ran a campaign based upon the principles of restorative practices, so I financially supported her.

When Joe Biden and Kamala Harris appeared together the next day, Joe Biden said:

This morning, all across the nation, little girls woke up, especially little Black and brown girls, who so often feel overlooked and undervalued in their communities. But today maybe they're seeing themselves, for the first time, in a new way: as the stuff of president and vice-presidents (NYT, *Biden and Harris Make First Appearance as Running Mates as Trump and Allies Launch Attacks.* Last updated Aug. 13, 2020).

These words are significant. That they are being uttered by a white male who is a presumed nominee for his political party is huge. Clearly, he has advisors, not the least of whom is his wife, Dr. Jill Biden, who is a former high school teacher and current professor at a community college.

The truth is that minorities do not see themselves reflected in our culture in a positive way often enough or maybe even ever. When we were four small schools at Crawford High School, the principals hired two consultants, a married African American couple, to do a two-day diversity training with our staff. I remember the hotel it was at. I remember one of the principals who was African American was in my breakout group. He was retired from the military and very much loved and respected by his students, his teachers, and staff. He shared that when he went out for a meal with anyone, he would never order fried chicken, or any cultural foods associated with African Americans, because he didn't want to awaken those stereotypes. He spoke about how careful he was about where he went, as a Black man. He was particularly protective of his children.

Acknowledging this highly respected leader openly share his experience as a Black man, successful, intelligent, experienced, but always looking over his shoulder, never able to really let his guard down, impacted me. To know that the safety and security I have been privileged to experience my entire life was nothing like this gentleman's experience, despite his successes and accomplishments, touched my soul.

But the most profound experience of the workshop was when we each individually took a survey of whether we saw ourselves represented in various aspects of life such as the media, including television, movies, magazines, advertisements, commercials, billboards, etc. We then added up the points which could total up to 100.

We were instructed to form a horseshoe shape around the room in the order of the score we got based upon how much we saw ourselves reflected in the culture. My score was a 94 or so, so I was probably the third person in the line beginning at 100. It was stunning to look around the room at our colleagues when we all found our place numerically.

The room began at 100 with white people and as the numbers went down the skin became brown. At the very end, those who saw they were not reflected in society, were our Black staff members.

There, across from me, was my colleague Debra Maxie. She had been the head counselor at Crawford before the small schools. She had an administrative credential and had been an educator for over 30 years, and there she was.

A woman named Angela spoke passionately as an African American—at the end of the line, physically and metaphorically. She stated that she so wished she was not at that place in the self-ranking; that she wanted to be able to say her experience was like those of us at the beginning of the line. But the truth was, her experience was that she did not see herself represented, particularly in a positive light, in our culture. She had also become a new administrator and her passion for students was palpable—but the pain she shared that day further opened my awareness to the inequities that dominate our culture and lives.

For Joe Biden to get this, to state that Kamala Harris, a woman of Indian and Jamaican descent, as his vice-presidential choice, means that the young Angela's and Debra's of our world can see themselves competing for the highest office of the land, is HUGE!

Those of us who score in the 90's and 80's on a survey on whether we see ourselves reflected positively in our culture are blind to our privilege until it is pointed out to us. The media validates us, confirms our worth, and reinforces our sense of currency as valued members of society. Yet, we neglect to recognize the impact of being a member of the dominant elite culture that is absent for our brothers and sisters of color, in this same media.

Things are changing and one of the greatest changes coming is "girl power." As our Platonic Year diagram of the 26,000-year cycle shows us, we are moving into the feminine principle era of our revolution around the Pleiadian star, Alcyone. The #MeTooMovement around women's rights to be respected by all men is a product of our planet's movement into this half of unified consciousness.

From being in the classroom at a multicultural school, I will tell you, "The girls are on fire!" I love to laugh at how those old white guys in Congress struggling to hold on to a past that no longer exists, especially after Covid-19, have no idea what's coming.

Kamala Harris isn't our future, she is our present and her selection as a vice-presidential candidate is an affirmation that we just took one step forward!

In the same week the September 2020 Issue of *O, the Oprah Magazine,* arrived in my mailbox featuring Breonna Taylor on the cover. The text on the cover is: "If you turn a blind eye to racism, you become an accomplice to it," signed, "Oprah." Also: "Breonna Taylor," then "Born June 5, 1993/killed by police/March 13, 2020/," followed in bold *Her Life Matters.* She is wearing her "Metro Louisville EMS" uniform. This woman was a first responder, professionals we have valued since 9-11 in 2001.

In the "behind the scenes," section of how the cover was done which is part of every monthly magazine, it reads: ***Honoring Breonna,*** in bold followed by this text, all in italics and with the first four words capitalized and in bold:

> ***AS OUR NATION CONFRONTS*** *the abhorrent reality of police brutality against Black Americans, one thing is incumbent upon us all: to bear witness. With this month's cover—the first in our history that hasn't featured Oprah— we pay tribute to 26-year-old Breonna Taylor, fatally shot by police who stormed into her Louisville home on March 13. The image was created by self-trained 24-year-old digital artist Alexis Franklin. We asked her to take us through her process of capturing not just a likeness, but a soul* (10).

Alexis Franklin's quote accompanies four photographs of the process. "There was a sparkle in Breonna's eyes—a young Black woman posing in her Louisville EMS shirt, happy to be alive" (12).

Breonna Taylor's selfie inspired the cover. The artist, also a Black woman, re-imagined this selfie and said, "I am so happy to play a small part in this long-overdue, world changing narrative on racial injustice and police brutality."

As the artist of the cover, Alexis describes her process to reveal the soul.

THE DEATHS of Alton Sterling and Philando Castile in 2016 hit me hard. I remember lying on my bed, tears streaming down my face, and just being … tired. Though I'm not proud of it, I began to guard myself. I quit paying such close attention to the news and deaths. It hurts too much. But when Breonna Taylor was killed, I couldn't even try to shut it out. I was uncontrollably angry and hurt. This time there was no shoving it down" (Ibid.).

Alexis then begins to describe her process as a digital artist:

The original photo is one Breonna took herself and has been featured in the news many times. Looking at it I see an innocence, simple but powerful. It was critical for me to retain that…

So many things were going through my mind— Breonna's life, mostly, and how it ended so abruptly and unnecessarily. Every stroke was building a person: each eyelash, each wisp of hair, the shine on her lips. the highlight on her cheek. I had that season when I chose to shut down my feelings around the killing of unarmed Black people because I couldn't take living day to day in such a state of awareness. Now I was as up close and personal as I could ever get to this woman and, consequently, to this very real problem. I felt a new level of determination and pressure to get it right, but I tried not to let that affect me. My greatest work happens when I simply enjoy it and let my hands do what they know how to do—ALEXIS FRANKLIN" (Ibid.).

In an August 13th 2020, article in the *New York Times,* by Richard
A. Open, Jr. and Derrick Bryon Taylor entitled; ***Here's What You Need
to Know About Breonna Taylor's Death,*** we learn the details of
Breonna's murder by police. The subtitle is: *Fury over the killing of
Ms. Taylor by the police fueled tense demonstrations in Louisville, Ky.,
and elsewhere.* The article begins:

> While the death of George Floyd in Minneapolis unleashed a
> wave of protests across the country, fury over the killing of
> Breonna Taylor, an African-American medical worker in
> Louisville, Ky., by the police also drove tense
> demonstrations in that city and beyond.
>
> Since the protests began in late May, Louisville officials
> have banned the use of no-knock warrants, which allow the
> police to forcibly enter people's homes to search them
> without warning, and, on June 23, fired one of the officers
> involved in the shooting.
>
> On Thursday, five months after Ms. Taylor's death, her
> family renewed their pleas for justice. "Right now in
> Louisville people are still waiting at 150 days for these
> officers to be arrested and charged," the family's lawyer,
> Ben Crump, said.
>
> "At this point it's bigger than Breonna, it's bigger than
> just Black Lives," Ms. Taylor's mother, Tamika Palmer,
> added. "We've got to figure out how to fix the city, how to
> heal from here" (Ibid.).

Under the heading ***What happened in Louisville,*** the article
continues by explaining the circumstances that Black citizens know
about and deal with as a reality that quite frankly is unknown, until now,
to those of us in the white community.

> Shortly after midnight on March 13, Louisville police
> officers executing a search warrant used a battering ram to
> enter the apartment of Breonna Taylor, a 26-year-old.
> Ms. Taylor and her boyfriend, Kenneth Walker, had been in

bed, but got up when they heard a loud banging at the door. After a brief exchange, Mr. Walker fired his gun. The police also fired several shots, striking Ms. Taylor.

Mr. Walker told investigators that Ms. Taylor coughed and struggled to breathe for at least five minutes after she was shot, according to the Louisville Courier Journal. She received no medical attention for more than 20 minutes after she was struck, the Courier Journal reported, citing dispatch logs.

… The police had been investigating two men who they believed were selling drugs out of a house that was far from Ms. Taylor's home. But a judge had also signed a warrant allowing the police to search Ms. Taylor's residence because the police said they believed that one of the two men had used her apartment to receive packages. The judge's order was a so-called no-knock warrant, which allows the police to enter without warning and without identifying themselves as law enforcement.

No drugs were found in the apartment, a lawyer for Mr. Walker said.

… In a 911 call just after the shots were fired, Mr. Walker told a dispatcher that "somebody kicked in the door and shot my girlfriend."

The police incident report contained several errors. It listed Ms. Taylor's injuries as "none," even though she had been shot at least eight times, and indicated that officers had not forced their way into the apartment—though they used a battering ram to break the door open.

Ms. Taylor's family also said it was outrageous that the police felt it necessary to conduct the raid in the middle of the night… But they "then proceeded to spray gunfire into the residence with a total disregard for the value of human life," according to a wrongful-death lawsuit filed by Ms. Taylor's mother (Ibid.).

Artist rendering of Breonna Taylor.
By MerlinFoof (reddit user).

These are the injustices many of our Black citizens deal with on a daily basis because of the history of this country embracing the slavery of fellow humans to drive the economy for those who assumed power.

The phrase "Black Lives Matter" is born out of the reality that for hundreds of years in America, Black lives didn't matter. Black people have unjustly been lynched, shot, incarcerated, villainized, discounted and rejected in our country. This reflects a lower consciousness based upon that fourth World of Separation. Here, the color of our skin separates us artificially, another man-made construct just like the story that we were born dirty.

Regarding the police, I want to say that there are elements of police work that are admirable. When former police chief of San Diego, Shelley Zimmerman, who my teaching colleague Ray Beattie worked with, heard about the death of George Floyd by the knee of a police officer she said: "This just set us back 35 years." As Police Chief she emphasized and revived community-based policing in San Diego where police become part of the community and are visible in the community.

When Ray came to Crawford High School to join the Academy of Law, from Lincoln High School, he brought his ties to the San Diego Police through a project called "Star Pal." I had the privilege and honor of having STAR/PAL work with the ninth-grade class I taught, the final period of the day. Ms. Portia, an African American and a retired probation officer, and Officer Carlos, came to my class and my colleague Jamie Davenport's ninth grade class, once a week for an entire school year.

Unruly ninth graders, during the last period of the school day, sat quietly in the circle set up in my classroom, where we convened before class began. "Why are you so well behaved when they are here?" I would ask, genuinely wanting to know. The answer was, "Because they say they will do a home visit if I cannot manage myself." One officer, Officer Denise, was tall, beautiful, Latin and always had a gun in a small and mostly hidden holster.

These officers loved these students. STAR/PAL provides tutoring programs for at-risk youth after school. On weekends they sponsor activities that are civic and community oriented for our students and others. Their purpose is clear:

The mission of STAR/PAL is to empower underserved
youth to build a safer and more prosperous community by

engaging with law enforcement and collaborative partners" (starpal.org).

With their offices located just a few blocks from Crawford High School, STAR/PAL worked with students at other schools in San Diego Unified. Each year, they took our ninth-grade students to the Holocaust Museum in Los Angeles—and when we got into the STAR/PAL van or a bus, Ms. Portia always had food for the students. Sadly, she passed away near the beginning of the lockdown.

Racism in America is systemic; from the judge who signed the warrant for the no-knock drug order, to police shooting first or literally suffocating a man with a knee in full broad daylight.

As we move deeper into the consciousness of the Fifth World of Peace, the dysfunction drops away because we can now see it so clearly. It is right in our face.

This is why Indigos are here—to make the transformation from the dark and unjust to the light of justice for all. Marianne Williamson advocates reparations. In an article by P.R. Lockhart on August 7, 2019, 4:20 p.m. on fox.com titled: "Marianne Williamson presents 2020 Democratic primary's first reparations plan," the subtitle reads; "The self-help guru wants to spend $200 billion to $500 billion on the plan, calling it 'payment of a debt that has never been paid.'"

This recalls Dr. Martin Luther King, Jr.'s famous speech at the Washington Mall on August 28, 1963, in the March of Washington D.C., where he stated with the Lincoln Memorial as his backdrop:

> Five score years ago, a great American, in whose symbolic shadow we stand today, signed the Emancipation Proclamation. This momentous decree came as a great beacon light of hope to millions of Negro slaves who had been seared in the flames of withering injustice. It came as a joyous daybreak to end the long night of their captivity.
>
> But one hundred years later, the Negro is still not free. One hundred years later, the life of the Negro is still sadly crippled by the manacles of segregation and the chains of

discrimination. One hundred years later, the Negro lives on a lonely island of poverty in the midst of a vast ocean of material prosperity. One hundred years later, the Negro is still languishing in the corners of American society and finds himself an exile in his own land. So, we have come here today to dramatize a shameful condition.

In a sense we have come to our nation's capital to cash a check. When the architects of our republic wrote the magnificent words of the Constitution and Declaration of Independence, they were signing a promissory note to which every American was to fall heir. This note was a promise that all men, yes black men as well as white men, would be guaranteed the unalienable rights of life, liberty, and the pursuit of happiness.

It is obvious today that America has defaulted on the promissory note insofar as her citizens of color are concerned. Instead of honoring this sacred obligation, America has given the Negro people a bad check, a check which has come back marked "insufficient funds." But we refuse to believe that the bank of justice is bankrupt, we refuse to believe that there are insufficient funds in the great vaults of opportunity of this nation. So, we have come to cash this check—a check that will give us upon demand the riches of freedom and the security of justice. We have also come to this hallowed spot to remind America of the fierce urgency of now. This is no time to engage in the luxury of cooling off or to take the tranquilizing drug of gradualism. Now is the time to make real the promises of democracy. Now is the time to rise from the dark and desolate valley of segregation to the sunlit path of racial justice. Now is the time to lift our nation from the quicksands of racial injustice to the solid rock of brotherhood. Now is the time to make justice a reality for all of God's children...

Let us not wallow in the valley of despair, I say to you today, my friends" (*npr.org*).

Dr. Martin Luther King, Jr. then launches into the famous part of this speech which we think of as the "I Have a Dream" speech. Although he "spoke about his dream during speeches in Birmingham and Detroit earlier that year, his initial drafts did not contain any references to a dream at all, according to his closest advisors' (AOL.com, *Dr. Martin Luther King's 'I Have a Dream' speech*: full text, Jan. 16, 2017, 11:00 AM).

The first part of this speech was Dr. King's prepared remarks. However, when you watch the video, the crowd is not resonating with his message. As a preacher he read his audience and shifted away from his written notes and spoke extemporaneously. This part of his speech is what has become known as his "I Have a Dream" speech.

But today, the prepared part of the speech addresses exactly where we are in American history/herstory. In 1963 people, Americans related to the "Dream" of equality. Today, we see we missed the first part of Dr. King's message. It is time to dust off the part of the message he prepared and pay up on our check marked "insufficient funds."

In the same Vox article titled *Marianne Williamson presents the 2020 Democratic primary's first reparation plan,* it states:

> Democratic presidential candidate and self-help guru Marianne Williamson has released a formal plan calling for reparations for the descendants of enslaved people in the U.S.
>
> The plan, released Wednesday, is similar to one she released in January on "racial reconciliation and healing," which argues that it is "morally incumbent" on America to take aggressive action to atone for centuries of slavery and discrimination, the vestiges of which continue to affect black communities. The formal rollout of Williamson's reparations plan is an indication that the candidate intends to keep reparations at the forefront of her campaign.

The article concludes with a quote from Williamson: "We need to realize that when it comes to the economic gap between blacks and whites in America, it does come from a great injustice that has never been dealt with," Williamson said at the July debate, pointing to the fact that the 1865 promise of "40 acres and a mule" to the formerly enslaved made in Union army Gen. William T. Sherman's 'Special Field Order 15' was never fulfilled. "That great injustice has to do with the fact that there were 250 years of slavery followed by 100 years of domestic terrorism" (*Vox,* by P.R. Lockhart on August 7, 2019, 4:20 pm)

Marianne Williamson's platform was based on "repairing the harm" done by our country to an essential segment of our citizenry. We have failed as a nation to meet our mission stated in the Declaration of Independence by our Founders.

> We hold these truths to be self-evident, that all men are
> created equal, that they are endowed by their Creator
> with certain unalienable rights, that among these are Life,
> Liberty and the pursuit of Happiness (*archives.gov*).

As some have pointed out, it is time to complete the revolution and hold these truths that are meant to be "self-evident" for every human being. This is the evolution of consciousness that is quickening during 2020, a year of great change and renewal.

According to the *New York Times*, *Black Lives Matter May Be the Largest Movement in U.S. History:*

> The recent Black Lives Matter protests peaked on June 6,
> when half a million people turned out in nearly 550 places
> across the United States. That was a single day in more than
> a month of protests that still continue to this day.
>
> Four recent polls—including one released this week by
> Civis Analytics, a data science firm that works with
> businesses and Democratic campaigns—suggest that about
> 15 million people in the United States have participated in

demonstrations over the death of George Floyd and others in recent weeks.

These figures would make the recent protests the largest movement in the country's history, according to interviews with scholars and crowd-counting experts.

"I've never seen self-reports of protest participation that high for a specific issue over such a short period," said Neal Caren, associate professor at the University of North Carolina at Chapel Hill, who studies social movements in the United States (by Larry Buchanan, Quoctrung Bui and Jugal K. Patel, July 3, 2020).

Fifteen million Americans were part of the George Floyd, Black Lives Matter protests just in the U.S. In Portland, Or. and Seattle, Wa., they continue to protest 80 days later. The model Trump resorted to in Portland, by sending in federal agents who were aggressive and hostile to the peaceful protesters was from the "*To*" quadrant of our "restorative practices discipline window." The intent is *to punish* and after thousands of years of punishing our fellow humans. America's unprecedented numbers of incarceration, particularly of Black and brown men, has nearly bankrupted us financially and socially.

The participation of 15 million Americans in these marches, and the millions of us supporting them from our shelter at home visage, are an acknowledgement by millions of Americans that great harm has been done to the African American community. This acknowledgement requires that we move to the next step and begin to organize around "repairing the harm." This is where reparations come in. We, as a society, have systematically denied African Americans, particularly men, equal financial opportunity.

We have kept the African American community in poverty through our societal institutions. There was no G.I. Bill for returning veterans who were African American after World War II. There was no Veterans Administration home loan program for them. All those benefits were reserved for and limited to white people by law.

I believe Marianne Williamson will be the Secretary of the Department of Peace in our next administration and I believe through reparations we can finally take responsibility for the cruelty and malice that the African American community continues to experience, on a daily basis.

I have seen what poverty looks like in America and it is not pretty. People live in constant fear of losing the little they have, of being evicted, having their car repossessed, not having money for food or diapers or even to do one's laundry or being deported. Poverty creates chaos in peoples' lives. Consider:

> The United States now had 630 billionaires whose wealth totaled $3.4 trillion, as of April 29. Meanwhile, the 400 richest Americans according to Forbes rankings, have as much combined wealth as the poorest 64% of American households (CNBC. 2020/05/01)

We are an amoral society.

At Centers for Spiritual Living, where we practice what our founder Ernest Holmes called Religious Science or Science of Mind, we know that we live in an infinite universe. These billionaire figures reinforce our belief. We just need to redistribute this wealth because it is clear there is plenty to go around. There is enough for everyone to have our basic needs met: of a safe home, universal health care, quality education and jobs that sustain a life of dignity and purpose.

All we lack is the will. But the Indigos are getting voted into government positions, and their peers are ready for radical change—based on their sense of justice for all. This makes them perfect stewards of this redistribution of wealth so that the dysfunction that is destroying our institutions is upgraded into new, bold policies that seek justice for all including "Life, Liberty and the pursuit of Happiness."

Let us not delay one more day.

Because this chapter is about girl power, the Democratic National Convention has been virtual and has been all about girl power this week.

The virtual convention began on Tuesday, August 18, with the keynote address by Michelle Obama. She spoke from the heart about empathy:

Empathy: That's something I've been thinking a lot about lately. The ability to walk in someone else's shoes; the recognition that someone else's experience has value too. Most of us practice this without a second thought. If we see someone suffering or struggling, we don't stand in judgement. We reach out because, "There, but for the grace of God, go I." It is not a hard concept to grasp.

It's what we teach our children.

And like so many of you, Barack and I have tried our best to instill in our girls a strong moral foundation to carry forward the values our parents and grandparents poured into us. But right now, kids in this country are seeing what happens when we stop requiring empathy of one another. They're looking around wondering if we've been lying to them this whole time about who we are and what we truly value.

They see people shouting in grocery stores, unwilling to wear a mask to keep us all safe. They see people calling the police on folks minding their own business just because of the color of their skin. They see an entitlement that says only certain people belong here, that greed is good, and winning is everything because as long as you come out on top, it doesn't matter what happens to someone else. And they see what happens when the lack of empathy is ginned up into outright disdain.

They see our leaders labeling fellow citizens enemies of the states while embodying torch-bearing white supremacists. They watch in horror as children are torn from their families and thrown into cages, and pepper spray and rubber bullets are used on peaceful protestors for a photo-op.

Sadly, this is the America that is on display for the next generation. A nation that's underperforming not simply on matters of policy but on matters of character. And that's not just disappointing, it's downright infuriating, because I know the goodness and the grace that is out there in households and neighborhoods all across this nation.

And I know that regardless of our race, age, religion, or politics, when we close out the noise and the fear and truly open our hearts, we know that what's going on in this country is just not right. This is not who we want to be.

So what do we do now? What's our strategy? Over the past four years, a lot of people have asked me, "When others are going so low, does going high still really work?" ...

But let's be clear: going high does not mean putting on a smile and saying nice things when confronted by viciousness and cruelty. Going high means taking the harder path. It means scraping and clawing our way to that mountain top. Going high means standing fierce against hatred while remembering that we are one nation under God, and if we want to survive, we've got to find a way to live together and work together across our differences" (cnn.com Transcript: Michelle Obama's DNC speech. (Updated 12:56 AM Tue. August 18, 2020).

Recall that the Earth's Precessional Cross has moved into the Feminine half of our 26,000-year revolution around Alcyone. On the following evening former Vice-President Joe Biden's wife of 43 years, Dr. Jill Biden, spoke in front of an empty classroom at Brandywine High School where she once taught. She also spoke from the heart.

We found that love holds a family together. Love makes us flexible and resilient. It allows us to become more than ourselves, together, and though it can't protect us from the sorrows of life, it gives us refuge, a home. How do you make a broken family whole? The same way you make a nation whole: with love and understanding and with small acts of kindness. With bravery, with unwavering faith. We show up for each other in big ways and small ones again and again. It's what so many of you are doing right now for your loved ones, for complete strangers, for your communities. There are those who want to tell us that our country is hopelessly divided, that our differences are irreconcilable, but that's not what I've seen. We're holding on to each other and coming together. We're finding mercy and grace in moments we might have once taken for granted. We're seeing our differences are precious, and our similarities infinite. We have shown that the heart of this nation still beats with kindness and courage. That's the soul of America Joe Biden is fighting for now (Vox.com.Read: *Jill Biden's moving DNC. Speech and Covid-19 and American Families,* by Anna North. Aug. 19 2020, 12:30 AM EDT).

The former First Lady and Secretary of State, Hillary Clinton's speech began:

One hundred years ago yesterday, the 19th Amendment was ratified. It took seven decades of suffragists marching, picketing and going to jail to push us closer to that more perfect union. Fifty-five years ago John Lewis marched and bled in Selma because that work was unfinished.

Tonight I'm thinking of all the girls and boys who see themselves in America's future because of Kamala Harris— a Black woman, the daughter of Jamaican and Indian immigrants, and our nominee for Vice-President of the United States. This is our country's story: breaking down barriers and expanding the circle of possibility (Transcripts: *Hillary Clinton's DNC speech.* Updated 1:19 AM, Thu. August 20, 2020).

Senator Elizabeth Warren, a previous presidential candidate shared a personal story in her speech which she gave from an Early Childhood Education Center in Springfield, Massachusetts.

Let me tell you about one of Joe's plans that's especially close to my heart: child care.

As a little girl growing up in Oklahoma, what I wanted most in the world was to be a teacher. I loved teaching. When I had babies and was juggling my first big teaching job down in Texas, it was hard. But I could do hard. The thing that almost sank me? Child care.

One night my Aunt Bee called to check in. I thought I was fine, but then I just broke down and started to cry… I had tried holding it all together, but without reliable childcare, working was nearly impossible. And when I told Aunt Bee I was going to quit my job, I thought my heart would break.

Then she said the words that changed my life. "I can't get there tomorrow, but I'll come on Thursday." She arrived with seven suitcases and a Pekingese named Buddy and she stayed for 16 years. I get to be here tonight because of my Aunt Bee.

I learned a fundamental truth: nobody makes it on their own.

And yet, two generations of working parents later, if you have a baby and don't have an Aunt Bee, you're on your own.

… It's time to recognize that childcare is part of the basic infrastructure of this nation—it's infrastructure for families.

Joe and Kamala will make high-quality child care affordable for every family, make preschool universal, and raise the wages for every child care worker (cnn.com

Transcript: Elizabeth Warren's DNC speech; updated
1:14 AM, Thu. August 20, 2020).

With Covid-19, every parent now needs an Aunt Bee. It is clear we have no infrastructure for childcare, just an expensive hodgepodge where every parent is on their own to find quality care for their children while they work.

Right now, as schools open virtually, mostly, around the country, teachers along with health care workers are bearing the brunt of having to teach their students and help their own children with the online schooling at the same time. All I can do is hold the light for each teacher knowing that they have the talent, strength and alacrity to make learning more relevant and more fun, because school is a drag and it shouldn't be.

Our schools and universities are built and organized on 18th century models. This pandemic is an excellent opportunity to shake up the systems and create individualized self-guided instruction where students work in small groups/pods to solve real-world problems across the curriculum. Educators have been wanting to tear those walls down, and Covid-19 has been the catalyst.

We can educate our children in new ways that engage them. There is research that directs us to the most effective instruction. With technology students can literally explore the world. We all are born with Spirit-given gifts. Provided with a tablet or laptop and access to the internet—kids can teach kids and hook up across the planet, with adult support.

In 1992 in Cardiff-by-the Sea, parents came together to form a non-profit foundation to help bring more funds to our small school district with a lower and upper elementary school. Out of 43 districts in San Diego County, Cardiff was ranked 42nd in funding per student.

Once formed, we chose to purchase technology to put in the hands of kids. As I said at the time, "They can eat cake." That was 28 years ago and we have used technology largely to support traditional instruction rather than to innovate the delivery of instruction to our 21st century children.

We saw the promise in 1992 of students collaborating around the world via the internet. I even remember two parents from Australia who taught the parents to "surf the net," one evening at one of our school events sponsored by the Foundation. I also remember Harvey White, a co-founder of Qualcomm and then Chairman and President of Cricket, speaking to Cardiff parents. As one of the first supporters of the Cardiff Educational Foundation, along with his wife, Frances, he told us that, "There will come a time when people will not believe that the phone was once connected to a wall." In that moment, my friends and I looked at each other, like "Wow!"

Let me tell you, just about every teenager in America has a phone— a personal computer that they love so much they sleep with them. Perhaps we should engage them in recreating public education so that it is purposeful to them and empowers them rather than disempowering them with stale curriculum and 18th Century learning modalities.

Eliminating the SAT and ACT for college admission, along with standardized testing in public schools is an admission that there is more than a one-size-fits-all curriculum in this country. We can do so much better if we co-create with our youth and college students to make education accessible for all, fun, empowering, self-motivating and even inspirational!

In Kamala Harris' acceptance speech as the Democratic nominee for vice-president of the U.S. at the Democratic National Convention on August 19, 2020, she recognized those who helped to make the crooked path straight enough for her to be nominated:

Greetings, America. It is truly an honor to be speaking with you. That I am here tonight is a testament to the dedication of generations before me: women and men who believed so fiercely in the promise of equality, liberty and justice for all. This week marks the 100th anniversary of the passage of the 19th Amendment. And we celebrate the women who fought

259

for that right. Yet so many Black women who helped secure that victory were still prohibited from voting, long after its ratification.

But they were undeterred.

Without fanfare or recognition, they organized, testified, rallied, marched and fought—not just for their vote, but for a seat at the table. These women and the generations that followed worked to make democracy and opportunity real in the lives of all of us who followed.

They paved the way for the trailblazing leadership of Barack Obama and Hillary Clinton.

And these women inspired us to pick up the torch, and fight on. Women like Mary Church Terrell and Mary McCleod Bethune. Fannie Lou Hamer and Diane Nash. Constance Baker Motley and Shirley Chisholm.

We're not often taught their stories. But as Americans, we all stand on their shoulders (Los Angeles Times, *Kamala Harris' speech at the Democratic National Convention: Read the full transcript.* Aug 20, 2020 6:40 AM PT).

The Speaker of the House, Nancy Pelosi pointed out in her speech that "Democrats in the House—the most diverse majority in history, more 'than 60 percent women, people of color, and LGBGT'" (cnn.com *Transcript: Nancy Pelosi's DNC Remarks.* Updated 1:18 AM ET, Thur. August 20, 2020), highlighting the diversity in the Democratic caucus. The Democratic Party, though it is not consciously esoteric, is in tune with the shift from a focus on the masculine to a greater empowerment of the feminine as we go into a new 13,000-year cycle. In contrast, the Republican Party is represented almost exclusively by white males.

As Van Veen says somewhere in the novel *Ada,* by Vladimir Nabokov, "When you reject the feminine principle you get the logic of insanity." We have lived with the logic of insanity for too long and these brilliant, talented and powerful women show us that we are in the shift.

Mature, intelligent, empathetic and compassionate, these women leaders in our country are showing and staking out the way forward.

As Star Mother stated, "It's women's time!"

Chapter 29

All Lives Matter Isn't Possible Until Black Lives Matter

8/23/2020

Oprah's book club featured *The Sun Does Shine, How I Found Life and Freedom On Death Row,* by Anthony Ray Hinton, in 2018. It took me almost three months to get through this book because I was so horrified by the level of cruel and negligent racism reflected in Ray's story that I had to set it aside for periods of time. That this level and depth of racism was taking place in America, not in the 1950s, '60s, or '70s, but that it was taking place in 2014, I found to be incredulous.

I grew up in Scarsdale, New York until I was nine and then my family moved to Westport, Connecticut. I went to Kenyon College in Gambier, Ohio for one year. I took a year off, got married to Jim Sadler and went to Europe for three weeks on what I refused to call a honeymoon. Jim and I then packed up our Volvo 122S sedan named Emily, rented a U-Haul car-top carrier and drove across the country in 1974 with a McGovern sticker on the back bumper, to Cardiff-by-the-Sea, California, where Jim's sister and brother-in-law lived. We then drove up the California coast and at Grants Pass, Oregon, cut over to the I-5 because the u-joints were going out in the car. Once in Portland, our destination, we drove to check out Reed College, which I had applied to and where I was accepted, sight unseen.

After I graduated from Reed, we moved to Cardiff-by-the-Sea, where we continue to live 43 years later.

I had no idea that the injustices of Tom Robinson in *To Kill a Mockingbird,* were still active and alive in part of the American South *today.* In this novel, Tom Robinson, a Black man, was falsely accused by Mayella Violet Ewell of raping her because when she came on to him sexually and tried to kiss him, he made her stop, and he ran away. She told a different story over a year after she said it happened in the Maycomb, Alabama courtroom.

Though a fictional novel, author Harper Lee grew up and lived in Alabama and her father was a lawyer who sometimes defended Black people. She understood the plight of Blacks in the South in the 1940's and 1950's and published this seminal book in 1960.

As part of the Academy of Law, I taught this novel to my tenth graders though this grade level English curriculum is focused on foreign or international writers. The Law teacher's classroom included a separate room set up as a courtroom. It was here our students did Teen Court, after school.

My tenth-grade classes would take time each year to write the script of the trial from the novel and then re-enact the trial in the courtroom. I had some fabulous Atticus Finches. I believe *To Kill a Mockingbird* is the greatest American novel. To see the look on students' faces when they finished the book was wonderful. We would spend six weeks reading the novel in class because in my class students read right in front of me. I am under no delusion that they are going to go home and read an assigned novel, unless they are in an Honors or AP class.

Of course, Tom Robinson is tried in Maycomb, Alabama (a fictional town) in front of an all-white jury. Folks come from miles away to see the spectacle. They fill the courtroom to standing room only so that when Atticus' children, Jem and Scout along with their friend Dill want to see the trial they ask Reverend Sykes, a Black minister if they can sit with him upstairs in the balcony with the "negro" people, which they do. Atticus' displeasure of their attendance at the trial is displayed when their maid Calpurnia comes into court to tell Mr. Finch that she doesn't know where the children are, just before the jury returns with a verdict, and he sees them in the balcony.

Tom Robinson, a gentle, kind, helpful worker and family man is found guilty by the all-white jury. Later we learn he ran from the guards at the prison he was taken to, and they shot him dead. Atticus, Jem, Scout and their neighbor and friend Miss Maudie are crushed.

Well, I was crushed all the way through Ray's story. The outrage I felt at the systemic racism of the state of Alabama into the 21st century, opened my eyes to some of the severity of racism that remains institutionalized not just in the South, but across our nation.

It was and remains a painful eye-opener.

In an article "As told to Fran Singh," in The Guardian titled, *I spent 28 years on death row,* dated Fri. 21, Oct 2016 08:59 EDT (EJI.com), Anthony, who goes by the name of Ray in his memoir, tells some of his story.

> I was 29 and mowing the lawn at my mother's house in Birmingham, Alabama on a hot day in July 1985 when I looked up and saw two police officers. When my mom saw the handcuffs, she screamed. They asked me whether I owned a firearm, and I said no. They asked if my mother owned one, and I said yes. I asked the detective 50 times why I was being arrested. Eventually, he told me I was being arrested for a robbery. I told him, "You have the wrong man." He said, "I don't care whether you did it or not. You will be convicted."
>
> At the station, it became clear I'd been at work when the robbery occurred. The detective verified this with my supervisor, but then told me they were going to charge me with two counts of first-degree murder from two other robberies. They said my mother's gun was the same kind as the one used at the crime scene, and that I matched the description of the man they were looking for. That was enough for them to pursue charges.

When I met my appointed lawyer, I told him I was innocent. He said, "All of y'all always say you didn't do something." I might have seen him three times in the two years I waited for trial. The only evidence linking me to the crime was the testimony of a ballistics expert who said the bullets from the murder weapon could be a match to my mother's gun. They found me guilty and on 17 December 1986 I went to death row.

On death row, the day starts at 2:45am. At 10am they bring you lunch. Dinner was at 2pm. And that was it. They don't care about actual mealtimes: they say they have to get through everyone, so they start early. The cell was 5ft. X 7ft. You spend about 24 hours in there.

For three years I didn't say a word to another human. I had to watch 54 men walk past to be executed. My cell was 30ft from the chamber and I could smell the burning flesh. There were 22 who took their own life. Going into my fourth year, I heard the man in the cell next to me crying. He told me his mother had died. I said, "Well, now you have someone in heaven to argue your case." The next morning, it was as though a light had come on: my sense of humour was back.

I let my mind travel. I visited the Queen; I married Halle Berry. My mind went everywhere, and at night I'd come back and check on my body.

Without lawyer Bryan Stevenson and the Equal Justice Initiative (EJI), I wouldn't be where I am now. I wrote to him after seeing him on TV one day while being walked back to my cell. I got to meet him in 1995 and finally had someone to fight for me.

Bryon Stevenson, who is the founder and executive director of "Equal Justice Initiative," did assign lawyers to defend Ray Hinton, but in the end, Bryan took on the case himself.

In an article posted on the Equal Justice Initiative EJI.com website titled, *United States Supreme Court Grants Relief to EJI Client Anthony Hinton,* they describe the charges against Mr. Hinton:

> Anthony Hinton was arrested in 1985 and charged with two separate shooting murders that occurred during robberies at two fast food restaurants near Birmingham, Alabama. The only evidence linking Mr. Hinton to the murders was testimony from state lab technicians who stated that bullets recovered from the murders and a third uncharged crime were fired from a weapon recovered from Mr. Hinton's mother. The State conceded at trial that without testimony linking gun evidence from the three separate crimes, Alabama could not convict Mr. Hinton of capital murder.
>
> The trial judge appointed one lawyer to Mr. Hinton who had to defend against three distinct crimes and whose out-of-court compensation was limited by statute to $1,000. That lawyer recognized that Mr. Hinton's defense required an expert witness who could effectively rebut the State's gun experts, but he mistakenly thought $1000 was the maximum he could get under Alabama law to hire an expert. He could only find one person willing to testify for the pay he could offer—Andrew Payne—and he believed Payne was inadequate, but nonetheless put him on at trial. As the Supreme Court found, "the prosecutor badly discredited Payne" and Mr. Hinton was convicted and sentenced to death.

In another article on the EJI website under the heading, "Anthony Ray Hinton," titled, *Mr. Hinton spent 30 years on death row for a crime he did not commit,* they provide the background of the crimes Mr. Hinton was charged with:

Background

In 1985, two Birmingham area fast-food restaurants were robbed and the managers, John Davidson and Thomas

Wayne Vason, were fatally shot. There were no eyewitnesses or fingerprint evidence; police had no suspects and pressure to solve the murders grew as similar crime continued.

On July 25, 1985, a restaurant in Bessemer was robbed and the manager was shot but not seriously wounded. Anthony Hinton was arrested after the manager identified him from a photo lineup, even though he was working in a locked warehouse fifteen miles away at the time of the crime.

Police seized an old revolver belonging to Mr. Hinton's mother, and state firearm examiners said that was the gun used in all three crimes. The prosecutor—who had a documented history of racial bias and said he could tell Mr. Hinton was guilty and "evil" solely from his appearance—told the court that the State's experts' asserted match between Mrs. Hinton's gun and the bullets from all three crimes was the only evidence linking Mr. Hinton to the Davidson and Vason murders.

Anthony Ray Hinton, 29 years old with no history of violent crime, steadfastly maintained his innocence. A polygraph test given by police exonerated him, but the judge (now-retired Circuit Judge James Garrett) refused to admit it at trial.

Mr. Hinton was appointed a lawyer who mistakenly thought he could not get enough money to hire a qualified firearms examiner. Instead he retained a visually-impaired civil engineer with no expertise in firearms identification who admitted he could not operate the machinery necessary to examine the evidence. With no credible expert to challenge the State's assertion of a match, Mr. Hinton was convicted and sentenced to death.

After almost 30 years, and through the hard work of the EJI and personal commitment of Bryan Stevenson, justice was served.

EJI attorneys engaged three of the nation's top firearms examiners who testified in 2002 that the revolver could not be matched to crime evidence. State prosecutors never questioned the new findings but nonetheless refused to re-examine the case or concede error.

For more than 15 years, EJI attorneys repeatedly asked state officials to re-examine the evidence in this case, but former Jefferson County District Attorney David Barber, and Attorneys General from Troy King to Luther Strange, all failed to do so (Ibid.).

After another decade of time, Bryant Stevenson and his staff threw a Hail Mary at the Supreme Court. "In 2014, The Supreme Court unanimously overturned his conviction based on his attorney's deficient representation, and Jefferson County Circuit Court Judge Laura Petro ordered a new trial."

This piece continues:

After 12 more years of litigation, the U.S. Supreme Court reversed the lower courts, and a new trial was granted. The judge finally dismissed the charges after prosecutors said that scientists at the Alabama Department of Forensic Sciences tested the evidence and confirmed that the crime bullets cannot be matched to the Hinton weapon.

After 30 years in custody for crimes he did not commit, Mr. Hinton's release is bittersweet. "We are thrilled that Mr. Hinton will finally be released because he has unnecessarily spent years on Alabama's death row when evidence of his innocence was clearly presented," said his lead attorney, Bryan Stevenson. "The refusal of state prosecutors to re-examine this case despite persuasive and reliable evidence of innocence is disappointing and troubling" (Ibid.).

The State of Alabama had new and correct evidence that the gun that was Mr. Hinton's mothers was not the weapon used in the two murders he was convicted of. But for 15 years the State refused to provide him a retrial. Keeping folks on death row is very expensive and an hour or two of trial time could have saved the state of Alabama a lot of money. Yet no Attorney General would provide any court time to hear this new and correct evidence that proved a man's innocence. In the end, the U.S. Supreme Court recognized that though he was innocent, the State of Alabama was going to execute Anthony Ray Hinton.

In an article in The New York Times titled, *Alabama Man Freed After Decades on Death Row,* by Alan Blinder, April 3, 2015, he writes:

BIRMINGHAM, Ala. – Nearly 30 years after the Alabama authorities relied on analyses of a handgun and bullets to send him to death row, Anthony Ray Hinton was freed on Friday after experts undermined the state's case.

Mr. Hinton's release from the Jefferson County jail, where he was being held awaiting a new trial that was ordered last year, came close to three decades after a court-appointed lawyer mounted such a feeble defense that the United States Supreme Court ruled it was "constitutionally deficient." ...

Despite pleas by Mr. Hinton's lawyers, who cited conclusions by newly enlisted specialists, the state refused for years to reconsider the evidence. And so it was not until Friday at 9:30 a.m., one day after a Circuit Court judge ordered his release, that Mr. Hinton exited the jail to hugs, tears and wails of "Thank you, Lord!"

"The State of Alabama let me down tremendously," Mr. Hinton said in his first interview after his release. "I have no respect for the prosecutors, the judges. And I say that not with malice in my heart. I say it because they took 30 years from me." ...

"He was convicted because he's poor," Mr. Stevenson said. "We have a system that treats you better if you're rich and guilty than if you're poor and innocent, and his case proves it. We have a system that is compromised by racial bias, and his case proves it."

"We've gotten into a culture," he said in a separate interview, "where the pressure to convict and to achieve these outcomes is so great that owning up to mistakes is less frequent than you'd like to imagine."

According to the Death Penalty Information Center, Mr. Hinton is the 152nd person exonerated from an American death row since 1973.

"Cases like Anthony Ray Hinton's give the public pause about the death penalty," said Robert Durham, the center's executive director. He added that "from the outset, this case exhibited many of the classic signs of innocence."

The piece concludes with a quote from Mr. Hinton:

"I've got to forgive," he said. "I lived in hell for 30 years, so I don't want to die and go to hell. So, I've got to forgive. I don't have a choice."

Ray's mother and his friend Lester were his rocks over the nearly three decades that Ray was on death row in an Alabama prison. Ray repeats many times throughout the book that he just wanted to go back to his mother's home and cook for her. Lester visited him in prison— as did Ray's mother, as long as she could, accompanied by Lester's mother, every month for the nearly 30 years Ray was locked up. His mother died during the time he was incarcerated.

Before he leaves his jail cell for freedom, Ray speaks to the inmates to give them hope.

It reminds me of the lyrics of the song *Hurricane,* by Bob Dylan about a man named Hurricane Carter:

"How can the life of such a man
Be in the palm of some fool's hand?
To see him obviously framed
Couldn't help but make me feel ashamed

To live in a land
Where justice is a game" (azlyrics.com).

Anthony Ray Hinton's story speaks for itself. His book, *The Sun Does Shine: How I Found Life and Freedom on Death Row,* written with Lara Love Hardin, is a harrowing, frustrating, maddening and ultimately redeeming story about the depths of injustice deep in our American systems. Propped up by our taxpayer dollars, whatever state justice is meted out, we have been fooling ourselves if we do not see and recognize the disparate treatment of the rich and the poor and white and Black in our justice systems across our nation.

Mr. Hinton tells what his life is now that he is no longer sitting on death row:

> I've spent the year since my release telling my story to anyone who will listen. I was asked to come to Necker Island—Richard Branson's private island—and tell my story to a group of celebrities and others who are working hard to end the death penalty. I go where I am asked to go—churches, colleges, small meeting rooms, private islands. I'm a curiosity—the man who survived death row—but I'm also a voice. I'm a voice for every man who still sits on the row. "I believe in justice," I tell crowds of people. "I'm not against punishment. But I don't believe in cruelty. I don't believe in useless punishment" (237–238).

But my favorite part comes with the beautiful heartfelt reflection:

> I have lived a life where I have known unconditional love. I learned on the row how rare that is. My mother loved me completely, so does Lester. Our friendship is rare and precious, and everytime I'm invited somewhere to speak—like Necker Island or London—I bring Lester with me. It's the least I could do, and every once in a while, we look at each other and smile at the craziness of it all. We are two poor boys from the old coal mining town of Praco, and they just shut down Buckingham Palace to give us a private tour.

I got to see a Yankee game.

We went to Hawaii (Ibid. 240).

Ray may have not met the Queen, but he did manifest a private tour of Buckingham Palace. This is the power of thought in action. Ray concludes for all of us individually and collectively:

Every single one of us wants to matter. We want our lives and our stories and the choices we made or didn't make to matter.

Death row taught me that it all matters.

How we live matters.

Do we choose love or do we choose hate? Do we help or do we harm?

Because there's no way to know the exact second your life changes forever. You can only begin to know that moment by looking in the rearview mirror.

And trust me when I tell you that you never, ever see it coming (241).

We did not see this pandemic coming. But here we are. We can take the model of Ray and begin to visualize and nourish thoughts about a more just and balanced world; more empathetic and compassionate, where masculine and feminine principles are balanced. Here everyone has a safe home, healthy food to eat, health care, basic income for dignity, quality jobs that pay a living wage, a clean environment, new technologies that clean our air and soil, social breakthroughs that break down barriers, and politicians and public servants whose primary concern is for the least of us.

Our country spends our resources on our military and our criminal injustice system and neglects everything else including ourselves. We need to reverse our funding from fear-based expenditures to love-based investment in ourselves, our families, our communities, our states and our nation.

We have seen the humans we have been, but we also see the New Human of love and grace and forgiveness emerging out of the darkness of our histories into the light of our infinite possibilities. Anthony Ray Hinton is a symbol of this metamorphosis taking place, in, through, and as, us. We are shifting and raising consciousness. It is a good thing, as we move into a greater presence of light. Let us rejoice in the emergence out of our barbaric past into a benevolent world of peace and joy as our focus, leaving war and punishment in our rearview window.

We may not have seen it coming, but it's obvious from what is going on in and around us in the year 2020 that the New Human is upon us.

Social Justice is upon us, and Anthony Ray Hinton gives us hope that we can redeem ourselves, our society, our culture, our country to a more just and equal place with the promise of our founders that:

> "We hold these truths to be self-evident, that all men are created equal, that they are endowed by their Creator with certain unalienable Rights, that among these are Life, Liberty and the pursuit of Happiness" (Declaration of Independence).

Chapter 30

Conscious Creation

8/27/2020

The Science of Mind: A Philosophy, A Faith, a Way of Life, by Ernest Holmes, the founder of Science of Mind, is the textbook Religious Science uses in Centers for Spiritual Living. Ernest Holmes found great truths in the writings of many, but Ralph Waldo Emerson's writings kept him coming back for more throughout his life

The first chapter of this seminal book is titled: *The Thing Itself.* It begins: "We all look forward to the day when science and religion shall walk hand in hand through the visible to the invisible" (25), predicting that eventually the study of the unseen will join the reality or perceived reality of the seen. This is coming through technology that will confirm the energy field surrounding absolutely everything and the unity, the universal oneness behind it all—which Ernest Holmes calls "The Thing Itself." He writes:

> We see abundance in the Universe. We cannot count the grains of sand on a single beach. The earth contains untold riches, and the very air is vibrant with power. Why, then, is man weak, poor and afraid? The Science of Mind deals with these questions. The Divine Plan is one of Freedom; bondage is not God-ordained. Freedom is the birthright of every living soul. All instinctively feel this. The Truth points to freedom, under Law. Thus, the inherent nature of man is forever seeking to express itself in terms of freedom. We do well to listen to this Inner Voice, for it tells us of a life wonderful in its scope; of a love beyond our fondest dreams; Of a freedom with the soul craves" (25–26).

Holmes continues:

> The study of Science of Mind is a study of First Cause,
> Spirit, Mind, or that invisible Essence; that ultimate Stuff
> and Intelligence from which everything comes, the Power
> back of creation—The Thing Itself.
>
> We accept this "Thing" and believe in It. What we desire
> is to know more about It, and how to use It" (26).

In Science of Mind, we accept several names for this Thing. Many call it God, Spirit, Intelligence, Allah, Source, Creative Source, the Presence, or even The Force. But in Science of Mind—this Thing—that is the power back of or beyond creation is a power, it is an intelligence, it is an energy that we call "Life." Therefore, we see Spirit as a unified power, and we refer to it as "It."

We do not see a vengeful, authoritarian God outside of us looking down from some mythical cloud handing out punishment. We see a Universe that is intelligent, all-knowing, all connected that moves "in, through, and as, us." We see Spirit incarnated. Spirit is not outside of us but resides in each piece of DNA in every cell of our body.

We are Spirit incarnate. We are powerful, we are intelligent, we are magnificent!!! Ernest Holmes explains:

> This is the simple meaning of true metaphysical teaching,
> the study of Life and the nature of the Law, governed and
> directed by thought; always conscious that we live in a
> spiritual Universe; that God is in, through, around and for us.
> There is nothing supernatural about the study of Life from
> the metaphysical viewpoint. That which today seems to us
> supernatural, after it is thoroughly understood, will be found
> spontaneously natural (27).

Ernest Holmes wrote and published this book in 1938. The technology he refers to is very close at hand in 2020; to see the energy fields that are presently invisible to us and therefore hidden; to see the quantum field and the unity or oneness of the ALL. Science is on the cusp of validating metaphysics; beyond the four dimensions that limit our thinking and our life experiences.

Ernest Holmes provides hope for us in 2020. The breakdown of our systems and institutions grants us an opportunity to create new healthy paradigms.

In a passage under the subtitle, *Learning to Trust Will Make Us Happy,* Holmes writes:

> All men seek some relationship to the Universal Mind, the Over-Soul, or the Eternal Spirit, which we call God. And Life reveals itself to whoever is receptive to it. That we are living in a spiritual Universe, which includes the material or physical universe, has been a conclusion of the deepest thinkers of every age. That this spiritual Universe must be one of pure Intelligence and perfect Life, dominated by Love by Reason and by the power to create seems an inevitable conclusion (32).

It is a comfort and a reassurance in these times of dysfunction and imbalance that the Universe is governed by Love and Reason. The chaos and havoc we are experiencing in 2020 will lead us ultimately to "Love" and "Reason" of a higher vibration. As we move into unity consciousness and the honoring of the Divine Feminine in this cosmic shift to a new 26,000-year cycle, we find balance and harmony.

In the second chapter, entitled *The Way It Works,* Holmes recaps:

> The Science of Mind is not a special revelation of any individual; it is, rather, the culmination of all revelations. We take the good wherever we find it, making it our own in so far as we understand it. The realization that Good is Universal, and that as much good as any individual is able to incorporate in his life is his to use, is what constitutes the Science of Mind and Spirit.
>
> We have discussed the nature of The Thing as being Universal Energy, Mind, Intelligence, Spirit-finding conscious and individualized centers of expression through

us—and that man's intelligence is this Universal Mind, functioning at the level of man's concept of It. This is the essence of the whole teaching (35).

Science of Mind is not a revelation of Ernest Holmes but a combination of various belief systems and modalities that he found made sense including religion, psychology, and sociology along with biology.

Under the subtitle *Universal Mind, or Spirit or God,* Holmes writes:

There is a Universal Mind, Spirit, Intelligence, that is the origin of everything: It is First Cause. It is God. This Universal Life and Energy finds an outlet in and through all that is energized, and through everything that lives. There is One Life back of everything that lives. There is One Energy back of all that is energized. This Energy is in everything. There is One Spirit back of all expression. That is the meaning of that mystical saying: "In Him we live, and move and have our being" (Acts 17:28).

The life which we live is the Universal Life expressing through us, else how could we live? Our thought and emotion are the use we make—consciously or unconsciously—of this original creative Thing that is the Cause of everything (35–36).

We are One with Creative Source. There is One Universal Mind, and we are a part of it. Through our thoughts and emotions, we use this power either consciously knowing we are Spirit expressing, or most commonly, unconsciously, believing we are separate from Spirit as we have been told and trained to believe for millennia.

Our thoughts create our lives, along with the emotions they evoke. As we say at Seaside Center for Spiritual Living; "Change Your Thinking, Change Your Life." A huge banner with this phrase by Ernest Holmes hangs on one side of the sanctuary.

Kryon says that the Precession of the Equinoxes that occurred on December 21, 2012, was the point of the centering of the 26,000-year wobble. As we move into this new, fresh cycle with no paradigm before us, we take the notion of evil from the realm of duality and place it into the museum of consciousness as an old relic, a thing of the past.

This is the shift.

Holmes finishes this message:

> Let us realize and work with this sound knowledge and perfect faith: That as high as we shall make our mark in Mind and Spirit, so high shall be Its outward manifestation in our material world (39).

Welcome peace, prosperity, wholeness, beauty, love, compassion, and empathy for ALL!

This is the principle upon which Science of Mind is based: that our thoughts, our beliefs, our convictions literally create our lives—focusing on freedom and the truth as a mental exercise brings that about through the quantum field. We don't focus on the how, we focus on the thought, the belief, the vision and the more we nurture it the sooner it transpires.

Throughout his time on death row, Ray used his imagination to maintain his sanity. He dated Sandra Bullock and Kim Kardashian. He made the winning touchdown at Super Bowls. He hit baseballs out of the park for home runs. He even started a book club with the blessings of a warden to help the men get out of their prison environment into their imaginations. The first book he chose for the book club was *To Kill a Mockingbird,* to help his fellow inmates.

But beyond that, Ray used his imagination to create a completely separate life of his dreams. In writing about his case in his book, he shares his visions of being escorted out of prison on death row to a private plane awaiting him. He would be flying on this plane to visit the Queen of England. He created every detail of the private flight and the meeting with the Queen including that her dress color matched his blue tie. The meeting was accompanied by tea and crumpets and a wonderful visit with Her Highness, before Ray returned to the U.S. on the luxury jet provided to him.

There is a Universal Law of cause and effect. What we put out into the quantum field or Universal Intelligence returns to us. In this way, by managing our thoughts, our feelings, our words, and actions we consciously create our reality rather than leaving our life to what Ernest Holmes calls the "law of averages."

Ray spent his decades on death row visualizing a life outside of prison that included dating celebrities and seeing himself as a heroic figure in various sports. He did this to maintain a positive mental state. But when he got out of prison, he wrote about being at Richard Branson's private island with Richard Branson and George Clooney along with his friend Lester.

When I read this, I did a double take. Was Ray still in his imagination after his release? But then I reread the passage and focused on "… but I'm not traveling in my mind" (*The Sun Does Shine*, 237), Ray explains. Following his release Ray did not get to meet the Queen of England, but authorities did shut down the tours of Buckingham Palace so that Ray and Lester could have a private tour.

The end to Ray's book is so beautiful because it so matches his visions in his imagination over almost thirty years on death row. Anthony Ray Hinton planted the seeds of celebrity and fame and he nurtured them in the soil of his mind. Watering them with new visions, fertilizing and keeping his seeds of hope growing below the surface, they popped out of the dirt to become the plant, the flower where he gained his freedom and did mix with the rich and famous in real life. Ray created these encounters in his mind on death row, and he actually realized them in his life. Visualizing his freedom and cavorting with the famous while on death row resulted in these events taking place in his real life. Believe and you will achieve!

This is how we describe the creative process in Science of Mind. We plant the seed with a thought which comes from the infinite, the One Mind, or Spirit. We nurture these thoughts with love, compassion, information, feeling, hope and faith until, voila, our thought becomes the thing. This is how we can, like Ray, consciously create our lives, one thought at a time. This is why it is essential to monitor and manage our thoughts. We must learn to not focus on what we don't want, that gives us anxiety, worry and stress, but to shift in the moment of the negative thought to its polar opposite. We do this by reminding ourselves we live in an infinite soup of love which we call our universe. This takes effort. Yet, it is an effort worth exerting personally and collectively.

Anthony Ray Hinton practiced these principles of Science of Mind, and he realized the visions he spent his time imagining and nurturing. By focusing on what we want, we create it, literally. Ray's story affirms this universal law, that what we put out returns to us, in most cases multiplied. Where are we placing our focus and energy? For this is what we are creating whether we realize it or not.

A new Platonic Year is upon us. The lessons are all around us. Do we choose love or hate, cooperation or competition, peace, or war? It is up to us. We literally create our lives with our thoughts, our words, and our actions. Mindfully choosing love moves us into the field of unity that is our new home in the universe.

Kryon reminds us over and over; we made it past the marker of December 21, 2012. We are on the unity side of the cycle, though we are just at the sunrise of our central sun, Alcyone. The promise of the coming together of humanity into the recognition and realization of our Oneness is upon us. Let us embrace a future that is full of light, peace, harmony, and love, and leave our barbaric past behind us, where it belongs.

Welcome to a New Human and a New Earth where Peace and Love are everyone's birthright! Welcome to the Age of Aquarius where we honor ALL Lives!

In Gratitude

Like so many of you, I did not realize when the pandemic began that I would begin a new career. But this pause, extended as it has become, has been an opportunity for humanity. It has provided us with the space to change who we are. We get to choose what we do with our days and nights, weeks, and months, and now, years.

I want to thank the reader Maryann at the monthly psychic fair at Harmony Grove Spiritual psychic fair. She told me I would be writing a book and it would be based on common sense, because, in her words, "There is no common sense on this planet right now." I did not comprehend the depth of her message at the time.

What began as a guided writing activity in a class by Marilyn Harper and her partner Joeuex Robey morphed into a trilogy that kept me writing every morning for almost 400 days. I want to thank both of them for their powerful class. I am also grateful for the admonitions of Adironnda that action is necessary. Just being spiritual is not enough.

This trilogy would not have been possible without the generosity of Lee Carroll and Monika Muranyi who gave me permission to use all the work I requested from their books. Without this gesture, the multidimensional aspect of this trilogy would be missing, along with the bigger picture of what we are going through as a planet and its inhabitants.

I want to thank Kryon for his clarity, and excellence as a teacher. Channeled by Lee Carroll for over 30 years, Kryon's lesson plans are clear, direct and on target. He uses no paralanguage, which for me is a sign that this work is channeled. Ordinary humans say "um," "ah," while we think of the next words. Channels don't. Their message is straightforward and direct. In the case of Kryon the messages are also revolutionary and blasphemous.

Kryon's message is simple: we are born magnificent! We are part of the divine matrix of the universe and our divinity lies within each of us. This challenges our notions that we are random products of chance and have no purpose beyond living one life; a life where we compete for limited resources. It also challenges the organized belief systems that insist we are born sinners and need to obey the rules of our belief system or we will be subject to an eternal life in hell.

I want to thank Cheryl Pauchuk, who at the time was with Park Point Press, the publishing arm of Centers for Spiritual Living. She hosted a virtual symposium where I learned one could write a book in 90 days. Though she did not accept my manuscript to publish, she did connect me with Eric D. Groleau in an email with the subject line: "To a beautiful writer, meet an awesome publisher."

Eric, of Strategic Edge Innovations, lives close to Lake Ontario in Canada. He and I have been collaborating weekly on Zoom. His skill in developing my book and diagrams into the professional and polished products you hold in your hands is magical. Together, we worked the puzzle to describe the 26,000-year cycle that is the overall theme of the trilogy.

Harmony Sedona cheered me on every step of the process and "held space."

Bobbie Walton stepped in at the end and volunteered to edit the work. "I hope you know you can't fire me until we complete Book 3," she told me early on. We laugh that her "coin of the realm" as she calls it, is two 99 cent fish tacos at the taqueria at the local gas station a mile from my house.

I also want to thank my esoteric team whom I ask to join me every morning before I begin writing. This team is comprised of entities that include writers, musicians, visionaries, channelers, as well as spiritual energies such as Jaspar and the Illuminated Ones, who guide this writing. One funny aspect is that the group has grown as certain individuals ask to be put on "The Team." One such request came from Jerry Garcia. That cracked me up!

I knew I wanted Michael Bernard Beckwith to write the forward because so much of this book is about Black Lives Matter. As a leader in the New Thought movement, I am so grateful for his insightful and hopeful vision for all of humanity. I am honored by his inclusion in this book. Kudos also to Jacquelyn Brown-Benefield, the Media Coordinator for Agape International Spiritual Center, for her sacred correspondence in this matter.

Much thanks to my dear friend and colleague from Crawford High School, Brenda Bell, for providing the photo of Congressman John Lewis. Eric and I could not find an image that was not copyrighted. Brenda dove into her archives and found the perfect photo from taking students to see him at a One Book One San Diego event in 2018.

Thank you to my Power of 8 partners who meet weekly and have set intentions for a successful launch of *Words of the Temple, Book 1*, since the beginning of 2021. Together we continue to support the vision for world peace.

Bobbie and I set up our final date to complete our editing and selected the next Saturday. It was Lily Rose's 32nd birthday. I froze, as we know certain dates are sacred in our lives. Later, I realized that Lily Rose and I had come full circle. Lily Rose is the conduit or channel for the *Words of the Temple*. I am the one who "needs to put it into writing." Thank you to my Pleiadian Angel. To my brilliant lights, Jesse, Brendon and Ada, thank you for making the world a brighter place!

Finally, I want to thank my husband Jim, who watched me sit at the dining room table writing first by hand (Book 1) and then typing on my iPad using wireless keyboard, every morning for over a year. Bobbie calls him "Thesaurus." He hopes this is a best-seller and we can go on a fabulous trip!

November 20, 2021
Cardiff-by-the-Sea, California

Works Cited

Alter, Charlotte. "Youth Quake: How the World Will Change When A New Generation Leads." *TIME,* 3 Feb. 2021, pp. 40, 42, 48, 49.

"Ancient Lemuria." *The Women of Lemuria: Ancient Wisdom for Modern Times,* by Kryon et al., Ariane Books, 2018, pp. 24, 25, 46, 78–79, 80, 82, 83, 84, 202, 203, 211, 212, 213–214.

Astrolada. "The Astrological Ages." *Astrolada,* www.astrolada.com/articles/astrology-techniques/the-astrological-ages.html.

Felsenthal, Edward. "2019 Person of the Year Greta Thunberg." *Time,* 23 Dec. 2020, pp. 48–65.

Franklin, Alexis. "Honoring Breanna." *O The Oprah Magazine,* 1 Sept. 2020, pp. 10–12.

"Gaia and the Universe." *The Gaia Effect: The Remarkable System of Collaboration between Gaia and Humanity,* by Kryon et al., Ariane, 2015, pp. 80, 82, 199, 212, 213, 213–214, 219, 220, 235, 236, 237.

George, Llewellyn. *A To Z Horoscope Maker and Delineator: An American Textbook of Genethliacal Astrology.* Llewellyn Publications, 1973.

Khan, Matt. *The Universe Always Has a Plan: The 10 Golden Rules of Letting Go.* Hay House, Inc, 2021.

Nabokov, Vladimir, *Ada or Ardor: A Family Chronicle,* McGraw-Hill International, Inc. 1969.

The New Human: The Evolution of Humanity, by Kryon and Lee Carroll, Kryon Writings, 2017, pp. 16, 161–162, 209–210, 198, 199, 46, 78.

SCIENCE OF SELF-EMPOWERMENT: Awakening the New Human Story, by GREGG BRADEN, HAY House UK LTD, 2019, pp. xvii-xviii, 43, 44, 46, 47, 48–50, 51, 52.

"Self-Reliance." *Essays: First and Second Series Complete in One Volume*, by Ralph Waldo Emerson, Perennial Library, 2010, pp. 45–49.
"Spirit." *The Science of Mind*, by Ernest Holmes et al., Tarcher Perigee, 2012, pp. 79–83.

"The Sun Does Shine." *The Sun Does Shine: How I Found Life and Freedom on Death Row*, by Anthony Ray Hinton et al., St. Martin's Press, 2019, pp. 237–238, 240, 241.

The Twelve Layers of DNA: An Esoteric Study of the Mastery Within, by Kryon and Lee Carroll, Platinum Pub. House, 2010, pp. 156, 157, 159, 160, 161, 162, 52–54, 101–102, 103.

About The Author

DEBORAH SADLER

In addition to being a licensed Religious Science Practitioner, teacher, astrologer, metaphysician and student of Kryon, Deborah is a cutting-edge leader in restorative justice. She knows raising consciousness is the key to world peace and delights that young people are leading the way.

For more information about Deborah, please visit her website:

wordsofthetemple.com

Additional Materials
& Resources

Access your Additional Materials & Resources here:
wordsofthetemple.com/additional

Made in the USA
Middletown, DE
24 February 2022